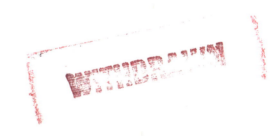

EconoPower

*How a New Generation
of Economists Is
Transforming the World*

Mark Skousen

WILEY

John Wiley & Sons, Inc.

Published by John Wiley & Sons, Inc., Hoboken, New Jersey
Published simultaneously in Canada

For general information on our other products and services or for technical support, please
contact our Customer Care Department within the United States at (800) 762-2974,
outside the United States at (317) 572-3993 or fax (317) 572-4002.

Wiley also publishes its books in a variety of electronic formats. Some content that appears
in print may not be available in electronic books. For more information about Wiley
products, visit our web site at www.wiley.com.

Library of Congress Cataloging-in-Publication Data:

Skousen, Mark.
    Econopower : how a new generation of economists is transforming the world/
Mark Skousen.
      p. cm.
    Includes index.
    ISBN 978-0-470-13807-6 (cloth)
      1. Economics. 2. Economics—philosophy. 3. Economics. I. Title.
HB71.S594   2008
330—dc22
                                                        2007045588

Printed in the United States of America

10 9 8 7 6 5 4 3 2 1

Dedicated to John O. Whitney, Columbia's B.M.O.C.
"A noble man cannot be lost in a crowd"

Contents

Foreword

There was a time not too long ago when most economists were pessimistic about the future. However, the great British economist Alfred Marshall was an exception. At the beginning of World War II, he was extremely upbeat about the next generation of economists, who he predicted would change the world for the better. He wrote a friend, "A thousand years hence 1920–1970 will, I expect, be *the* time for historians. It drives me wild to think about it."[1]

Then, in 1930, at the beginning of the Great Depression, famed economist John Maynard Keynes—Alfred Marshall's most illustrious student—wrote a little essay chastising his fellow colleagues for being overly negative about the depressed economy. In his essay, "Economic Possibilities for Our Grandchildren," Keynes lambasted his friends for their pessimism, declaring that they were "wildly mistaken" about the future. According to Keynes, the Great Depression was a "temporary maladjustment," and "in the long run mankind is solving its economic problem." (You thought I was going to quote Keynes's famous remark, "In the long run we are all dead," didn't you?) He anticipated a "far greater progress" than we had ever imagined, that within a hundred years the human race would be so far advanced economically that the real problem would be simply this: "how to use his freedom from pressing economic cares, how to occupy the leisure, which science and compounded interest will have won for him, to live wisely and agreeably and well."[2]

The positive predictions of Alfred Marshall and John Maynard Keynes have proven to be correct, thanks in large measure to the next generation of economists who have helped transform the way the world works through improved policies and exciting new empirical studies. Since World War II, the world economy has been booming, entrepreneurship has been unleashed with a torrent of new inventions and technological advances, and, despite a few recessions and crises here and there, we have avoided another Great Depression and world war.

Mark Skousen does a wonderful job in this book, *EconoPower,* explaining how economists played an important role in this postwar boom and how a new generation of these movers and shakers is making a difference. Even I am amazed at what economists are doing today— making it easier to save, stay out of debt, and invest prudently; bringing millions of people out of poverty through private-bank micro credits; reducing crime and improving public education; saving governments lots of money and taking companies public through more efficient auctions; alleviating traffic congestion through peak pricing techniques; making corporations more profitable while rewarding workers and shareholders; and helping countries achieve their own economic miracles and avoid future international conflicts.

I note with particular pride that many of the economists Mark mentions in this book were faculty or students at the University of Chicago, including such luminaries as Milton Friedman, who more than anyone has shown us how to create the right environment for a stable, noninflationary growth economy (by controlling the money supply, cutting taxes, and limiting the growth of government); James Buchanan, father of the public-choice school, who shifted the emphasis from "market failure" to "government failure" and introduced ways to limit state power; Gary Becker, who was the first to apply economic principles to sociology and other disciplines; and Robert Mundell, one of the founders of supply-side economics, touting the benefits of free trade, tax cuts, and deregulation.

Back in the 1960s and 1970s, these Chicago academics were treated as fringe economists, even though they considered themselves the true intellectual descendants of Alfred Marshall. This small group advocated limited government, sound money, decreased regulations, investing in stock index funds, and cutting taxes. Many in the profession called them kooks. Today they are instead called Nobel laureates.

I was privileged to be a part of that Chicago group in the 1960s and 1970s, participating firsthand in the birth of supply-side economics. At that time, our nation stood at a crossroads deciding whether to continue a policy of high taxes, rising inflation, and slow growth, or to change course and cut taxes and regulations to foster more growth, less inflation, and more savings. It was at this time that the Laffer curve (highlighted in Chapter 26) was born—the idea that a sharp cut in high marginal tax rates could so encourage savings, productivity, and economic growth that government could enjoy more revenues, not less. Welfare spending and income-support programs are also commensurably less as the economy expands. Indeed the best form of welfare will always be a good, high-paying job. In short, not only do tax cuts cost a lot less than anyone currently believes, but they are also often the best way to help the poor. Tax cuts can cure all manner of maladies!

The supply-side revolution thus spawned the Thatcher-Reagan revolution and a new paradigm in economic science. The Reagan-era tax cuts spurred not only excellent economic growth but also enormous savings. Just look at the economy that supply-side economics has ushered in. I've never seen a major economy that comes even close to the current U.S. economy. I've never even read about an economy, modern or ancient, near or far, large or small, that can hold a candle to the United States of today. While the country isn't perfect, it is the closest thing this old planet has ever created.

Today, the U.S. economy is the only developed economy that is also a growth economy. I believe this is true because of the incredible policies put in place over the past 25 years. Over that time, fiscal policy has been improved dramatically—lower marginal tax rates have encouraged work and investment. Monetary policy has been improved greatly so we now have stable, low inflation, translating into much lower interest rates for borrowers. Trade has gotten freer, creating more wealth for the United States and its trading partners. Finally, economic restrictions and union membership are lower, allowing markets to function more freely.

If you want to see the effect of these changes, just look at the stock market. From January of 1966 through July of 1982, the average annual compound real rate of return of the S&P 500 was negative 6.1 percent.

Really think about that. Due to poor economic policies, the stock market barely appreciated in nominal terms, and returns were actually negative due to the huge increase in price levels. Since pro-growth policies were instituted under President Ronald Reagan, though, the S&P 500 has delivered an average annual compound real rate of return of 8.1 percent from July of 1982 through today. In short, supply-side economics has hugely improved the economic lot of our country, and it is sweeping across the globe, as well.

Furthermore, through the trailblazing work of the Chicago school and elsewhere, a new generation of economists is entering a golden age of discovery—in such diverse fields as law and criminology, behavioral finance and the stock market, and even the economics of religion, happiness, and sports. Economists have even improved their ability to predict! I am glad to see Mark Skousen draw upon the successes of economists from all parts of the political spectrum. We should favor good economics no matter who advocates it, whether Keynesian or Austrian, and equally criticize bad economics, whether it comes from Republicans or Democrats.

There remains to this day economic naysayers forecasting doom and gloom, but I am not one of them. Granted, mistakes are being made, such as in California, where progressive taxation and excessive regulations are stifling a once-great state. (Disclaimer: I decided to move my family and business from California to Tennessee, which has no income tax.) But there's much progress as we begin the twenty-first century. If the United States can move toward pro-growth policies such as a low flat tax, Social Security privatization, school choice, increased trade with foreign countries, and less military interventionism, Keynes's vision could be even brighter. Much remains to be done and discovered, but giant market forces are at work that will be hard to reverse.

Mark Skousen is to be congratulated for putting together a blueprint for an advancing cadre of economic experts spreading their gospel to broader and broader spheres. As Mark indicates, economics is no longer the dismal science, but an upbeat, universal science fulfilling ever-expanding needs, and I'm glad to be part of it.

—ARTHUR B. LAFFER
Founder and Chairman, Laffer Associates

Acknowledgments

*E*conoPower describes a new generation of economic entrepreneurs who are creatively applying their theories to solve many of the world's problems. These are exciting, heady times for applied economists. In preparing this book, I've interviewed and consulted with many of them. I would like to especially thank the following:

- José Piñera, a Harvard-trained economist who became minister of labor in Chile and is now president of the International Center for Pension Reform.
- John Mackey, CEO of Whole Foods Markets and creator of a new brand of business called "conscious capitalism."
- Muhammad Yunus, president of the Grameen Bank, and co-winner of the 2006 Nobel Peace Prize.
- Gary Becker, professor of economics, University of Chicago.
- Paul Milgrom, professor of economics, Stanford University.
- Paul Klemperer, Edgeworth Professor of Economics, Nuffield College.
- Robert W. Poole, Jr., Director of Transportation Studies, Reason Foundation.
- David Swensen, chief investment officer of the Yale endowment fund.
- Jeremy Siegel, professor of economics at the Wharton School.

- Richard Thaler, professor of economics, University of Chicago.
- Briggitte Madrian, professor of public policy at Harvard University.
- Robert Shiller, professor of economics, Yale University.
- Charles Koch, president of Koch Industries.

I'd also like to thank Kenna C. Taylor (Rollins College); Steve Moore (*Wall Street Journal*); David Colander (Middlebury College); Larry Wimmer (Brigham Young University); Burton Malkiel (Princeton University); William G. Shipman (State Street Global Advisors); John O. Whitney (Columbia Business School); William Easterly (New York University): James Gwartney (Florida State University); Larry Iannoccone (George Mason University); Art Laffer (Laffer Associates); and Greg Mankiw (Harvard University). I also benefited from a series of papers and lectures presented at the American Economic Association meetings held in January, 2008, in New Orleans. This program, entitled "Better Living through Economics," was organized by Professor Charles Plott (CalTech) in preparation for an edited volume of the same title.

And finally, I want to thank my wife, Jo Ann, who helped edit and restructure this book to make it suitable for publication. She is the perfect combination of criticism, witticism, and encouragement.

In prosperity, AEIOU,
Mark Skousen
New York

January 2008

Introduction

A Golden Age of Discovery

Economics is experiencing . . . a golden age of discovery. This is not an exaggeration. Empirical economists are charting the economy and society with a wealth of detailed applied results that truly bear comparison with other epochs of discovery in other sciences.

—Diane Coyle
The Soulful Science[1]

In 2006 the Nobel Peace Prize was awarded for the first time to an economist. Since the 1960s, the Nobel committee has awarded dozens of Nobel prizes in economics, but only one Nobel *Peace* Prize has gone to an economist. It is a watershed event, symbolic of the new prowess of the profession. Muhammad Yunus, a former head of the economics department at Chittagong University in Bangladesh, was honored for starting a private commercial bank (Grameen Bank) that has helped over 2 million people climb out of poverty in Bangladesh. Establishing peace through commerce and microcredit is a new solution to eliminating severe poverty, one of the world's most persistent challenges, and the Nobel committee recognized the connection between commerce and peace. (See Chapter 21 for the extraordinary story of Muhammad Yunus and his role in reducing extreme poverty in the world.)

When British economist John Maynard Keynes wrote his optimistic essay "Economic Possibilities for our Grandchildren," in 1930, at the beginning of the Great Depression, he hoped economists would come down from their ivory towers and become useful, competent people "on the level with dentists." Many economists have indeed become useful practitioners, but Keynes did not realize how far-reaching and influential the new frontiers of economics would expand. He had no idea that, for example, beyond his lifetime, economists would be telling investors to reduce their risk and maximize their returns by diversifying into a variety of stock index funds, that government officials could save millions by changing the way they auction off their debt, that religious fanaticism and strife could be curtailed through free competition among a large number of rival faiths, that legislators could reduce crime by authorizing concealed weapon permits, that they could clean up the environment by auctioning off pollution permits, or that murder-mystery novelists could solve their crimes by using elementary economic principles!

From the Dismal Science . . .

Welcome to the new world of economic imperialism. During the twentieth century it was popular to label economics the "dismal science," a term of derision coined by English critic Thomas Carlyle in the 1850s. Carlyle lashed out against the classical economists who predicted poverty, crisis, and the iron law of subsistence wages. Even a century later, in the 1970s, when global economies suffered from a combined bout of rising inflation and rising unemployment, economists were criticized for having a terrible record of forecasting interest rates, inflation, or the next recession. In accepting his Nobel Prize in Economics in 1974, Friedrich Hayek reflected the somber mood of most economists when he confessed, "We have indeed at the moment little cause for pride: as a profession we have made a mess of things."[2]

During the early 1990s, economists went through a period of narcissistic self-incrimination. For example, during the 1991–1992 recession, Harvard professor Robert J. Barro had this to say about the economy: "Why is the economy weaker than expected? How will the economy do over the next year? What should the government do to help? As a first approximation, the right answers to questions like these are: 'I don't know,' 'I don't know,' and 'nothing.' "[3] Not to be outdone, Herbert Stein, a former chairman of the Council of Economic Advisors, admitted, "I am more and more impressed by my ignorance. . . . I don't know whether increasing the budget deficit stimulates or depresses the national income. I don't know whether it is M2 or M1 that controls the level of spending. I don't know how much a 10 percent increase in the top rate of individual income tax will raise the revenue. . . . I do not know how to pick winning stocks."[4] A year later, Princeton professor Paul Krugman, who won the coveted John Bates Clark Medal (given bi-annually to the brightest economist under the age of 40), asserted that economists "don't know how to make a poor country rich, or bring back the magic of economic growth when it seems to have gone away. . . . Nobody really knows why the U.S. economy could generate 3 percent annual productivity growth before 1973 and only 1 percent afterward; nobody really knows why Japan surged from defeat to global economic power after World War II, while Britain slid slowly into third-rate status."[5] And this quote comes from a man whom *The Economist* has called "the most celebrated economist of his generation."

. . . To a New Imperial Science

Fortunately, this professional self-defeatism has been reversed in the past decade. The twenty-first century has given way to a more optimistic can-do attitude. Economics, no longer dismal, has come a long way toward reinventing itself and expanding into new territories so rapidly that another phrase is needed to describe this new golden age of discovery. Like an invading army, the science of Adam Smith is overrunning the whole of social science—law, finance, politics, history, sociology, environmentalism, religion, and even sports. Therefore, twenty-first-century economics might appropriately be dubbed the "imperial science."

Who started this trend? Some historians point to Kenneth E. Boulding, long-time professor at the University of Colorado in Boulder, who died in 1993, as the father of interdisciplinary science. Boulding published over 1,000 articles on more than two dozen eclectic subjects, ranging from capital theory to Quakerism. But Boulding's vision of interdependence between disciplines isn't exactly what has happened. Instead, economics has started to dominate the other professions. In my judgment, much of the credit for this new imperialism should go to Gary Becker, the Chicago economist who appropriately holds positions in the departments of sociology, business, and economics. Becker, who won the Nobel Prize in 1992, was one of the first economists to branch into what were traditionally considered topics in sociology, including racial discrimination, crime, family organization, and drug addiction. He is cited repeatedly in this book.

This introduction will give you a taste of what economists have been doing to solve the world's numerous problems and advance the standards of living everywhere. Happily, you will see that the contributions of economists in this new age are relatively nonpartisan. Solutions to real issues are coming from both sides of the political spectrum, from neoclassicists, Chicago school market economists, and Keynesians alike. Reflecting this nonpartisanship, Jeremy Siegel, one of the financial economists highlighted in this book, dedicated his bestseller, *Stocks for the Long Run,* to both Milton Friedman and Paul Samuelson, economists who represent two extremes of the political spectrum. Siegel's approach symbolizes the healthy cooperative advances economists are making today.

In this next section, I outline the basic tools that economists are using to transform how we live. These tools of analysis can be used to explain phenomena of ordinary business life, such as why restaurants charge a higher price at dinner for the very same meal at lunchtime. But that is not the purpose of this book. Many books, such as Steven Levitt's *Freakonomics,* have already been written to explain unconventional and everyday economic phenomena. But this book is different; it is especially geared toward introducing ways economists are solving the world's problems, both individually and as a nation—in transportation, economic growth, environment, crime, health care, retirement plans, terrorism, and even how to achieve happiness. In many cases, these economists have gone beyond writing abstract academic papers and books; they are applying their theories in the real world by running businesses, consulting companies, and taking positions in government.

Not all economists are engaged in practical advice. In fact, I would guess that only a minority of economists are attracted to applied economics. The majority of academicians, especially in the graduate schools and Ph.D. programs at major universities, focus largely on highly abstract mathematical modeling, divorced from real-world problems. Economists refer to this abstract thinking as the Ricardian vice, named after the nineteenth-century economist David Ricardo who developed unreal and oversimplified models without testing them against factual evidence. In my judgment, it took economics down the wrong road. French economist J.-B. Say referred to Ricardo and other abstract thinkers as "idle dreamers, whose theories at best only gratify literary curiosity [and are] wholly inapplicable in practice."[6] After surveying the graduate programs at six Ivy League schools, Arjo Klamer and David Colander concluded that "economic research was becoming separated from the real world."[7] Fortunately, this disconnection is gradually disappearing, as you will see in this book. Many departments in economics and business are establishing problem-solving research centers, such as the new Applied Economics Workshop at Chicago's Graduate School of Business. Economists are becoming more empirical than ever before.

Seven Power Tools of Economics

In writing about economics over the past decades, I've been amazed by the powerful and diverse ways in which economic analysis can influence the worlds of finance, business, law, religion, politics, history, and the other social sciences. Economics can change people's and nations' lives, for better or for worse, depending on how closely they adhere to or violate basic principles. Economic policy can change the course of history.

What are these basic concepts? Below are seven essential principles that, when applied to a wide variety of problems, can transform the world.

1. **Accountability:** Economics is all about accountability. In a market economy, those who benefit from the fruits of labor ought to pay for them. The user-pay concept encourages discipline, industry, thrift, and other virtues. If someone else pays, the user doesn't pay much attention to the cost. When consumers don't pay for the products they use, the results are high costs, waste, and fraud. Ownership rights, therefore, are essential to accountability. Nobody spends someone else's money as carefully as he spends his own. What belongs to you, you tend to take care of; what belongs to someone else, or to no one, tends to fall into disrepair or is overused. As William Graham Sumner states, "A fool is wiser in his own house than a sage is in another man's house." This principle applies at home, in the workplace, and in the halls of government.

2. **Economizing and cost-benefit analysis:** In a world of scarcity and choice, one must economize. The most successful households, businesses, and governments are those that invest for a better tomorrow, live within their means, and avoid excessive debt. Thrift is a virtue. Competition and the profit motive are the best systems ever devised to keep costs low and avoid losses. Measuring costs and benefits helps determine the best, most efficient use of resources.

3. **Saving and investment:** Saving and investment are critical elements in achieving long-term success in business and life in general. As a sign posted outside one business states, "You can't do today's work with yesterday's machines if you expect to be in business tomorrow." It's time to discourage the consumer-society mentality of excessive debt, overspending, and waste, and to encourage thrift and the productive use of investment resources.

4. **Incentives**. Incentives matter. The law of the downward sloping demand curve demonstrates that if you encourage something, you get more of it; if you discourage something, you get less of it. The profit motive promotes economic growth by creating better products at cheaper prices. A freely competitive price system is also the best solution to an economic crisis. Shortages are eliminated more quickly

because higher prices discourage consumption and encourage the expansion of new supplies naturally, without government interference. Taxes can also have a significant impact on incentives. As Calvin Coolidge stated, "You can't increase prosperity by taxing success."

5. **Competition and choice:** Economic freedom leads to choice and opportunity—the freedom to move, obtain a better education, compete in a new business, find a new job, hire and fire, and buy and sell. The best way to achieve prosperity is to produce what people want. In Latin the phrase is *do ut des,* "I give in order that you should give." The fastest way to earn more is to produce more of what the customer wants, as a worker or as a business entrepreneur.

   On the other hand, monopoly leads to higher prices and less service. Competition levels the playing field—it leads to lower prices and even the principle of "one price," that is, everyone paying the same low price for a product, no matter what your financial or social status (known as the principle of nondiscrimination). The secret to ending poverty is equal opportunity, not state-mandated equality of wealth or income. Free people are not equal in wealth or income, and equal people are not free. As Winston Churchill once said, "The inherent vice of capitalism is the unequal sharing of blessings; the inherent virtue of socialism is the equal sharing of miseries."

6. **Entrepreneurship and innovation:** Success for individuals as well as for nations depends on entrepreneurial skills and strategies that often go contrary to the conventional wisdom. Where will technological advances originate from? Joseph Schumpeter wisely contends that "economic progress, in capitalist society, means turmoil," the "creative destruction" of the marketplace—and it is the entrepreneur who performs this essential function in search of excessive profits. Society must embrace change, sometimes dramatic change that comes with innovation and entrepreneurial skills.

7. **Welfare:** The welfare principle states that you should try to help those who need help. This is the virtuous principle of all good religions, and good economists. Nobel laureate Muhammad Yunus put this into practice through his Grameen Bank loans. But they were not handouts. We must not forget the other side of the welfare principle: Officials have an obligation *not* to help those who don't need help. To help the independent is to destroy their initiative. This policy

applies to households, churches, and government programs. If a government institutes a welfare program for everyone, irrespective of their financial condition, it opens the community up to slothful behavior, and costly and inefficient operations on a massive scale. Imagine if everyone in a parish, rich or poor, were eligible for church assistance. A government program that concentrates on helping the needy demonstrates a caring society, but one that offers benefits to everyone for free or at a very low cost discourages self-discipline and makes things worse.

The principles of accountability, economy, competition, incentives, investment, opportunity, and welfare apply to all peoples and all nations. As Leonard E. Read, founder of the Foundation of Economic Education (FEE), stated, "Let everyone do what they please as long as it's peaceful." The role of government in every nation is to keep the peace and to defend everyone's right to life, liberty, and property. Good government enforces contracts, prevents injustice, provides a stable monetary and fiscal system, and encourages good relations with its neighbors. Benjamin Franklin correctly observed, "No nation has ever been ruined by trade." Moreover, a sound economy cannot be founded on an unsound monetary system. Keynes rightly stated, "There is no subtler, no surer way of overturning the existing basis of society than to debauch the currency." Sound policy also requires that government officials consider the economics of legislation on all people in the long run, and not just in the short run. Frederic Bastiat observed, "Countries which enjoy the highest level of peace, happiness and prosperity are the ones where the law least interferes with private affairs." And the great Chinese philosopher Lao-Tzu wisely noted, "Governing a large country is like frying a small fish. You spoil it by too much poking." In the following chapters, I demonstrate repeatedly the virtue of these seven great principles. They constitute the power of economic thinking. The future belongs to sound economics.

Economists' Powerful Methods

Economists have developed powerful tools of investigation that have led to many discoveries. Their toolbox includes empirical work, data mining, simulations, experiments, institutional incentives, and the use of statistical methods to test the validity of theories. Empiricism and econometric work are relatively new phenomena that have gradually changed the profession, especially with the availability of cheap computer power for calculations of complicated mathematical models. There has always been a lively debate about the best tools for achieving new knowledge and building better policies. Should economists engage in the abstract methods of pure deductive reasoning and high theory, or should they engage in concrete testing of hypotheses and the mining of data? Those who have chosen the latter have made, in my judgment, the most significant contributions.

The new field of behavioral economics has also created valuable tools, largely borrowed from the principles of psychology, to achieve the goals of individuals and society. This is one of the few examples where economics has borrowed from another social science, rather than the other way around. As we shall see in Part I, the results have been impressive.

By focusing on solving many of the world's problems, applied economists are being recognized as never before. Let's look at some historical examples of the triumph of economics.

Can Investors Beat the Market?

One of the first breakthroughs in applied economics came in finance theory. Harry Markowitz, a graduate economics student at the University of Chicago, wrote an article on portfolio theory in the March 1952 issue of *The Journal of Finance*. It was the first attempt to quantify the economic concept of risk in stock and portfolio selection. Out of this work came modern portfolio theory, which advances three principles: (1) investors cannot expect to achieve above-average profits without taking higher risks; (2) diversification will increase returns and reduce risk; and (3) the markets are relatively efficient, that is, short-term changes in stock prices are virtually unpredictable, and it is extremely difficult if not impossible to beat the market averages over the long run. This view, known as the Efficient Market Theory, was a revolutionary but now accepted doctrine among academics, although as we shall see in the first part of this book, behavioral economists are finding ways to improve on these initial findings and have discovered a few ways to beat the market—for now anyway.

These ivory tower ideas were greeted with scorn by Wall Street professional managers, but numerous studies by financial economists since Markowitz's initial paper have confirmed modern portfolio theory. Stock market index funds, the economists' favorite way to profit from the efficient market theory, are now the largest type of mutual fund sold on Wall Street.

Public Choice Theory:
New and Improved Government

James Buchanan and Gordon Tullock, both at the University of Virginia, published *The Calculus of Consent* in 1962 and forever changed how political scientists view public finance and democracy. Today public-choice theory has been added to the curriculum of every economics class.

Buchanan and other public-choice theorists contend that politicians, like businesspeople, are motivated by self-interest. They seek to maximize their influence and set policies in order to be reelected. Unfortunately, the incentives and discipline of the marketplace are often missing in government. Voters have little incentive to control the excesses of legislators, who in turn are more responsive to powerful interest groups. As a result, government subsidizes vested interests of commerce while it imposes costly, wasteful regulations and taxes on the general public.

The public-choice school has changed the debate from "market failure" to "government failure." Buchanan and others have recommended a series of constitutional rules to require the misguided public sector to act more responsibly by protecting minority rights, returning power to local governments, imposing term limits, and requiring supermajorities to raise taxes.

Economics Enters the Courtroom

In 1972 Richard A. Posner, an economist who teaches at the University of Chicago Law School and serves on the U.S. Seventh Circuit of Appeals (chief judge 1993–2000), wrote *Economic Analysis of Law,* which synthesized the ideas of Ronald Coase, Gary Becker, F. A. Hayek, and other great economists at the University of Chicago. Today centers of "law and economics" are found on many campuses. Judge Posner states, "Every field of law, every legal institution, every practice or custom of lawyers, judges, and legislators, present or past—even ancient—is grist for the economic analyst's mill."[8]

Economists apply the principles of cost-benefit and welfare analysis to all kinds of legal issues—antitrust, labor, discrimination, environment, commercial regulations, punishments, and awards. In Chapter 15, I discuss the work of several economists on the relationship between crime and punishment, the efficacy of capital punishment, and whether concealed weapon permit laws and gun ownership deter crime. Economists are frequently called on to testify in court cases, a lucrative new source of income.

Chicago's Gary Becker has been in the forefront of applying price theory to contemporary social problems, such as education, marriage and divorce, race discrimination, charity, and drug abuse. Not surprisingly, he calls his book for the general public *The Economics of Life*. But Becker warned, "This work was not well received by most economists," and the attacks from his critics were "sometimes very nasty."[9] Now, decades later, Becker's work is being imitated everywhere by those who seek ways to solve social problems.

The Outline of *EconoPower*

Economists have made significant improvements in other disciplines—in accounting, history, religion, management, public infrastructure, sociology, and even auction design. This book offers dozens of examples of how these tools are being applied to solve problems for individuals, communities, and the nation.

Part One deals with personal financial matters, probably the most useful information on a personal level. I begin this section highlighting the breakthrough contributions of the behavioral economists (Richard Thaler, Robert Shiller, Jeremy Siegel, David Swensen, and Brigitte Madrian) to improve people's finances—increasing savings, reducing debt, and getting a better return on investments. I also tell the story of Chile's privatization of its public pension system, and whether the United States and other nations should adopt radical reform of their social security programs. This part also includes a review of "happiness" economics, a fascinating new area of economic research.

Part Two reports on the influence of economists on business management and the accounting profession, especially the introduction of "economic value added" (EVA), the economist's new tool of measuring investment value and company performance. I also tell the story of Koch Industries, the world's largest private company, and how the creative genius of Charles Koch and other libertarian CEOs has been influenced profoundly by "Austrian" economists like Ludwig von Mises, Friedrich Hayek, and Joseph Schumpeter.

Part Three reveals exciting discoveries by economists to solve domestic problems, such as road congestion, health care, public education, crime, and other issues high on the public list. I also reveal the remarkable ways in which economists have designed auctions for Google, eBay, and government agencies that have benefited both buyers and sellers. On the lighter side, I discuss three mystery novels where economists have helped to solve the crime.

Absent from Part Three is a chapter on the drug war. I intended to write on this controversial subject, which has attracted the attention of economists for several decades, particularly Milton Friedman, Gary Becker, Steve Levitt, and other members of the Chicago school. Most economists studying the debate fall on the side of decriminalization. Admittedly, there has been some progress in drug policy, including legalization of medical marijuana in some states, a reduction in teenage arrests for illicit drug use, and more flexibility in mandatory sentences for drug crimes. But economists have apparently had little to do with these changes. I asked Jeffrey A. Miron, a professor of economics at Harvard University who specializes in drug issues and author of *Drug War Crimes* (Independent Institute, 2004), whether economists have had any influence in the drug war. His answer: "Not so far." Perhaps a future edition of *EconoPower* will include a chapter on drug policy.

Part Four looks at how economists are working successfully on international issues—extreme poverty, inequality, pollution, global warming, population growth, globalization, military conflict, and religious wars. I also update you on the new flat tax revolution that is spreading in Europe and elsewhere. One of the most intriguing new fields of study is the economic freedom indexes being developed and refined by various think tanks, and how they relate to economic growth, legal institutions, trade and tax policy, and efforts to achieve peace in politically unstable areas. Finally, I take a look at the relatively new field of religion and economics, with some surprising results about religion and competition.

Part Five highlights new ways to forecast the future. Economists are famous for making bad predictions, but that's changing, as demonstrated by recent accurate forecasts by behavioral economists Jeremy Siegel at the Wharton School and Robert Shiller at Yale on the stock market and real estate. I also include chapters on the increasing importance of gold as a single indicator of global instability and inflation, whether another Great Depression is possible, and whether consumer spending is really a good leading indicator (my own contribution). My final chapter looks toward the future and what kind of new dynamic economic philosophy will dominate the new millennium. If the chapters in this book are any indication, the future for economics and economists looks bright.

Readers will note that I have not spent much time in this book on traditional areas where economists have had an impact on public policy, such as international trade agreements, price indexes, monetary and fiscal policy, and anti-trust. Instead, I have tried to focus on new and supprising fields where economists have made a difference.

Part One

PERSONAL FINANCE

EARNING, SAVING, INVESTING, AND RETIRING

The new behavioral economists have made exciting advances in the area of personal finance, discovering how to improve people's ability to earn, save, invest, retire, budget, and get out of debt.

I start this important section with a simple but powerful plan that has the potential of tripling workers' savings rates. It's already become law (the 2006 Pension Protection Act), due to the ingenuity of Chicago economist Richard Thaler, who is a leader in the new field of behavioral economics.

We also look at radical new proposals to improve Social Security and other welfare plans. These huge social programs have provided a safety net for retirees and the poor, but they have a serious downside. For most Americans, Social Security does not deliver the goods at retirement. It is a lousy and inflexible savings program and a heavy tax on low-income workers and minorities. Many economists characterize public retirement plans as defective and counterproductive, and favor replacing them with some form of personal investment accounts similar to those offered to federal employees (the thrift accounts) or the personal savings accounts that Chilean citizens now enjoy. In this section, I tell the story of a Chilean labor economist, José Piñera, who has made a major difference in his own country and the rest of the world.

Interestingly, major corporations faced the same problem facing Social Security today—the unfunded liability problem. Fortunately, business has largely solved its pension problem by switching from defined-benefit plans to defined-contribution plans, such as 401(k)s or IRAs.

Chapter 1

Economist Discovers a Painless Way to Triple Your Savings Rate

The $90 Billion Opportunity

I come bearing good news. By incorporating simple lessons of psychology, and a little common sense about human nature, it is actually quite easy to help Americans save.

—RICHARD H. THALER
UNIVERSITY OF CHICAGO[1]

This is the most important contribution in human welfare in the last five years.

—ROBERT SHILLER
YALE UNIVERSITY

In 1999, a study by two British economists, Wynne Godley and Bill Martin, warned that the United States was headed for serious trouble. They point to three unsustainable imbalances: an overvalued stock market, the collapse in private saving, and an alarming increase in debt.[2]

In 2000–2001, the booming U.S. economy suddenly fell into recession, America was struck by Islamic extremists, and the robust stock market began a long descent that took blue chip stocks down 30 percent and technology stocks down more than 70 percent. The Federal Reserve stepped in to prop up the economy by slashing interest rates and expanding the money supply, and the economy and the markets recovered.

Yet serious problems remain. Most economists and political leaders recognize that easy money cannot solve long-standing issues, such as the saving crisis. Saving, investing, and capital formation are the principal ingredients of economic growth. Recent studies by the World Bank conclude that countries with the highest growth rates (most recently in Asia) are those that encourage saving and investing: that is, investing in new production processes, education, technology, and labor-saving devices. Such investing in turn results in better consumer products at lower prices.[3] Harvard's Greg Mankiw concludes, "Higher saving leads to faster growth."[4]

The United States Is Living on Borrowed Time

That's why America faces a potential crisis. Private net saving in the United States has hit alarmingly low levels. Given this positive relationship between saving and economic performance, what are we to make of the gradual decline in private net saving in the United States? The latest data indicates that private net saving—the gap between disposable income and spending—has fallen to record lows as a percentage of GDP for most industrial countries. (See Figure 1.1.)

What is the primary cause of the gradual decline in private savings in the United States and elsewhere? Many economists note that private savings figures don't include appreciation from real estate and stocks owned by Americans, and thus the saving crisis has been postponed by higher prices in real estate and stock market holdings. But with the recent collapse of the credit markets in real estate and a shaky stock market, a financial crisis may appear around the corner.

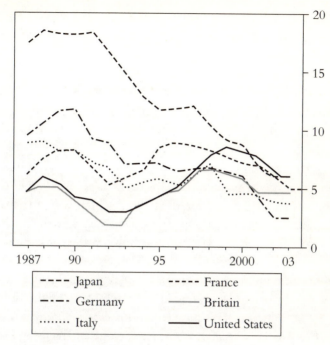

Figure 1.1   Decline of Savings Rate in the United States and Other Countries: 1987–2003

Other economists contend that Social Security and income taxes discourage saving. With FICA taxes squeezing more than 15 percent of all Americans' wages and salaries off the top, the government's mandatory welfare system makes it difficult for most Americans to make ends meet. Social Security taxes especially hurt the poor who are deprived of the necessary funds to buy a home or start a business. (See Chapters 5 through 8 for radical solutions to the Social Security crisis.)

Of course, millions of Americans continue to save for retirement, investment, and other reasons, but lately the debtors have outnumbered the savers. Who makes up for the imbalance? Foreign investors (as reflected in the growing current-account deficit) are pouring billions into U.S. debt and equity securities, bank accounts, and real estate. As long as foreign investors make up the difference, America will survive and prosper. But what happens when they stop?

Behavioral Economics Enter the Workplace . . . with a Little Help from Washington

To head off a potential financial savings crisis, in 2006 President George W. Bush signed into law the Pension Protection Act. A major part of this law known as "autosave" encourages companies to sign up employees for 401(k) plans automatically. For the first time, employers will automatically enroll workers in their 401(k) plans. Workers can choose not to participate, but they must specifically request exemption. This is the opposite of what was the norm in employee benefits. In the past, workers had to sign up for their 401(k) plans to participate, and, on average, only a third did. Before, no action was the same as choosing "no." Now, no action is the same as choosing "yes." Consequently, even procrastinators will be invested in a 401(k)!

In addition, there is a mechanism to increase gradually the amount saved, and employers are encouraged to match some of the dollars that workers invest each year. This new rule is known as "contribution escalation." When workers receive a pay raise, some of that wage or salary increase will automatically go into their 401(k) investment plan.

This small change in the law will have a big impact. According to *Business Week,* "the new rules could bring investment managers an extra $90 billion in retirement assets."[5]

The Economist behind the SMART Plan

Who's behind this new law? These two new pension ideas are the brainchild of Brigitte Madrian, professor of public policy at Harvard University, and Richard Thaler, professor of economics at the University of Chicago Graduate School of Business and a leader in the hot new field called "behavior economics." Madrian earned her Ph.D. in economics at MIT in 1993, and Thaler earned his Ph.D. from the University of Rochester in 1974 and considers himself a maverick from the standard rational approach to economics. He is also the founder of an asset management firm.

Consider the titles of two recent books by behavioral economists on the subject: *Irrational Exuberance* by Robert Shiller of Yale University (who correctly warned investors that the bull market on Wall Street in 2000 was not sustainable) and *Why Smart People Make Big Money Mistakes* by Gary Belsky and Thomas Gilovich.

To understand behavioral economics, consider the following four questions:

1. Are you constantly surprised by the size of your credit card bill?
2. Do you live in fear that you haven't saved enough for retirement?
3. Do you often find yourself buying stocks at the top and selling at the bottom?
4. Have you failed to update your will?

If you answered "yes" to any of these questions, join the crowd. Most of your fellow citizens are in the same boat. Two-thirds of Americans think they are saving too little. Fortunately, help is on the way, at least for two of the problems listed above: overspending and not saving enough for retirement.

Essentially, the behavioral economists take issue with a fundamental principle of economics—the concept of rational predictable behavior. They argue that investors, consumers, and businesspeople don't always act according to the "rational economic man" standard of the textbooks, but instead suffer from overconfidence, overreaction, fear, greed, herding instincts, and other "animal spirits," to use John Maynard Keynes's term.[6]

Their basic thesis is that people make mistakes all the time. Too many individuals overspend and get into trouble with credit; they don't save enough for retirement; they buy stocks at the top and sell at the bottom; they fail to prepare a will. Economic failure, stupidity, and incompetence are common to human nature. Robert Shiller observes that "a pervasive human tendency towards overconfidence" causes investors "to express overly strong opinions and rush to summary judgments."[7] As Ludwig von Mises noted, "To make mistakes in pursuing one's ends is a widespread human weakness."[8]

Fortunately, the market has a built-in mechanism to minimize mistakes and entrepreneurial error. The market penalizes mistakes and rewards correct behavior. As Israel Kirzner states, "Pure profit opportunities exist whenever error occurs."[9]

But the new behavioral economists go beyond the standard market approach. They argue that new institutional measures borrowed from the principles of psychology can be introduced to minimize error and misjudgments, without involving the government. The Pension Protection Act helps those who make the mistake of saving too little of their income. The government persuades without force.

At the American Economic Association meetings in Atlanta in January 2002, Richard Thaler of the University of Chicago presented a paper on his "SMART" savings plan, a systematic way to increase dramatically and painlessly the savings rate of American workers. "By incorporating simple lessons of psychology, and a little common sense about human nature, it is actually easy to help Americans save," he told Congress in 2004. His findings were reported in an academic article in a 2004 issue of the *Journal of Political Economy*. Thaler, author of *The Winner's Curse* and a pioneer in behavioral economics, has developed a new institutional method to increase workers' savings rates.

Thaler noted that the average workers' savings rates are painfully low. Many blame the low rate on high withholding taxes for Social Security and Medicare and a national proconsumer, antisaving mentality. But Thaler suggested that part of the problem is the way retirement programs are administered. Most corporations treat 401(k) plans as a voluntary program, and, as a result, only a third of their employees choose to sign up. He convinced five corporations in the Chicago area to adopt his SMART plan and have their employees enroll in an "automatic" investment 401(k) plan.

Thaler's plan, developed with his collaborator Shlomo Benartzi of UCLA, is threefold: (1) employees are automatically invested in 401(k) plans unless they choose to opt out; (2) they commit to increasing their savings in the future, although most refused to commit to increasing their savings immediately; and (3) employees agree to automatically invest a portion of any pay increase in higher contributions to their 401(k) plans, without reducing their take-home pay.

From Reluctant to Enthusiastic Savers

Here were the results: Instead of 33 percent signing up (as they do in a typical corporate investment plan), 86 percent participated in 401(k) plans. In just 14 months from the time the SMART plan was instituted, the participants increased their savings rate from 3.5 percent to 9.4 percent, and after two more years they were saving 13.6 percent of their salary. Their savings rates nearly quadrupled! And this was from a group that had been reluctant savers.

Thaler's SMART plan is simple, but effective. Having authored several investment books advocating "automatic investing" and dollar-cost-averaging plans,[10] I applaud Professor Thaler (and Professor Madrian) for taking the concept of automatic investing to a new level. It works on three levels to achieve high levels of saving over time: (1) it encourages high saving rates; (2) the saving rates tend to increase automatically over time; (3) savings are invested on a tax-free basis. Retirement plans are ideal for growth because the funds stay invested over the long run.

If companies everywhere adopted this plan, it could indeed revolutionize the world and lead not only to a much more secure retirement for workers but to a higher saving and investment rate. The result could be a higher economic growth and standard of living throughout the world. With the encouragement of the 2006 Pension Protection Act, we could already be benefiting with higher economic growth, especially if the new savings are invested in the stock market. The idea appeals to both the public and private sector. Government agencies have adopted this automatic growth thrift plan, which is increasing the saving and investment rates of thousands of public workers. Vanguard, the country's largest mutual fund company, is offering the idea to their employer customers.

Most important, automatic enrollment is a private-sector initiative that does not require government intervention. In short, through innovative management techniques and education, individuals can solve their own financial and business problems without the help of the state. A new generation of economists is indeed changing the world.

Where Will You Invest Your 401(k)?

If you save regularly and automatically, you will have a lot of savings to invest. How best to invest those funds? How can you make good profits on your retirement funds without taking undue risks? That's the subject of the next chapter.

Chapter 2

Modern
Portfolio Theory

Can You Beat the Market?

*A blindfolded monkey throwing darts at a newspaper's financial pages
could select a portfolio that would do just as well as one carefully selected
by the experts.*

—Burton Malkiel
A Random Walk Down Wall Street (1973)

The next three chapters will show you how sound economic
principles can help you improve your investment skills. As you
will see, academic economists have been skeptical of promises
by stockbrokers, money managers, mutual funds, and financial newsletter writers that you can get rich quick in the stock market. But they also
offer some excellent solutions.

25

We begin by discussing what economists call the "efficient market theory" of investing.

There was a time when Wall Street analysts and money managers hated economists. In the 1960s, ivory-tower academic professors had the gall to come to Wall Street and denounce the value of stock market analysis. Known as "efficient market theorists" and "random-walkers," these academic economists boldly declared that expensive, painstaking security analysis and active money management were "useless," maybe even worse than useless, because individual stock pickers are likely to underperform a broad-based portfolio of stocks that are bought and held for the long term. Some economists even claimed that a monkey could do a better job of stock selection.

The academic economist who started this monkey business was Eugene Fama, an American economist who earned his MBA and Ph.D. in economics and finance from the Graduate School of Business at the University of Chicago. He continues to teach at Chicago. His Ph.D. thesis, which concluded that stock prices are unpredictable and random, was published as "The Behavior of Stock Market Prices" in the *entire* January 1965 issue of the *Journal of Business*.

Fama's thesis has become known as the "efficient market hypothesis" and is not unlike the "perfect competition model" in microeconomics. Unbridled competition and entrepreneurship make it difficult to beat the market, he says. Burton G. Malkiel, a professor of economics at Princeton, popularized the efficient market theory in his 1973 work called *A Random Walk Down Wall Street,* which has now gone through nine editions. Malkiel sums up the efficient market, or random walk, theory as follows:

"Short-run changes in stock prices cannot be predicted. Investment advisory services, earnings predictions, and complicated chart patterns are useless. . . . Taken to its logical extreme, it means that a blind-folded monkey throwing darts at a newspaper's financial pages could select a portfolio that would do just as well as one carefully selected by the experts."[1]

The efficient market proponents were labeled "random walkers" because of their belief that short-term movements in the stock market appeared unpredictable and random, like a drunken sailor meandering down Wall Street, and that security analysts and fund managers are not likely to beat the market.

Taking a cue from Malkiel's book, editors of the *Wall Street Journal* engaged in a contest every six months between the editors who picked stocks by throwing darts at the NASDAQ stock listings and professional analysts who carefully selected their favorite stocks based on fundamental or technical analysis. The contest lasted for 14 years, from 1988 until 2002. Interestingly, the pros won most of the contests, with an average return of 10.2 percent for the experts and 3.5 percent for the dart throwers.

However, Malkiel argued that the contest was rigged. "There's a publicity effect," he said, explaining that, by advertising the stocks that the experts picked, the *Journal* influenced the market. "Because the *Journal* talks about the experts' picks and the experts describe why they picked certain stocks, the stocks get publicity boost," Malkiel said. He added that, when he recalculated the returns from experts' stocks using the value from the day before the article was released instead of the day of, the experts do not fare any better than the dart throwers.

Economists Create a Modern Portfolio Theory

There are a number of reasons why traditional Wall Street is rigged against the average investor. Malkiel and others point to the transaction costs of actively managed portfolios: commissions, performance fees, bid-ask spreads, and taxes, for example. It also becomes extremely difficult to overperform all the other thousands of security analysts who are trying to find undervalued investments.

If you are not likely to beat the market, what do Fama, Malkiel, and other efficient marketers propose? Should you avoid stocks entirely and just concentrate on bank savings accounts and CDs? On the contrary. They came up with an ingenious, simple solution: Be a passive investor in the market. Buy a large portfolio of individual stocks, or a stock index fund, and hold for the long run, taking dips and bear markets in stride. As simplistic as it may seem, such a strategy has been highly profitable during the past 50 years, with the S&P 500 Index returning approximately 12 percent compounded annualized return (including dividends).

In the beginning on Wall Street, the efficient market theories of academia created a furor. Highly paid security analysts and fund managers felt that their careers were threatened by evidence that they were underperforming the market averages. Nevertheless, it's hard to contradict the evidence. Economists have conducted numerous studies that confirm Malkiel's claim. (See Figure 2.1 below for a study made by *The Economist* in the 1990s.) Few professional investors or mutual funds have been able to achieve returns comparable to the S&P 500.

Eventually, however, Wall Street joined the efficient market theorists by creating stock market index funds. John C. Boyle created the first index fund at Vanguard group of funds in Valley Forge, Pennsylvania, in 1976, and the Vanguard 500 Index Fund (symbol, VFINX) is now the largest stock market index fund in the world, with $72 billion in assets. Today there are thousands of index funds of every stripe imaginable.

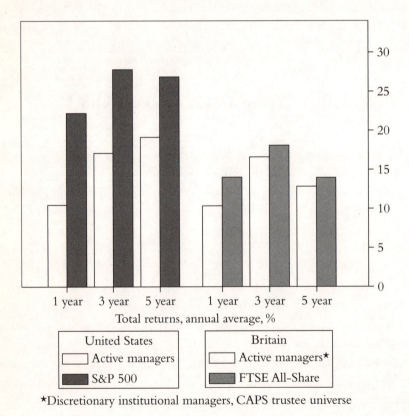

Figure 2.1   Index Funds Tend to Outperform Money Managers
SOURCE: *The Economist* (May 29, 1999). Reprinted by permission.

Who Can Beat the Averages?

Despite the above caveats, active money managers and mutual funds still try to beat the indexes, and a few have been successful, including Warren Buffett, Peter Lynch, Michael Price, and Value Line. Warren Buffett's closed-end investment company, Berkshire Hathaway, is without question the most successful fund to outperform the indexes over the long haul. Berkshire Hathaway (symbol BRK.A) traded for $20 a share in the early 1970s and today is selling for over $100,000 a share (no stock splits or dividends). The Omaha billionaire has been a sharp critic of the efficient-market theory. Prior to creating the Berkshire Hathaway company, Buffett was involved with his mentor, Benjamin Graham, the father of fundamental analysis, in a partnership that engaged in arbitrage techniques. He states:

> The continuous 63-year arbitrage experience of Graham-Newman Corp., Buffett Partnership, and Berkshire illustrates just how foolish EMT is. While at Graham-Newman, I made a study of its earnings from arbitrage during the entire 1926–1956 life-span of the company. Unleveraged returns averaged 20% a year. Starting in 1956, I applied Ben Graham's arbitrage principles, first at Buffett Partnership and then Berkshire. Though I've not made an exact calculation, I have done enough work to know that the 1956–1988 returns averaged well over 20%. Over the 63 years, the general market delivered just under a 10% annual return, including dividends. That means $1,000 would have grown to $405,000 if all income had been reinvested. A 20% rate of return, however, would have produced $97 million. That strikes us as a statistically-significant differential that might, conceivably, arouse one's curiosity.[2]

Buffett concludes, "Observing correctly that the market was frequently efficient, they [the efficient market theorists] went on to conclude incorrectly that it was always efficient."

There are other historical examples of individuals or strategies that have beaten the markets. Some floor traders on the New York Stock Exchange have consistently outperformed their peers. *Fortune's* 100 Best Companies to Work For have beat the averages. And some futures and options traders have knocked the socks off their competition. In his book, *Market Wizards,* Jack Schwager tells the story of a commodity trader who turned $30,000 into $80 million; a former securities analyst who during seven years had a realized average annual monthly return of 25 percent (over 1,350 percent annualized), primarily from trading stock index futures; and an MIT electrical engineering graduate who earned 250,000 percent return over a 16-year period.[3] Schwager tells similar amazing stories of superior investors in the stock market.[4]

In response, traditional economists argue that (a) only a minority of investors have consistently beaten the market, and (b) strategies that outperform can never last because, as they become more popular, the strategy will stop working. As an example, the Dogs of the Dow strategy was a popular vehicle to beat the market in the 1990s. In 1991, Michael O'Higgins and John Downs wrote *Beating the Dow,* outlining the Dogs of the Dow strategy: Buy the 10 Dow stocks with the highest dividend yield. This mechanical technique proved successful for several years, but became so popular in the late 1990s that it failed to best the Dow averages into the 2000s.

Is there a beat-the-market strategy that the new generation of economists recommend? That's the subject of our next chapter.

Chapter 3

Yes, You Can Beat the Market . . . with Less Risk

Dividends are the critical factor giving the edge to most winning stocks in the long run.

—JEREMY SIEGEL
THE FUTURE FOR INVESTORS (2005)

F inancial economists have made it easier for investors to maximize returns while minimizing losses. The efficient market hypothesis and its suggested strategy, investing in a broad-based index fund, have great merit. But the question remains: Is there a way to beat the market with less risk?

Economists continue to search for this alchemy of finance. One economist who has made a possible breakthrough is Jeremy Siegel, professor of finance at the Wharton School at the University of Pennsylvania. Siegel earned his Ph.D. in economics from MIT in 1971, and taught macroeconomics and finance at the University of Chicago from 1972 to 1976. His two mentor economists are Paul Samuelson (MIT) and Milton Friedman (Chicago). He is most famous for his book, *Stocks for the Long Run,* but his most recent book, *The Future for Investors* (2005), presents a significant discovery. In his studies, he uncovered what he calls "The Growth Trap." Professor Siegel and his staff engaged in a massive research project: dissecting the entire history of the Standard & Poor's famous S&P 500 Index since its inception in 1957. He wanted to test the established theory that the addition of new vibrant companies to replace older, slower performing companies is the secret to the S&P 500 Index's strong long-term track record.

Efficient market theorists contend that investors will do well if they just buy and hold a basket of stocks. That's what the Dow Jones Industrial Average and the S&P 500 do, right? Well, not quite. Actually, stock indexes are constantly changing. Public companies must meet specific requirements in order to be included in an index, and stocks that no longer qualify are occasionally being delisted or replaced by other stocks that qualify. As a result, the S&P 500 and other indexes are not really a constant, unchanging list of stocks. The S&P 500 is constantly being updated and tinkered with, based on Standard and Poor's criteria for market value, earnings, and liquidity. By definition, the companies added are performing substantially better than the ones being deleted. The walk isn't so random after all. Interestingly, in 2000, at the peak of the technology bubble, 49 new firms were added to the index; in 2003, near the bottom of the bear market, S&P added only eight new firms. These annual changes transformed the composition of the index from largely industrial stocks to largely financial and technology companies. It's all part of the creative destruction process of capitalism.

Siegel's project was a mammoth undertaking that required tracing the complex corporate histories of hundreds of successive firms that were acquired or distributed over several decades. He then compared the performance of two portfolios over nearly a 50-year period: the

"Survivors" portfolio, consisting of all the original S&P 500 stocks, and the "Total Descendants" portfolio, consisting of companies that have been added over the years. He came to a startling conclusion, reported in his book, *The Future for Investors:* "The returns on the original firms in the S&P 500 beat the returns on the standard, continually updated S&P 500 Index and did so with lower risk. . . . The shares of the original S&P 500 firms have, on average, outperformed the nearly 1,000 new firms that have been added to the index over the subsequent half century."

How is this possible? According to Siegel, the reason is clear: Standard & Poor's waits too long before adding these new growth companies to this index. Investors had already bid up the price of these bold, new companies to an excessively high level, and by the time they were added to the S&P 500, investors were paying too much. Standard & Poor's reflected this expensive habit in their S&P 500 Index.

Admittedly, Standard & Poor's was correct in noting that the new candidates for the index had better earnings, sales, and market values than the older firms. But they fell into the "growth trap" of adding too late the bold and the new to their index.

By the same token, the S&P waited too long to cut the losers from the list. By the time the companies were finally eliminated from the index, they were ready for a turnaround. After being cut from the index, these stocks usually started to rally. They tended to recover and return to their true value. This is an example of what statisticians call "recession to the mean." Undervalued stocks will eventually make a comeback, just as overvalued stocks eventually fall back down to their intrinsic value. Siegel discovered that the S&P tends to chase the stock price rather than anticipate it.

Peter Lynch warns that the growth trap is fairly universal. Individuals and institutions alike suffer from it. In his book, *One Up on Wall Street,* he notes that institutions wait to "buy Wal-Mart when there's an outlet in every large population center in America, fifty analysts following the company, and the chairman of Wal-Mart is featured in *People* magazine as an eccentric billionaire who drives a pickup truck to work. By then the stock sells for $40." Lynch was buying Wal-Mart when it was $4. He points out that most institutional buyers are restricted from buying small growth companies because the market capitalization is below their minimum. But once the price of the stock doubles or triples, the market capitalization is sufficiently high to qualify for purchase. "This results in a strange phenomenon: Large funds are allowed to buy shares in small companies only when the shares are no bargain."

IBM ("Big Blue") versus Exxon ("Big Oil")

Professor Siegel creates an example of the growth trap by comparing the total returns over a 53-year period (1950–2003) of the technology giant International Business Machines (symbol, IBM, known as "Big Blue") with Standard Oil of New Jersey (now Exxon/Mobil, symbol XOM, known as "Big Oil"). He calls it a classic case of the new versus the old. By every growth matrix used by security analysts, IBM beat out Standard Oil in terms of earnings, sales, cash flow, book value, and so on. Over a 53-year period, Big Blue's earnings per year—the key indicator of long-term growth—outperformed Big Oil's earnings growth by more than three percentage points per year. During this time, technology as a sector grew much faster than the energy complex.

The results, however, are shocking. While IBM beat out Standard Oil in terms of internal company statistics, Standard Oil returned a better profit for investors. Assuming reinvestment of all dividends, $1,000 invested in IBM would be worth $961,000 at the end of this 53-year period, while $1,000 invested in Standard Oil (Exxon) would have reached $1,260,000—31 percent more. This return assumes reinvestment of all dividends, a key factor.

Why did this happen? Because investors consistently paid too much for IBM stock and underpaid for Standard Oil. Investors made the fundamental mistake of pushing IBM's price up excessively in relation to true value, and neglecting Standard Oil's relatively low price to value.

It all goes back to price-earnings ratios, a key to sound investing. P/E is defined as the price of the stock divided by the earnings per share. Investors tend to bid up the price of fast-growing new economy stocks, so that growth stocks have high P/E ratios. Siegel's study demonstrates a behavioral weakness: Investors consistently make the mistake of chasing the high P/E stocks, while avoiding the low P/E stocks. Inevitably, regression to the mean takes place. High P/E stocks like IBM eventually come back down to earth, despite their high earnings, and low P/E stocks like Standard Oil climb up to their true value. This is why *Forbes* columnist and investment manager David Dreman contends that the best contrarian approach to making money is to buy companies with low price-earnings ratios.

Beware of Technology Stocks

In many ways, the growth trap is a paradox. The new economy stocks are providing economic growth in the global economy, yet they continually disappoint investors. For the few high profile winners, like Microsoft or Dell, there are hundreds of losers. And even the winners are usually overpriced. "Our fixation on growth is a snare," warns Professor Siegel. "The most innovative companies are rarely the best place for investors," because investors constantly overpay for the privilege of owning shares in the bold and the new. Siegel warns in particular against buying any stocks with P/E ratios exceeding 100, which inevitably fall out of favor. In contrast, investors typically neglect the familiar older companies that are selling at low multiples and offering bargain opportunities.

Jeremy Siegel's study found few technology or telecommunications stocks in any lists of the top 20 performers over a decade or more. Interestingly, Peter Lynch came to the same conclusion as Siegel. In his bestseller *Beating the Street,* Lynch wrote: "Finally, I note with no particular surprise that my most consistent losers were the technology stocks."

Siegel's Positive Strategy

Siegel suggests a strategy that can overcome the growth trap and beat the market with lower risk. The technique can be found in Siegel's comparison between IBM and Standard Oil. We noted that despite IBM's better growth data year after year, old-fashioned Standard Oil earned a higher total return than the new-economy stock IBM. What made the difference?

Dividends! IBM's market price was simply too high to overcome the gains earned from the hefty dividends Standard Oil/Exxon paid out over the years. "Standard Oil's high dividend yield made a huge difference in boosting its return," declares Professor Siegel. Despite lower sales and earnings than IBM, Standard Oil's regular dividend checks, if reinvested, made the difference in outperforming the giant tech company. Studies show that 97 percent of stock appreciation comes from dividends.

While IBM was constantly pushed from its relative value by overzealous investors who would impatiently push its price up to above-average levels, Standard Oil stayed true to its nature and provided steady profits to its shareholders.

Growing evidence indicates that companies that pay regular dividends show better long-term growth and lower risk patterns than non-dividend-paying growth companies. Because they tend to be large and mid-market cap stocks that have been around for many years, dividend stocks are not normally subject to the extreme valuations that apply to new growth and technology companies. They stay married to their true values.

Dividend Weight versus Market Capitalization

You don't have to sacrifice profits to invest in dividend stocks. Recent academic studies find that stock indexes linked to dividends tend to outperform market cap index funds. *Smart Money* recently reported, "Independent research appears to back the fundamental indexers. Constructing portfolios based on earnings, dividends, sales or book value going back five, ten and twenty years across markets in the U.S., U.K., Europe, Southeast Asia and Japan, a London research firm, Style Research, concluded that fundamental indexing outperformed cap weighted index funds an average 2–2.5% a year."[1]

Jeremy Siegel's work indicates that dividend-weighted index funds beat market cap indexes by 300 basis points each year.[2] That's a huge difference. See Figure 3.1 that shows the difference in total returns over a 44-year period.

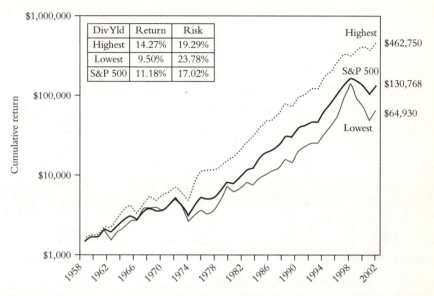

Div Yld	Return	Risk
Highest	14.27%	19.29%
Lowest	9.50%	23.78%
S&P 500	11.18%	17.02%

Figure 3.1   Long-Run Returns of Dividend-Weighted vs. Market-Weighted Stock Indexes

Show Me the Money

Dividend stocks are an excellent investment strategy for investors for a number of reasons.

First, dividends don't lie. A cash dividend is the only real evidence that a company is doing its job, providing a useful product or service to its customers, working for the shareholder as well as company executives and its employees. Following the many corporate scandals and questionable accounting schemes and fictitious earnings reports, there's nothing like a check in the mail or cash deposit in your brokerage account to assure yourself that the company is doing something right. It's comforting to know that the company actually earned enough money to pay the shareholders. Cash dividends are not subject to revisions, like past earnings. Earnings are always suspicious, due to creative accounting. Revenues can be booked in one year or several years. Capital assets can be sold and the value listed as ordinary income. Liabilities can be written off as immediate expenditures, or spread out over time. But cash paid into your account is a sure thing, a litmus test of the company's true earnings. It's tangible evidence of the firm's profitability. Admittedly, there have been a few dividend scandals, but these are extremely rare. It's not a financial trick or Ponzi scheme. Dividends must be paid out of earnings. In the words of Geraldine Weiss's classic book title, *Dividends Don't Lie*.

Second, regular dividend payouts impose fiscal discipline on a company. It's similar to investors who have a mortgage on their home. Home owners are motivated to earn enough money to pay the monthly mortgage. Or as Patrick Dorsey, head of stock analysis at Morningstar, states, "A company that pays a dividend is like an investor who commits to a 401(k) or savings plan—because the money isn't in your pocket, it can't be wasted elsewhere."

Third, dividend stocks beat the market. As noted earlier, over the long run dividend-weighted indexes surpass market-weighted indexes by 300 basis points each year. A diversified portfolio of dividend stocks tends to outperform nondividend stocks. Studies support this finding in international markets as well.

In essence, dividends give investors the chance to buy stocks at attractive valuations. Seldom do you find a high-flying stock that has a large market capitalization and pays a healthy dividend.

Fourth, dividend stocks are less risky. Studies show that not only do dividend stocks outperform nondividend stocks, but they do so with less volatility. That's the nature of large cap stocks that pay regular dividends. By investing in these stable companies, you completely avoid the high risk ventures of aggressive growth stocks, such as the technology bubble that burst in the early 2000s. You avoid the Enrons or eToys of the future. At the same time, dividend stocks will rise in a bull market, though admittedly not as spectacularly as growth stocks. It is during bear markets that they shine. The dividend payout provides a cushion when growth stocks are crashing all around you; they are often a safe haven for speculators. That's not to say they won't decline; they often do decline with the rest of the market, and are not immune to the machinations of Federal Reserve policy and geopolitics. But they do tend to hold up better than the hot stocks of the recent past.

Figure 3.2, courtesy of Ned Davis Research, demonstrates that dividend-paying stocks outperform growth stocks with less volatility.

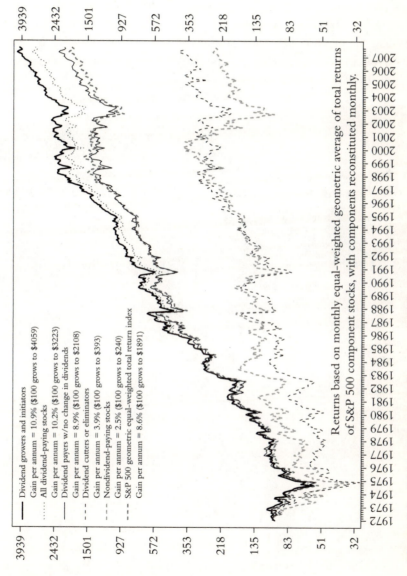

Figure 3.2 Dividend-Paying Stocks Outperform Growth Stocks
SOURCE: Ned David Research.

Legend (within figure):

Dividend growers and initiators
Gain per annum = 10.9% ($100 grows to $4059)
All dividend-paying stocks
Gain per annum = 10.2% ($100 grows to $3223)
Dividend payers w/no change in dividends
Gain per annum = 8.9% ($100 grows to $2108)
Dividend cutters or eliminators
Gain per annum = 3.9% ($100 grows to $393)
Nondividend-paying stocks
Gain per annum = 2.5% ($100 grows to $240)
S&P 500 geometric equal-weighted total return index
Gain per annum = 8.6% ($100 grows to $1891)

Returns based on monthly equal-weighted geometric average of total returns of S&P 500 component stocks, with components reconstituted monthly.

39

Recently Jeremy Siegel joined forces with legendary fund manager Michael Steinhardt to create the WisdomTree group of dividend-linked stock market funds. For information, go to www.wisdomtree.com. Two exchange-traded funds (ETFs) that invest in the top 100 dividend-paying stocks are: WisdomTree Dividend Top 100 Stock Index Fund (symbol DTN) and the WisdomTree International Dividend Top 100 Stock Index Fund (symbol DOO). Both have outperformed the S&P 500 Index since their inception in June 2006.

Chapter 4

High-Return Investing

Lessons from Yale's Endowment Fund

True diversification represents a contrarian alternative. High expected return asset classes of domestic equity, foreign developed equity, emerging market equity, and real estate . . . provide the free lunch of improved return and risk characteristics.

—David F. Swensen
Chief Investment Officer, Yale University

In 2001–2002, I was president of the Foundation for Economic Education in Irvington, New York. FEE had a grand history as one of the oldest educational foundations in the country, teaching students and adults about the basic principles of sound economics. When I came aboard, I also became responsible for an endowment fund worth a couple million dollars. Endowment funds are created by institutions such as FEE from individuals who make unusually large donations, often as legacies in a will. In a way, endowments are like rainy-day funds. They are highly desired by nonprofit organizations because the fund gives the organization a cushion to draw upon during lean times when fundraising efforts are slow. In addition, most nonprofit boards allow the organization to use a small percentage of the endowment fund to pay for current operations.

Endowment funds have the benefit of tax-free accumulation. Any interest, dividends, and capital gains earned in the endowment accumulate without federal and state taxation. These funds are typically invested in a very conservative manner. When I came aboard as president of FEE, I noted that 70 percent of the portfolio was invested mostly in government bonds, and 30 percent was invested in high-quality stocks. Endowment funds are cherished in the nonprofit world, and no one wants to see an endowment decline in value. I was told in no uncertain terms that, even though I had the power to manage the FEE endowment fund, I was not to alter this extremely conservative 70:30 ratio.

As a result, the FEE endowment fund has hardly kept up with inflation over the years. This is the main drawback to most endowment funds held by universities, foundations, corporations, churches, and think tanks. They are simply too conservative and tend to underperform the broader stock market indexes.

Along Comes the New Yale Model

Challenging this traditional view is David F. Swensen, who was hired as chief investment officer of Yale University's endowment fund in 1985. Under his leadership, Yale investments increased from $6 billion to $18 billion, returning an annualized profit of 17.2 percent over the past 10 years. That's two percentage points above the market averages, and well beyond more conservative endowment funds. Moreover, Yale's fund did not suffer a single down year during the difficult 2000–2003 bear market. Swensen is considered the Babe Ruth of endowment funds.

After earning his Ph.D. in economics under Nobel Prize winner James Tobin, Swensen worked for Lehman Brothers and Salomon

Brothers in Wall Street before returning to Yale to create the "Yale model" of multi-asset class investing. Swensen's market-beating investment approach employs the market principles of competition, incentives, entrepreneurship, and economy. And so far it has worked superbly.

What made the difference? First of all, Swensen was not impressed with the conventional approach to endowment investing: the conservative portfolio of investing in U.S. stocks (preferably large blue-chip companies) and U.S. bonds (preferably U.S. Treasuries). The mix varies—some endowments have more stocks than bonds, and others, like the FEE endowment, had more bonds than stocks. Either way, Swensen recognized that such a conservative portfolio is doomed to mediocre performance, below the market averages.

As an alternative, Swensen devised a program involving greater diversification into other asset classes, including foreign markets, natural resources, and alternative investments in hedge funds and private equity funds. In his book, *Unconventional Success,* Swensen outlines the following multi-asset class of an investment portfolio, consisting of six asset classes in the following sample:

Domestic stocks	30%
Foreign developed stocks	15%
Emerging market stocks	5%
Real estate and natural resources	20%
U.S. Treasury bonds	15%
U.S. Treasury Inflation-Protected Securities (TIPS)	15%

Note how vastly different this multi-asset portfolio is from the conventional corporate, university, or charitable endowment fund. Instead of 70 percent in bonds, Swensen reduced the bond component to 30 percent, half of that in TIPS. Instead of 30 percent in stocks, he increased his position in equities to 50 percent, with a large exposure in foreign markets. Swensen argues that such an unconventional asset fund can beat the market with less volatility if the assets inside the fund are "noncorrelated." By that, he means that the various assets move in different directions when market trends change. For example, if inflation rises, domestic stocks might decline, but real estate and natural resources—known as inflation hedges—might counterbalance stocks and keep the portfolio from declining significantly.

Even though the vast majority of you reading this book will not run an endowment fund, Swensen's approach can apply equally to your own self-managed 401(k), IRA, or other retirement program. You can achieve superior market returns by investing in multi-asset "noncorrected" investment areas along the lines Swensen has developed.

In *Unconventional Success,* Swensen makes three general recommendations:

1. Diversify into the six asset classes listed above.
2. Rebalance your portfolio to the original weightings of the six asset classes above on a regular basis (once or twice a year).
3. Emphasize low-cost index funds and indexed exchange traded funds (ETFs).

He is critical of actively managed mutual funds, which are not likely to beat the markets (as noted above) because of high fees, taxes, and the superiority of competitors. The Yale investor sets high standards: "Of the 9,000 or 10,000 mutual funds in the United States, a mere several dozen merit the consideration of thoughtful investors."[1]

"Eating Your Own Cooking"

Swensen contends that you can win at the active-management game, but it is extremely difficult. Where can you find a "small subset of truly talented investors" whose characteristics include "integrity, passion, stamina, intelligence, courage, and competitiveness" and whose interests are aligned with yours? Above all, he would like to see high levels of "co-investment," that is, investment managers who invest a large percentage of their own net worth in their own funds or managed accounts. "Many high-quality investment managers pride themselves in 'eating their own cooking.'"[2]

Most fund and money managers enjoy little co-investment. In fact, the vast majority of mutual funds contain precious little side-by-side investing. One of the unique features of the Yale investment fund is that its directors seek out specialized money managers who have "concentrated portfolios" in only a handful of stocks and often own out-of-favor positions. They compete against each other for Yale's investment accounts, and selected managers are dropped if they don't perform as well as their peers—another example of the "creative destruction" process in the new global economy.

Other Ivy League Schools Adopt Yale's Model

Swensen's unorthodox model has not gone unnoticed. Other elite schools such as Stanford and Harvard are following his lead. As a group, the top performing university endowments have gained approximately 15 percent during the past decade, easily surpassing the average pension plans and U.S. stock market indexes. Harvard University's endowment, managed under Mohamed El-Erian, is the world's biggest. Twenty years ago, approximately 80 percent of its portfolio was invested in domestic stocks and bonds. Today under El-Erian, it looks very different: 31 percent in foreign and domestic stocks; 35 percent in U.S. bonds and other fixed income; 17 percent in hedge funds; and a whopping 31 percent in hard assets including real estate, timber, and energy. By diversifying into foreign stocks, especially emerging markets, the Harvard endowment fund grew 23 percent to $35 billion last year, beating the S&P 500 Index by 3 percentage points. It benefited in particular from the emerging markets portfolio, which advanced 44 percent.

Beating the Market Is Highly Improbable, but Not Impossible

Swensen and his coinvestors have been able to achieve superior returns, but Yale, Harvard, and any other Ivy League schools have access to managers with better skills and knowledge than the average investor. In *Unconventional Success,* Swensen recommends that most investors are better off limiting themselves to stock market indexes. According to Jeremy Siegel and his firm WisdomTree, you can improve your returns with slightly lower risk by investing in dividend-linked stock indexes (see the previous chapter).

The extreme version of the efficient market theory denies the ability to find undervalued bargains in the financial markets, based on the belief that the markets are always efficient and information is available cost-free to the general public. But the fact is that information is not cost-free and is not always available to the public. Big money can be made in small, obscure stocks because of the public's lack of information. Insiders and floor specialists find out about companies before the public knows, and therefore can profit accordingly. Moreover, the general public is woefully ignorant of economic trends and therefore is incapable of acting profitably on events in the world economy. There are plenty of false theories that investors and analysts act on that result in financial loss, leaving the door open for shrewd individuals who understand current trends and gain accordingly.

The behavioral economists have done wonders in discovering ways to increase our savings and use our retirement funds more wisely. Can the same be done with the public retirement program—Social Security? In the next few chapters, I address that controversial issue, beginning with the remarkable success of pension reform in Chile. But can it be duplicated in the United States? Let's find out.

Chapter 5

How Chile Created a Worker-Capitalist Revolution

We are creating a worker-capitalist revolution through Social Security privatization.

—José Piñera
ARCHITECT OF CHILE'S PENSION SYSTEM

I n the 1950s, under the guidance of Theodore Schultz and Arnold C. Harberger, the University of Chicago began a scholarship program for students from the Catholic University of Chile. Dozens of Chilean economists sat at the feet of Milton Friedman, George Stigler, and other giants of the Chicago school to learn about the advantages of markets and democratic capitalism. Known as the "Chicago boys," they returned to Chile to implement a promarket approach to Latin American issues.

Out of small things come great rewards. This small program has led to a worldwide worker-capitalist revolution that would astonish Karl Marx. Because of the incredible success of tiny Chile's privatized retirement program, today over 30 countries have followed Chile's lead and converted their own style of social pension systems into genuine pro-growth personal retirement accounts. Major developed nations, including the United States, are now debating whether to adopt the Chilean pension model.

The primary architect of this worldwide revolution, José Piñera, was a student at Catholic University of Chile in the late 1960s. After graduating in 1970, Piñera did graduate work at Harvard University, where he received his M.A. and Ph.D. in economics. Piñera returned to Chile in 1975 as a professor at the Catholic University of Chile, and found himself in the midst of a political crisis. Chile had suffered a major economic disaster in the early 1970s under the first democratically elected Marxist, Salvador Allende. Allende's socialist policies of nationalization, high wages, and price controls created shortages, black markets, and runaway inflation. After a series of public protests, the military, led by General Augusto Pinochet, staged a coup d'état in September 1973. Allende committed suicide. When the global inflationary recession exacerbated the problems in Chile, General Pinochet called in Piñera and the Chicago Boys to reorganize the economy. They urged drastic cuts in government spending, denationalization, tax reform, expanded trade, and strict control of the money supply. Pinochet was favorably impressed by Piñera's economic reform plans that would, he promised, dramatically increase Chile's growth rate.

Piñera was appointed Minister of Labor and Social Security (1978–1980), and then Minister of Mining (1980–1981), in the Pinochet cabinet. He carried out four major reforms in Chile: the world's first privatized retirement system, a private health insurance program, the reestablishment of democratic trade unions, and a constitutional law establishing property rights in the mining industry. He also was a leading advocate for the new 1980 Constitution that established a bill of rights and a gradual transition path to a return to democracy.

Piñera is most famous for his radical reform of social security in Chile, a program that has been imitated around the world. Today Piñera is the president of the International Center for Pension Reform, and speaks and consults full-time around the world on this subject. He has personally met with most of the world's leaders to convince them to change their public pension programs.

How Does Chile's Private Pension System Work?

As Chile's labor secretary, Piñera recognized that the traditional pay-as-you-go retirement system was bankrupt. The Chicago Boys decided to go in a different direction, to link individual benefits to individual contributions (the accountability principle). Under the new scheme, funds invested by workers would go into individual accounts owned by the workers. Employees were required to contribute 10 percent of their wages, but could invest up to 20 percent voluntarily. As in other countries, contributions are tax deductible, and returns earned in the private accounts are untaxed until withdrawal at retirement. When workers reach retirement age, determined by the worker, as there is no set age for retirement in Chile, workers can transfer the value of their account into an annuity through an approved insurance company that pays them a fixed amount of income for the rest of their lives. Thus, the retiree who lives a long life does not have to worry about running out of money, but he has the advantage of directing his investments during his saving years.

Employees can manage their own retirement accounts by choosing among 20 mutual funds, which are managed by private investment companies known as AFPs (from the Spanish for pension fund administrators). They can choose among stocks, bonds, government debt, and most recently foreign stocks. They are free to change from one AFP to another. AFPs are highly regulated, and none have gone bankrupt. Workers are required to be well diversified and cannot have too heavy a position in one fund. "Our plan was to be radical (even revolutionary) in approach but conservative and prudent in execution," Piñera states. "We trust the private sector, but we are not naive. We knew that there were companies that might invest in derivatives and lose a lot of money. We didn't want the pension funds investing workers' money in derivatives in Singapore."[1]

How did the Chicago Boys come up with the idea of a competitive privately run pension system? Surprisingly, it was not Milton Friedman's idea. In his 1962 book, *Capitalism and Freedom,* he argued against Social Security on economic and ethical grounds, but did not offer an alternative.[2] According to Chicago professor Arnold Harberger, the idea of privatization originated from the teacher's annuity plans, known as TIAA-CREF, or Teachers Insurance and Annuities Association/College Retirement Equities Funds, at the University of Chicago, where the faculty was offered a choice of stock and bond funds. Chilean graduates and professors saw how well the teachers' annuities worked, and Piñera adopted the idea.[3]

There was a transition period to the new system. The Chilean government offered a minimum guarantee on every retired worker's pension. Workers already in the workforce who had contributed to the state system for many years were given the option of staying in the system. Those who moved to the new system received a recognition bond, which acknowledged their contributions to the old system. When those workers retired, the government cashed their bonds.

The privatized social security plan opened on May 1, 1981, which was Labor Day in Chile and most of the world. It was supposed to open May 4, but Piñera made a last-minute change to May 1. "When my colleagues asked why," he said, "I explained that May 1 had always been celebrated all over the world as a day of class confrontation, when workers fight employers as if their interests were completely divergent. But in a free-market economy, their interests are convergent. I told my colleagues, 'Let's begin this system on May 1, so that in the future, Labor Day can be celebrated as a day when workers freed themselves from the state and moved to a privately managed capitalization system.'"[4]

The Benefits of Following the Chilean Model

Chile was the first country in the world to privatize Social Security. The results have been astounding. Today 93 percent of the labor force is enrolled in 20 separate private pension funds. Annual real returns on pension investments averaged over 10 percent since 1981 (compare that to the average 1 percent in the U.S. Social Security system). Just as importantly, Chile's private pension plan deepened the nation's capital market and stimulated economic growth. Its domestic savings rate has climbed to 26 percent of gross domestic product, and the economic growth rate averaged over 5 percent annually from 1984 on. Today the total funds in Chile's private pension system exceed $120 billion, 80 percent of Chile's GDP.

In short, Chile provides a role model for successful privatization of the U.S. Social Security system. According to Piñera, converting the pay-as-you-go system into a genuine savings program would dramatically increase capital formation and economic growth in the United States even though it would admittedly involve serious transition problems much greater than those experienced in tiny Chile. Some economists still oppose privatizing Social Security, but most are willing to experiment with a small percentage of the FICA tax to see what happens. For example, President George W. Bush proposed that two percentage points be assigned to personal investment accounts, but so far the bill has not been adopted. A wide variety of media have endorsed the Chilean model, including *Time* magazine and *BusinessWeek*. According to *BusinessWeek* (cover story, "Economic Growth: A Proposal," July 6, 1996) converting Social Security into a fully funded pension plan, complete with individual savings accounts, could boost national savings and increase U.S. plant and equipment by 25 percent by 2020, and would dramatically increase the economic growth rate. The massive flow of funds into the equity markets would substantially reduce the cost of capital and encourage investment. The late MIT professor Rudi Dornbusch, no friend of supply-side economics, endorsed privatizing Social Security and education as two key sources of growth. According to Dornbusch, the resulting capital formation would support rising real wages and therefore offer a long-term answer to the eroding standard of living.[5] José Piñera thinks that the biggest boost to Social Security reform will come if China adopts private accounts. "Then the United States will have to act; otherwise, they will be left behind in rather dramatic fashion."

Now let's take a closer look at the U.S. Social Security system, and why some economists are urging radical surgery.

Chapter 6

The Call for Social Security Reform

There is a strong case for reducing the role of the government budget in providing health services beyond a minimum.

—Vito Tanzi and Ludger Schuknecht[1]

At a recent financial conference, I asked an audience of several hundred investors, "By a show of hands, how many of you receive food stamps?" Not a single hand went up. Then I asked, "How many of you receive Social Security or Medicare?" Half the audience raised their hands. (Most investors at financial conferences are over 65 years old.)

Then I asked, "How many of you will eventually receive Social Security and Medicare?" Every hand went up. Finally, I asked, "How many of you think you will enroll in the food stamp program during your lifetime?" Suddenly, every hand went down!

Table 6.1   U.S. Social Welfare Programs

Program	Total Coverage (in Millions)	Current Recipients (in Millions)	Total Annual Expenditures
Social Security	153.8	52.2	$491.5 billion
Medicare	157.5	40.0	$297.4 billion
Food Stamps	23.9	23.9	$27.0 billion

SOURCES: Social Security Adminstration; US Department of Agriculture; US Budget. Coverage data for Social Security and Medicare is for 2002. All other data is for 2004.

It was a dramatic moment, and I've thought about it many times. Every person in the room was either receiving Social Security and Medicare, or expected to do so in their lifetimes. Yet none of them thought they would ever sign up for food stamps.

Why not? The reality is that these wealthy investors don't qualify for food stamps. The food stamp program is a social welfare program limited to the very poor; there's a means test to qualify (currently around $25,000 for a family of four), and most Americans attending investment conferences don't need food stamps. On the other hand, Social Security and Medicare are universal social insurance plans. All people pay taxes for the programs, and at age 65 (sometimes earlier) they all collect benefits, even though most Americans can afford their own pension program and health insurance. Is there any wonder voters are more worried about Social Security and Medicare than they are about food stamps?

Table 6.1 shows the stark contrast between the food stamp program and Social Security and Medicare.

Why Not "Foodcare"?

Suppose the president of the United States proposed a new welfare program called "Foodcare." Since food is even more vital to each American citizen than health care or retirement money, he theoretically argued, the food stamp program should be expanded and universalized, like Social Security and Medicare, so that everyone qualified for food stamps and paid for the program through a special food stamp tax. Suppose Congress agreed and passed new welfare legislation. Thus, instead of 24 million Americans taking food stamps, suddenly 158 million or more would begin paying the food stamp tax and collecting food stamps, representing perhaps 10 percent of household budgets.

What effect do you think this universal Foodcare plan would have on the food industry? Would we not face unprecedented costs, red tape, abuse, and powerful vested interests demanding a better, more comprehensive Foodcare? And suppose snacks were not covered by Foodcare—wouldn't the general public start demanding that the government cover the cost of this new entitlement? Would they complain that the costs of snacks were rising too fast? In other words, once you go down this road, it's inevitable that government would become more and more involved in the food business. Ludwig von Mises was right: "Middle of the road policies lead to socialism."[2]

Fortunately, there is no nightmarish foodcare program. Granted, there have been abuses and waste in the food stamp program, but the problems of efficiency are few compared to, say, Medicare, which is notorious for costly fraud and waste. Interestingly, since 1995 the number of Americans on food stamps has declined from almost 27 million to under 24 million, while the costs have risen only slightly, from $22.8 billion to $27 billion. Yet have the cost and scope of Social Security or Medicare declined? Never.

Safety Net or Dragnet?

Our conclusion is clear. Government welfare systems—if they should exist at all—should be limited to helping those who really need assistance. They should be safety nets, not dragnets that capture everyone. It was a tragic mistake to create a Social Security and Medicare system where everyone at some point became a ward of the state. I'm convinced that if President Roosevelt had conceived Social Security in 1935 as a retirement plan for only the less fortunate who could not plan ahead financially, it would be a relatively inexpensive welfare program that would require taxpayers to pay at most 2 to 3 percent of their wages and salaries in FICA "contributions," not 12.4 percent as they do today. If President Johnson had proposed Medicaid in 1965 as simply a supplemental medical/hospital plan limited to the needy, today taxpayers would be paying 0.5 percent of their wages and salaries to medical welfare, not 2.9 percent as they do today. Instead, the systems were made universal, a clear violation of the welfare principle outlined in Chapter 1, and the duplication is horrendous—and unnecessary.

Because we all pay in and we all eventually benefit (until we die), we don't always think clearly about these entitlements. Example: A stockbroker recently told me about a client who called and complained bitterly about attempts by Congress to revamp Medicare. He angrily said, "They can cut spending all they want, but don't touch my Medicare!" While the stockbroker listened patiently to this man's tirades, he pulled up the client's account on his computer screen. The client had accounts worth over $1,000,000! If anyone could afford his own medical insurance plan, it was this man. He didn't need Medicare. Yet he saw Medicare as his right. He had paid into it all his life, and he deserved the benefits.

Imagine what this man would be saying about Congress and food prices if we had Foodcare.

Chapter 7

$4,000 a Month from Social Security?

*Social Security will remain nicely in balance for at least the next 20 years
... If it ain't broke, don't tinker.*

—Professor Robert Kuttner
Business Week, February 20, 1995

Robert Kuttner, a political commentator and former Harvard professor, is in a minority. According to most experts, Social Security is headed for trouble within the next 20 years. Money that should be escrowed in the Social Security Trust fund has been poorly managed. And because retirees are living longer, the fund is raided every year to pay current recipients' monthly Social Security checks. With insufficient buildup of reserves for future retirees, the system is likely to go broke sometime in the next 20 to 30 years.

Social Security works like this: It is funded through the FICA (Federal Insurance Contributions Act), a payroll tax paid equally by the employee (6.2 percent) and the employer (6.2 percent). Social Security is not a savings plan, however. It is known as a "defined benefit" system, where current receipts are used to pay current benefits. In each year since 1983, tax receipts and other income have exceeded benefits, and have been invested in the Social Security Trust Fund (now around $2.1 trillion). The accumulated surpluses are invested in U.S. Treasury securities. Since the surpluses are invested in U.S. Treasuries, it helps fund the federal deficit each year, and hides the actual level of deficits. Eligible workers are covered for retirement income and disability benefits; if a covered worker dies, his or her spouse and dependent children may receive survivors' benefits. But if an individual dies without a spouse or children under age 21, all Social Security checks stop—single or widowed individuals paying into the system all their lives will not receive a single penny of Social Security payments if they die before age 65.

Social Security faces tough times ahead. It is estimated that by 2018, Social Security will be paying more in benefits than it collects. We would need approximately $11 trillion in the bank today, earning interest, to pay all the program's estimated obligations. Economists have suggested several solutions: raise taxes, eliminate the salary cap, cut benefits, increase the national debt, cut other government programs, and implement personal retirement accounts (as discussed in Chapter 5).

Professor Robert Kuttner, the American Association of Retired Persons (AARP), and other apologists for the current Social Security system are opposed to any tinkering with the Social Security system. But the real issue is not whether the national pension program is solvent. It is not a question of whether to reduce Social Security payouts, defer retirements, assess a means test, or raise FICA taxes again. Congress has attempted all of the above, and the system is still fundamentally unsound.

The real problem is simple: Social Security is a lousy retirement program and, as a result, imposes a huge drag on the U.S. economy and every other nation with a similar plan. FICA taxes cut deep into the pockets of every worker and every business. Payroll taxes have increased 17 times, from 2 percent of wages up to a maximum of $60 in 1937, to 12.4 percent, up to a maximum $12,000 today. To cover future payouts beyond 2015, experts predict taxes will have to rise to 17 percent of gross income, further eroding a worker's ability to contribute to personal savings and investment accounts. When is this craziness going to stop?

The tragic irony of Social Security is that it is a forced savings plan that doesn't contribute one dime to real savings. That's because Social Security is a pay-as-you-go system. Contributions are immediately paid out in benefits. FICA taxes go either to (a) pay current Social Security retirees, who use the money to pay bills, or (b) the Social Security Trust Fund, which invests entirely in T-bills, in other words, government spending. In short, payroll taxes are consumed, not saved. As Professor Joseph Stiglitz states, "the Social Security program is a tax program, not a savings account."

Social Security versus Individual Retirement Accounts

Imagine what would happen if Social Security taxes were invested in Individual Retirement Accounts, so that wage earners could invest in stocks and bonds. In other words, what would be the effect if Social Security funds were invested in free-enterprise capitalism, that is, a stock index fund, rather than government transfer programs?

Such a study was made in 1995 by William G. Shipman, principal at State Street Global Advisors in Boston, Massachusetts.[1] He analyzed two workers, one earning half the national average wage (approximately $12,600 in 1995), and the other making the maximum covered earnings ($61,200). A low-income earner who retired in 1995 would receive $551 a month from Social Security. But if he had been allowed to invest his contributions in conservative U.S. stocks over his working years, he would be receiving an annuity of $1,300 a month for the rest of his life, almost three times his Social Security income.

A high-income earner would do even better. If he retired today, he would receive $1,200 a month from Social Security. Had he invested the money over the long run in stocks, he would be receiving an annuity of $4,000 a month. Now that's what I call retiring with dignity.

Furthermore, according to Shipman, if individuals born in 1970 were allowed to invest in stocks the amount they currently pay in Social

Security taxes, those individuals could receive nearly six times the benefits that they are scheduled to receive under Social Security, as much as $11,729 per month. Even a low-wage earner saving 12 percent of his income would receive nearly three times the return on Social Security. (This study assumed an historical return of approximately 10 percent on stock index funds.) In sum, he concludes that Social Security is a lousy retirement plan and a tragic waste of resources.

Even more outrageous, neither the low-income earner nor the high-income earner has true ownership of his Social Security benefits. True savings can be passed on to heirs, but if a person dies young, his preassigned "beneficiary" is the government. The Social Security system is touted as fair and equal, but how can it be considered fair if one worker receives payments for 30 years while another receives little or nothing because he dies young?

This year over $500 billion will be paid into Social Security. In addition, the Social Security Trust Fund, held for future payouts, is valued at $2.1 trillion and rising. Imagine if all that money had been invested in the capital markets. Imagine if the Social Security Trust Fund could be managed by Peter Lynch, Warren Buffett, or even an index fund.

Actually, the private sector faced a very similar problem to what Social Security faces today: billions in unfunded liabilities due to the fact that people are living long and their trust funds are being invested too conservatively. In the next chapter, we see how major private corporations solved this problem.

Chapter 8

How the Private Sector Solved Its Own Pension Crisis

Of all social institutions, business is the only one created for the express purpose of making and managing change. . . . Government is a poor manager.
—PETER F. DRUCKER[1]

I n the ongoing debate over privatizing Social Security, one story has been overlooked. The private business sector in the United States has already faced the pension fund problem and resolved it.

Here's what happened. After World War II, major U.S. companies added generous pension plans to their employee-benefit programs to save taxes. These "defined benefit" plans largely imitated the federal government's Social Security plan. Companies matched employees' contributions; the money was pooled into a large investment trust fund managed by company officials; and a monthly retirement income was projected for all employees when they retired at 65.

Management guru Peter F. Drucker was one of the first visionaries to recognize the impact of this unseen revolution, which he called "pension fund socialism" because this corporate Social Security look-alike was capturing a growing share of investment capital in the United States.[2] Drucker estimated that by the early 1990s, 50 percent of all stocks and bonds would be controlled by pension-fund administrators.

But Drucker (who doesn't miss much) failed to foresee a new revolution in corporate pensions—the rapid shift toward individualized defined contribution plans, especially 401(k) plans. Corporate executives recognized serious difficulties with their traditional defined benefit plans, the same problems Social Security faces today. Corporations confronted huge unfunded liabilities as retirees lived longer and managers invested too conservatively in government bonds and blue chip/old economy stocks. Newer employees were also angered when they changed jobs or were laid off and didn't have the required vested years to receive benefits from the company pension plan. Unlike Social Security, most corporate plans were not transferable. The Employment Retirement Income Security Act (ERISA), passed in 1974, imposed regulations on the industry in an attempt to protect pension rights, but the headaches, red tape, and lawsuits grew during an era of downsizing, job mobility, and longer life expectancies.

The New Solution: Individualized 401(k) Plans

The new corporate solution was a spinoff of another legislative invention—the Individual Retirement Account (IRA). The 401(k) rapidly became the business pension of choice, and there is no turning back. These defined contribution plans solve all the headaches faced by traditional corporate defined benefit plans. Under 401(k) plans, employees, not company officials, control their own investments by choosing among a variety of no-load mutual funds. Corporations no longer face unfunded liabilities because there is no guaranteed projected benefit. And workers and executives have complete mobility; they can move their 401(k) savings to a new employer or roll them over into an IRA.

According to recent U.S. Labor Department statistics, almost all the newest company pension systems are defined-contribution plans, not defined-benefit plans (see Figure 8.1). Almost all of the major Fortune 500 companies have switched to defined-contribution plans or hybrid "cash-balance" plans. Companies that still operate old plans include General Motors, Procter and Gamble, Delta Airlines, and the New York Times Company. IBM, a company that once guaranteed lifetime employment, switched to a cash-balance plan in the late 1990s, giving its 100,000 employees individual retirement accounts they can take with them in a lump sum if they leave the company before retirement. Meanwhile, long-time workers are still eligible for IBM's old defined-benefit plan. But virtually all "new economy" companies, such as Microsoft, AOL, and Home Depot, offer 401(k) plans only.

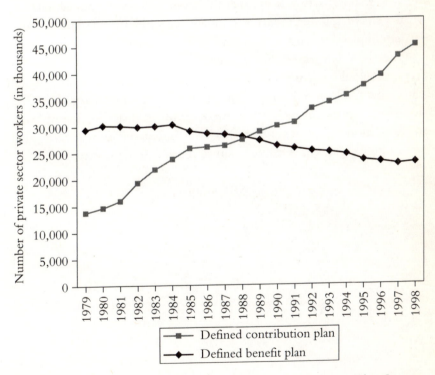

Figure 8.1 Defined Benefit Plans Decrease; Defined Contribution Plans Increase
http://www.epinet.org/Issueguides/retire/charts/dbdc_600.gif

Why Social Security Needs Reform

Congress could learn a great deal by studying the changes corporate America has made in pension-fund reform. In fact, Social Security is in a worse position than most corporate plans were. Since fewer than a fourth of all contributions go into the Social Security Trust Fund, the government program is more a pay-as-you-go system than a defined-benefit plan, where most of the funds remain in a corporate managed trust fund. As a result, the unfunded liability, or payroll-tax shortfall, exceed will $20 trillion over the next 75 years. To pay for so many current recipients, Congress has had to raise taxes repeatedly to a burdensome 12.4 percent of wages, and payroll taxes will need to be raised another 50 percent by the year 2015 to cover the growing shortfall.[3] Few corporate plans require such high contribution levels.

Moreover, the Social Security Trust Fund is poorly managed, so much so that experts indicate that the annual return on Social Security is 3.5 percent for single-earner couples and only 1.8 percent for two-earner couples and single taxpayers.[4]

Clearly, converting Social Security into personal investment accounts would not only be a step in the right direction, but in step with what Chile and 30 other nations are doing with their public pension plans. Unfortunately, government—unlike business—is not prone to innovation. As Drucker notes, "Government can gain greater girth and more weight, but it cannot gain strength or intelligence."[5]

Chapter 9

The Four Sources of Happiness

Is Money One of Them?

I'm tired of Love: I'm still more tired of Rhyme. But Money gives me pleasure all the time.

—HILAIRE BELLOC

I f we can better prepare for retirement by saving more and investing better, there is no doubt that Americans could look forward to their golden years. More money in retirement can be a good thing. But can money buy happiness? Economic research has drifted into some unusual corners. A growing subtopic for the new generation of economists is in the field known as "happiness economics." I came across a very interesting book called *Happiness and Economics: How the Economy and*

Institutions Affect Human Well-Being by economists Bruno S. Frey and Alois Stutzer. It's a technical book, with lots of graphs and mathematical regressions, but its purpose is not to measure tangible profits and losses but the more abstract sensation of happiness and well-being.

The authors' conclusions are pretty clear: "The general result seems to be that happiness and income are indeed positively-related."[1] In other words, money may not buy happiness directly, but it can provide many benefits, including greater opportunities, higher status in society, and the ability to travel and enjoy better food, housing, health care, and entertainment. Several studies indicate that wealthier people live longer. In short, money fulfills highly desirable wants.

I remember the day I discovered that I would be financially independent. It was a summer day in the late 1970s when I came home and presented my wife with over a dozen checks from a mail-order business I had started. Within a year, we had bought our first home, with 20 percent down, and by 1984, we had become successful enough that we could move our entire family (with four children) to the Bahamas to "retire." The experience of becoming financially secure gave Jo Ann and me an incredible feeling of satisfaction. Of course, we didn't really retire. We used our free time to read and write, go sailing, spend time with our children, and become involved in the local theater, a private school, and church work.[2] Eventually, we returned to the mainland, but continued our semi-retired status.

Why Most Poor People Are Unhappy

Figure 9.1 shows the relationship between income and happiness across nations. In general, people in poor countries are less satisfied than people in rich countries. One reason is that poor nations are often more subject to violence and uncertainty. As Frey and Stutzer state, "Countries with higher per capita incomes tend to have more stable democracies than poor countries have. . . . The higher the income, then the more secure human rights are, the better average health is, and the more equal the distribution of income is. Thus, human rights, health, and distributional equality may seemingly make happiness rise with income."[3]

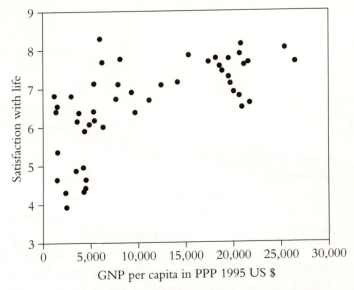

Figure 9.1   Relationship between Happiness and per Capita Income
SOURCE: Frey, Bruno S., *Happiness and Economics*. Reprinted by permission of Princeton University Press.

But the graph also indicates that money suffers from diminishing returns in happiness. Subjective well-being rises with income, but once beyond a certain threshold, income has little or no effect on happiness. Many wealthy people have experienced this law of diminishing returns and are not any more happy than middle-class people. In fact, some wealthy people are downright unhappy. Frey and Stutzer conclude, "Higher happiness with material things wears off."

Four Elements of Happiness

Years ago I read a sermon on the "Four Sources of Happiness." The minister spoke of work, recreation, love, and worship. What did he mean?

First, he said, you have to find rewarding and honest employment to be happy. Hard work and entrepreneurship offer the opportunity to create surplus wealth. Money in the bank gives you a real sense of security as well as freedom to do what you want to do. Moreover, studies show that unemployed people, believing they are not contributing to society or themselves, are generally unhappy.

Second, recreation is essential to your well-being. It helps to take a break from work from time to time. Relaxation and avocations are essential elements of a happy life. People who spend too much time at the office and can't relax with their family or friends at home need to learn the joy of recreation with a hobby, sports, travel, or other avocation. Some of my most memorable times have been playing softball or basketball with friends, traveling with family members on the weekend, or visiting a bookstore.

Third, love and friendship are also key elements of happiness. Everyone needs someone to confide in, to spend time with, to learn from, to reminisce with, to love and to be loved by. For most people, love and friendship take time and effort. You have to work at developing friendships, but the rewards are never-ending.

Finally, worship. According to the preacher, developing one's spiritual side is essential to happiness. Some of my friends say they don't need religion, but I think they are missing out on one of the joys of life—listening to a great sermon, singing hymns, meditating on the word of God, charitable work, and praying for God's help in solving business or family problems.

Let me conclude this essay with a delightful stanza by the Norwegian playwright Henrik Ibsen, who put the role of money in the proper perspective:

> Money may be the husk of many things, but not the kernel.
> It brings you food, but not appetite;
> Medicine, but not health;
> Acquaintances, but not friends;
> Servants, but not faithfulness;
> Days of pleasure, but not peace or happiness.

Part Two

ECONOMISTS ENTER THE CORPORATE BOARDROOM

C an economists contribute to the bottom line of corporate balance sheets? Absolutely. Economists have influenced corporations to adopt Economic Value Added (EVA) to measure the opportunity cost of capital; establish competitiveness within company divisions; encourage managers to motivate their employees with stock options, "decision rights," and other ownership strategies; and reduce waste and inefficiency in corporate retirement programs, health insurance, and other employee benefits. The next two chapters give details of how economists are changing corporate America.

Chapter 10

Improving the
Bottom Line with EVA

*Until a business returns a profit that is greater than its cost of capital, it
operates at a loss.*

—PETER F. DRUCKER

The English essayist (and economist) Walter Bagehot once
remarked, "No real Englishman in his secret soul was ever sorry
for the death of an economist."

Quite a few security analysts and fund managers on American
shores probably feel that way about the economists who came up with
the efficient market hypothesis and proved that 95 percent of profes-
sionals can't beat a blindfolded monkey in picking stocks. Highly paid
Wall Street analysts don't like being compared to sightless apes. Yet after
decades of heated exchange between Wall Street and academia, the

eggheads are winning the argument. Today index funds—the professors' favorite investment vehicle—are the fastest-growing sector on Wall Street, although as we noted in previous chapters, some economists have improved on the efficient market theory.

The latest group to sympathize with the words of Walter Bagehot are the accountants. Over the past decade, ivory-tower economists (mainly professors teaching modern finance theory at MBA schools) have taken on the accounting departments, damning them for not taking into account the full opportunity cost of capital, the amount the shareholders could earn simply by investing their money elsewhere.

Are Accounting Profits for Real?

For years, economists have complained that conventional accounting distorts the true economics of the firm by not including a charge for common stock values in its earnings reports and balance sheets. Generally accepted accounting principles treat stock equity as if it were free. Thus, publicly traded corporations release quarterly reports showing substantial earnings that in fact are losses. "True profits don't begin until corporations have covered a normal return on investment," declares Al Ehrbar, senior vice president of consultants Stern Stewart & Co., specialists in EVA—a new performance technique for business.[1]

What is EVA? It stands for "economic value added" (also called economic profit, or residual income). Essentially, EVA is a precise measurement of the opportunity cost of capital. For years, opportunity cost was a nebulous concept known only to professors. The term "opportunity cost," coined by Austrian economist Friedrich Wieser in the early twentieth century, refers to the universal principle that all human action involves giving up other opportunities. When you invest in a stock, lend money, or create a new product, you give up the opportunity to invest elsewhere. If you invest in a high-flying computer stock, you can't buy T-bills. If you build a new office building, your money is tied up for years in concrete and can't be invested in AT&T.

EVA is a practical application of classical economics and modern finance theory. The Austrians introduced the concept of opportunity cost, and Nobel laureates Merton H. Miller and Franco Modigliani applied it in their model of the firm to determine capital's real value. In the 1980s, G. Bennett Stewart III created EVA as a financial yardstick to measure opportunity costs in business.

EVA is fairly simple to determine: It is after-tax operating profits minus the appropriate capital charge for both debt and stock equity. If a company issues debt, the opportunity cost is linked to the Treasury rate (currently around 4 to 5 percent), plus the credit risk of the issuer. If the company issues stock, the opportunity cost is measured by the long-term annualized return on the stock market, approximately 10 to 12 percent. In short, EVA recognizes that investors must earn enough to compensate for the risk of their investment capital.

If a firm earns more than these opportunity costs, it has added value to its shareholders and created wealth in the world economy. Hence, the phrase "economic value added." If EVA is positive, shareholders and the economy are making real contributions to the bottom line. Otherwise, the business should shut down and invest shareholders' funds in Treasuries or an index fund. As British economist John Kay declares, "In the long run, firms that fail to add value in a competitive market will not survive, nor do they deserve to."[2]

Okay, so what good is EVA to corporate managers? EVA analysis helps evaluate potential acquisitions, expansion plans, and nonperforming assets, and assists to eliminate low-profit-margin operations that are clearly unprofitable when full costs are taken into account. EVA is also being used as an incentive system for managers and employees. Bonuses are linked to economic earnings, not just accounting earnings, and EVA has proven effective in boosting productivity.

EVA has made significant inroads into the business world. Already over 300 major corporations, including Coca-Cola, Eli Lilly, and Whole Foods Market, use EVA as a capital accountability tool to reinforce the idea that profits don't begin until corporations have covered their normal return. Wall Street analysts at Goldman Sachs and First Boston, among others, use EVA to evaluate stocks. According to Ehrbar, EVA predicts stock performance and market value better than any other accounting measure, including return on equity, cash flow, earnings per share, or sales. EVA makes company officers focus more clearly on creating shareholder value and a higher stock price. Stern Stewart, a firm that specializes in applying EVA, issues an annual EVA report on the top 1,000 U.S. corporations. For several years now, Intel has had the highest EVA ranking and GM the lowest.

EVA Wins the Battle

Accountants still have a dominant grip on the way corporate financial statements are submitted, but the success of EVA has forced them to take notice. All five accounting firms offer an EVA-type statistic to their clients. Most accounting textbooks now include a significant section on economic value added, economic profit, or residual income. Previous editions did not mention EVA or opportunity cost.

Want more? Check out Al Ehrbar's highly readable *EVA* or John Kay's brilliant *Why Firms Succeed*. See also www.eva.com.

I like EVA. Companies using it appear to perform better in creating wealth and shareholder value. But it may have potential drawbacks. EVA puts enormous pressure on company managers to overachieve and to create constant above-average profit centers. Imagine not earning a true profit unless your company or division beats last year's Dow Jones Industrial Average. It could be depressing. Wonder what your company's EVA will look like in the next recession? Heads could roll. Some managers may want to join Wall Street analysts and accountants in shooting those dismal scientists.

Chapter 11

How Ludwig von Mises Helped Create the World's Largest Private Company

As I learned introductory economic concepts, such as opportunity cost, subjective value, and comparative advantage, I instinctively began to apply them in our company.

—CHARLES KOCH, THE SCIENCE OF SUCCESS (2007)

The stone which the builders refused has become the chief cornerstone.

—PSALMS 118:22

Commenting on business leaders in *The Anti-Capitalist Mentality*, the Austrian economist Ludwig von Mises said bluntly, "There is little social intercourse between the successful businessmen and the nation's eminent authors, artists and scientists. Most of the 'socialites' are not interested in books and ideas."[1]

Mises would find an exception in Charles Koch, the 71-year-old CEO who transformed his father's oil and gas operation in Wichita, Kansas, into the world's largest private company, Koch Industries, by applying the big ideas of a select group of academic economists. His new book, *The Science of Success* (Wiley & Sons), quotes liberally from economists and social thinkers such as Adam Smith, Friedrich Hayek, Joseph Schumpeter, Albert Einstein, Daniel Boorstin, Michael Polanyi, and yes, a half dozen times from Ludwig von Mises's 900-page tome, *Human Action*. Ayn Rand would be proud of this modern-day John Galt.

John Maynard Keynes's dictum, "Practical men, who believe themselves to be quite exempt from any intellectual influences, are usually the slaves of some defunct economist,"[2] aptly applies to Charles Koch (pronounced coke). It takes a genius to transform arcane economic theory into a profitable enterprise, and Koch has done just that, using ivory-tower concepts of the Austrian school of economics to create a trademarked business style called "Market-Based Management."

Influence of the Austrian School

Why the Austrian school? I daresay that hardly any graduate from college or MBA school has heard of Mises, Hayek, and other members of this laissez-faire school of economics (except perhaps Joseph Schumpeter, famous for his "creative destruction" concept). The Austrians were railroaded out of academia during the Great Depression and are absent from most of today's textbooks (mine are an exception). Austrian economics, with its emphasis on disequilibrium, dynamic "creative destruction," heterogeneous capital, structural imbalances, and macro disaggregates, has found little place in today's world of Keynesian interventionism, monetary aggregates, and econometric model building.

Hence, business leaders who know about the Austrians are usually self-taught. Known as a voracious reader, Koch may well have discovered Mises and Hayek as a result of his engineering background (Koch earned three degrees in engineering at MIT), since the Austrian emphasis on the stages of production and dynamic "creative destruction" would appeal to engineers.

The Austrians are the rejected stone that has become Koch's chief centerpiece. Today thousands of Koch engineers and managers are being taught Mises and Hayek. Two years ago, Koch established the Market-Based Management Institute at Wichita State University (www.mbminstitute.org), where Austrian methodology is a central theme. Perhaps some day MBA students at Harvard and Stanford will be assigned Mises's *Human Action* or Hayek's *Individualism and the Economic Order.* There's nothing like a big success story to transform the B school's pedagogy.

And there's nothing bigger on the scene today than Koch Industries, which has transformed itself into a giant commodity and financial conglomerate. When Charles Koch became the chief executive of Rock Island Oil & Refining after the death of his father in 1967, the company was a moderately successful enterprise based in Wichita, Kansas. He renamed it Koch Industries in honor of his father—and over the next 40 years proceeded to transform Fred Koch's legacy into the world's largest private company through stupendous growth and active mergers and acquisitions. But Mr. Koch's rise hasn't come from simply investing in good companies (the Warren Buffett way); he runs them. Koch Industries produces such brands as Stainmaster, Lycra, and Dixie cups. With its acquisition three years ago of Georgia Pacific, Koch Industries now has 80,000 employees in 60 countries with $100 billion in revenues in 2007. In one generation, the book value of Koch Industries has increased over 2,000-fold. That's an 18 percent compounded annual return, comparable to the long-term track record of Warren Buffett's Berkshire Hathaway. Is the next paradigm shifting from Omaha to Wichita?

What's even more amazing is that he did it in the face of debilitating family and government lawsuits, numerous business failures, and mature industries not known for innovation or new technology like oil and gas, basic industrial commodities, textiles, and cattle. Many of his biggest gains have been in turnarounds.

So what is the secret to his firm's unprecedented growth in a non-growth market? Koch calls his technique Market-Based Management (MBM). For years, he and his colleagues have experimented with MBM as Koch Industries acquired new businesses (37) and exited others (42). Koch is famous for coming into new firms and increasing operating margins, cutting overhead, and introducing innovations that focus on five areas, what he calls vision, virtue and talents, knowledge processes, decision rights, and incentives. Concepts such as "vision" and "virtue" don't lend themselves easily to the precision suggested by the title of *The Science of Success.* But Mr. Koch approaches them with the analytic eye of an engineer. These key insights from Austrian economics have now invaded the MBA schools and business management courses. In Koch's MBM guidebook, the Austrian concept of opportunity cost of capital is now called "Economic Value Added (EVA)," property rights has become "decision rights," and Hayek's rules of just conduct translate into "principled entrepreneurship."

Charles Koch is perhaps the most successful businessman you've *never* heard of, even though his company is bigger in sales than Microsoft, Dell, and HP. That's because, unlike Microsoft or Berkshire Hathaway, Koch Industries is privately owned, a situation Koch prizes. He doesn't have to worry about Sarbanes-Oxley, quarterly earnings, or executive stock option compensations that distort the stock price. "Perverse incentives make managing a public company long term extremely difficult,"[3] he writes.

Teaching Market-Based Management at Columbia Business School

Of course, MBM didn't emerge like Athena, full grown and armed from the brow of Zeus. For years many businesses and business schools have developed ways to "create long-term value" by incorporating such MBM concepts as incentives, integrity, internal profit centers, local autonomy, economic value added, sunk costs, comparative advantage, and marginal price analysis. (See Jim Collins's book, *Good to Great,* for numerous case studies.) Clearly, Koch doesn't have a monopoly on these market concepts. But Koch is far ahead of the curve in his unrelenting systematic application of its principles, and his book is peppered with numerous real-world examples of his advanced formula. (In an appendix of his book, *The Science of Success,* Koch lists 89 aspects— "a partial list"—of MBM.)

He relates, for instance, how Koch Industries applied MBM to overhauling the Matador Cattle Co.'s Beaverhead Ranch in Montana.

An analysis identified the "key drivers of profitability"; they included costs, the weights of calves when they were weaned, and the weight, or "carrying capacity," of fully grown cattle. Eventually costs were reduced by 25 percent, Mr. Koch reports, weaning weights were raised 20 percent, and carrying capacity was increased by 8 percent. Not a bad upgrade. In revealing the story of Koch Industries, Charles gives credit to his brother David, whose leadership "has grown its process equipment and engineering business more than 500-fold."[4] Yet the boss still complains that his own company succeeds in practicing MBM only 50 percent of the time.

At Columbia Business School, John Whitney taught Market-Based Management for years, and I followed in his footsteps using Koch Industries, Whole Foods Market, and Agora Publishing as case studies. These companies are run by libertarian CEOs who apply economic strategies to create long-term value. Koch doesn't have a monopoly on these market concepts, but he has trademarked "MBM," and his MBM course books are peppered with numerous examples of successes and failures.

Is Koch's business indeed a science, as he contends in his book, *The Science of Success*? He goes to great lengths to prove that his MBM methodology can be universally and objectively applied. In his book, he reproduces a graph from the Heritage Foundation showing that national income per capita is directly correlated with economic freedom—countries that adopt free markets achieve higher economic growth. By the same token, Koch contends that applying MBM—the principles of a guided "invisible hand"—can save depressed companies and make profitable ones even more profitable.

Yet Koch's MBM techniques may face roadblocks. Can a long-term strategy work in a corporate world that focuses on quarterly earnings and CEOs who change every six to seven years? Can employees handle the competitive pressure? Will unions, companies, and governments embrace a deregulatory environment and slough off an entitlement mentality? The biggest challenge may be to convince the business world that MBM isn't mere ideology, but is a practical formula to create long-term wealth. My course at Columbia was rated highly by the MBA students, but an illiberal department chair refused to renew the course, calling it "too political." (At Columbia, can anything be "too political"?) Charles Koch is a political libertarian, and he is a major contributor to free-market foundations such as the Cato Institute and the Institute for Humane Studies at George Mason University. For many business schools, it's hard to separate science from politics.

Anti-Keynesian, Anti-State?

Koch is no Keynesian businessman. He is no fan of guaranteed lifetime employment, automatic pay raises, seniority, meaningless make-work projects, or the entitlement mentality that runs rampant in big business or heavily unionized companies. Most employees at Koch Industries are union members who must be flexible if they are going to survive. Koch aggressively searches for only "A" or "B" grade employees; those rated "C" either must improve or be let go. Koch Industries doesn't tolerate failure for long. I like his anti-Marxist slogan, "From each according to his ability, to each according to his contribution."

Though anti-statist to the core, Koch reveals in his book some things that will surprise libertarians. For example, most libertarians practice "minimum" compliance with state rules, but Koch teaches "maximum" compliance with environmental and other government regulations. In today's litigious society, it is suicide to act otherwise: Koch Industries faces 159,000 lawsuits and employs 125 full-time lawyers. At the same time, however, he is a fierce opponent of corporate welfare and trade subsidies.

Until now, Koch's Market-Based Management, Principled Entrepreneurship, and other trademarked management techniques were taught to company officials and employees, and there was always a shroud of mystery about his guiding principles. But now he has decided to share his economic applications to the world. If a company can follow Adam Smith's invisible hand doctrine of the "harmony of interests" by aligning the interests of its customers, workers, suppliers, and shareholders to create long-term value, the results can be explosive for both business and society. That's the powerful message of Charles Koch's business model. And I don't use the word *revolutionary* lightly. This new management strategy could revolutionize every corporation, government, and non-profit organization. But it's going to require strong medicine and a new entrepreneurial spirit. Can it happen? Mr. Koch is aided in this possibility by the fact that his company enjoys bigger sales than, oh, Microsoft.

Part Three

SOLVING
DOMESTIC PROBLEMS

E conomists often serve as consultants to government in solving domestic economic problems, such as taxes, spending, and the national debt. The next seven chapters demonstrate how the economics profession has spread its wings into new territories: health, education, transportation, crime, sports, auctions, and even literature.

Chapter 12

Look, Ma'am, No Traffic Jams!

Congestion is clogging the arteries of our cities . . . . HOT [High-Occupancy Toll] lanes and other pricing strategies hold the greatest promise of improving mobility of all Americans.

—ROBERT W. POOLE, JR., DIRECTOR OF TRANSPORTATION STUDIES, REASON FOUNDATION

The introduction of the London congestion charge is, in important respects, a triumph of economics.

—JOURNAL OF ECONOMIC PERSPECTIVES[1]

F reeways are supposed to be free, but often they can be expensive in terms of time, money, and stress. Inefficient use of roads and highways is also a major source of pollution and environmental misuse of scarce resources. Congestion is found everywhere these days, and it's getting worse. If there were a Freeway Hall of Shame, these interstate highways would make the list:

- The Los Angeles US-101 and I-405 Interchange, which results in more than 27 million hours of delay each year.
- Houston I-610 and I-10 Interchange, which costs more than 25 million hours of delay.
- Chicago I-90/94 and I-290 Interchange. Known as the Circle Interchange, it leads to 25 million hours of delay per year.
- Phoenix I-10 and SR-51 Interchange causes 22 million delay-hours annually.
- Los Angeles I-405 and I-10 Interchange. This San Diego Freeway interchange causes 22 million hours of annual delay.
- Washington I-495 beltway, which is in gridlock for hours in both morning and afternoon rush hour.

The Eisenhower Interstate Highway system, built largely in the 1960s and 1970s, has failed to keep pace with a tripling of the number of vehicles operating. Conservative estimates by the U.S. Department of Transportation say the United States loses $168 billion yearly from highway congestion. The nation's trucking system in 2004 lost 243,032,000 hours due to traffic delays, according to the Federal Highway Administration. Delays and traffic jams are also expensive for emergency and police vehicles in reaching their destinations on time. Lives are lost because of transportation gridlock.

Traffic delays are commonplace inside cities as well. Few signal-light systems work in an optimal manner at intersections. Road construction and repair are rated poor by citizens and engineers. In fact, an association of engineers recently graded our roadway system a "D" and our streets a "D−" for signal-light optimization to keep traffic flowing smoothly and safely.[2]

Table 12.1 demonstrates the growing problem of peak-hour congestion in the United States. In 1983, 30 percent of U.S. roadways were congested; in 2003, 67 percent were overcrowded.

Increasing mobility has many advantages and would make us more prosperous. Increasing average speed would reduce gas and car maintenance costs and make more productive use of our time. In sum, eliminating

Table 12.1 Urbanized Areas Experiencing Peak-Hour Congestion of 40 Hours or More per Traveler

1983	1993	2003
Los Angeles	Los Angeles	Los Angeles
Boston	Detroit	San Francisco-Oakland
Denver	San Francisco-Oakland	Washington, DC
New York	Seattle	Atlanta
Phoenix	San Jose	Houston
Seattle	Washington, DC	Dallas-Fort Worth
Tampa-St. Petersburg	Riverside (CA)	Chicago
Minneapolis-St. Paul	Dallas-Fort Worth	Detroit
Charlotte	Chicago	Riverside (CA)
Louisville	Phoenix	Orlando
	Tampa-St. Petersburg	San Jose
	Orlando	San Diego
		Miami
		Boston
		Austin
		Baltimore

SOURCE: 2005 Urban Mobility Report, Texas Transportation Institute.

congestion would make each one of us wealthier by several thousand dollars a year, and reduce pollution to boot.

Is there any solution to the annoying problem of congestion in our cities and highways? I work at home, so I don't have to worry too much about clogged streets and highways, or lengthy commutes. I suspect thousands choose to work at home for the same reason. Yet millions don't have that luxury and are forced to travel long distances to work. Roughly 3.4 million Americans endure three-hour commutes each working day. According to the Texas Transportation Institute, every year the average American spends 47 hours—more than an entire workweek—in congestion. Adding up the costs of time, gas, and wear and tear, Americans lose over $1,000 a year in gridlock.[3]

Why Isn't the Current System Working?

The standard solution—the government taxes consumers and then grants states the funds to build and maintain roads—is failing to keep up with increased traffic on our roads and highways, and does little to deal with gridlock. As cars have become more efficient (going more miles on a gallon of gas), the revenue from gas taxes (per gallon) has fallen relative to the need for more roads. Moreover, since the completion of the Interstate Highway System in the 1980s, the federal gas tax has been used increasingly to fund pork barrel projects.

But there's a more fundamental economic problem. The main drawback to the current highway use and funding system is that the road users aren't paying the true cost of using the freeways at peak hours. Here we need to apply consistently the principles of accountability and marginal pricing. The per-trip cost of getting on the freeway is always zero, unless there is a toll. Even then, the toll never varies with how crowded the freeway is. In short, the Interstate Highway System ignores the pricing mechanism. There is no effort to match supply and demand with a varying price. At zero price, rush hour means that demand exceeds supply, and there is a surplus of cars on the highway.

Solutions to Transportation Gridlock

Governments at all levels are attempting some solutions to the congestion problem: expanding the number of lanes, encouraging car pools by assigning a separate lane to cars with two or more occupants (High Occupancy Vehicle [HOV] lanes), building light rail and public transportation, and imposing tolls on some highways and interstates. Building more road capacity can keep up with demand in urban areas, but there is a limit to this asphalt jungle. Los Angeles is the land of endless freeways, but is still home to the worst congestion in America. Public transit and subway systems work reasonably well in New York, Chicago, Washington, and other big cities, but the percentage of people who use public transportation is relatively small (25 percent in New York, 11 percent in Chicago, but nationwide only 1.5 percent). Consequently, the per-traveler cost is prohibitive and must be heavily subsidized. Surprisingly, from 1960 to 2000, the United States added about 63 million workers, yet the total number of workers using public transit actually declined by nearly 2 million.

Eventually, despite all these efforts, the supply simply can't seem to keep up with ever-growing demand.

For years economists have been recommending a solution called "peak pricing" to help alleviate the surplus of cars during rush hour. By raising the price (toll) at certain peak times, marginal drivers would take other routes, or take the freeway at a different time, at off-peak hours. Commuters would work with their companies to go to work and get off work at off-peak times. At the same time, tolls would provide additional financing to maintain the highways and build new lanes and roads where necessary.

The Singapore Example of Peak Pricing

Singapore was the first country to try peak pricing on a national scale, starting in 1998. A toll system called Electronic Road Pricing (ERP) operates during peak hours in the central business district and along expressways and arterial roads going in and out of the city. The Land Transport Authority charges anywhere from S$0.25 to S$4.00, depending on time and location. Foreign-registered cars are charged S$5.00 a day. Each car is required to carry a Cash Card on its windshield, like an E-Z Pass, that is read electronically when the vehicle enters the city and deducted automatically from the car owner's Cash Card account.

Although the ERP toll system is unpopular with drivers who feel entitled to free road access, the results have been positive. The Land Transport Authority reported recently that road traffic has decreased by 13 percent during ERP operational hours, with vehicle numbers declining from 270,000 to 235,000 within the restricted zone. Carpooling has increased, and average road speeds increased by about 20 percent.

Because Singapore is a small island, it has also adopted a certificate of entitlement (COE) program to curb auto ownership. Bermuda has a similar program that limits each resident to one automobile. But Singapore's schedule is more flexible. The government limits the total number of automobile certificates of ownership in the country, and in effect, requires residents to bid for the right to buy a motor vehicle. Thus, a resident of Singapore can own more than one vehicle, but he must bid for it. Currently a subcompact costs S$45,000 and a full-size car costs around S$100,000, in addition to the price of the car itself.

The London Congestion Charge

London has also benefited from the imposition of a Congestion Charge. By the late 1990s, more than one million people were entering central London on an average workday. Traffic was getting so crowded in central London that the average speed had fallen more than 20 percent since the 1960s to 8.6 mph by 2002. A study showed that in 1998 drivers spent almost 30 percent of their time stationary during peak periods in inner London and more than half their time at less than 10 mph. In surveys, Londoners complained that "there is too much traffic in London" and rated solving the problem more important than fighting crime.

To respond to this crisis, Ken Livingston, the first mayor of London, proposed a congestion charge in May 2000. In 2003, the City of London began imposing a daily charge for driving or parking within central London between 7:00 A.M. and 6:30 P.M. on workdays, excluding public holidays. Video cameras and mobile units capture images of vehicle license plates entering, leaving, and parking within the zone, and if drivers have not registered, they are fined £100. The revenues from the daily charge remain earmarked for public transport.

Economists helped determine the daily charge, which started at £5 and has since been raised to £8. For a variety of reasons, they discovered, however, that it was neither feasible nor appropriate to charge a price equal to the marginal cost of congestion. But so far the £8 fee has proven workable.

The results have been impressive, showing reductions in traffic and congestion that exceeded expectations. The number of private cars, vans, and trucks coming into central London declined 27 percent. In other words, some 65,000 to 70,000 trips are no longer made. The use of private cars fell from almost half of central London traffic to just over a third. Surveys indicate that a large body of the public shifted to other forms of transportation: Taxi use is up 22 percent, buses are up 21 percent, and bicycles up 28 percent. Average travel speeds have increased to 10.4 mph, a rise of almost 17 percent, and congestion has dropped an average 30 percent.[4]

Moreover, higher traffic patterns did not materialize as expected outside the central London area. In fact, travel times decreased 27 percent during the morning peak and 34 percent on return journeys.

One of the most worrisome issues was the impact of the vehicle charge on central London retail sales. Some stores were hurt by the daily fee, as potential shoppers stay home or buy online, but surveys indicated that there was no significant effect on total sales. Most importantly, the public and local businesses appear to support the London fee scheme. Fifty-eight percent felt it improved London's image.

The only drawback has been the cost. The setup and operational costs of the program turned out to be considerably higher than expected, and net annual revenues have fallen short of expected levels. Instead of taking in an estimated £230 to 270 million a year, Transport for London actually took in net revenues of less than £100 million in 2004–2005.

The Nation's Pioneer HOT Lane: 91 Express Lanes in Orange County, California

The hottest scheme to reduce the high traffic load is the HOT (High-Occupancy Toll) lanes, where special lanes on a congested highway charge market prices (varying prices according to demand conditions) for the privilege of driving in uncongested bliss. The first expressway to offer HOT lanes was the SR 91 Riverside Freeway between Anaheim and Riverside, California.

Accelerated population growth in Riverside caused massive delays in each direction. To ameliorate "The Corona Crawl," as reporters often called it, the California Department of Transportation developed a 35-year lease agreement with the California Private Transportation Company (CPTC) to create a toll road in the median of SR 91 called the 91 Express Lanes. Open to the public on December 27, 1995, 91 Express was the first toll road to use a variable pricing system based on the time of day. It is not truly a congestion price system because toll rates are preset by time instead of based on actual congestion. But those rates are adjusted every few months based on actual measured traffic flow in the lanes. In 2007, the toll on the busiest hours (4:00–5:00 P.M. on Friday) is $9.50, the highest toll for any toll road in the nation. The highest toll in the morning (7:00–8:00 A.M.) is $4.05.

The HOT lanes on SR 91 Express have successfully eliminated traffic congestion in those lanes, while keeping other lanes on the same road available "free" for those who would rather spend time than money. After more than 10 years of operation, rush-hour traffic on the lanes speeds along smoothly at 65 mph, giving drivers in that corridor a kind of "congestion insurance." In 2003, Orange County purchased the 91 Express Lanes for $207.5 million. The County has continued the private sector's pricing scheme to eliminate congestion.

Other States Adopt HOT Lanes and Tolling

Other states have followed California's lead. High-Occupancy Toll (HOT) lanes have been created or are in development in Dallas and Houston, Texas; the Washington, DC, Beltway; Denver; Salt Lake City; Seattle; Minneapolis; Miami; and Atlanta. "We are out of money in our transportation trust funds throughout our region," said Lon Anderson, spokesman for the Mid-Atlantic AAA in 2004. "There's no money to make the wholesale changes many would like to see. HOT lanes offer that opportunity."[5]

Today's carpool (HOV) lanes were developed originally as express busways, but were opened to carpools because there was never enough bus traffic to use more than a small portion of their capacity. On the Washington Beltway (I-495) and other freeways (I-95 and I-395), the new HOT lanes will be free to carpools of three or more, van pools, and buses, but individual drivers can also use the lanes by paying a toll. The tolls will be collected electronically, and thus toll booths are avoided. Police will monitor the HOT lanes to catch and fine cheats.

Resistance has developed in some states that are considering or testing toll roads and HOT lanes. In Texas, a protestor founded the Texas Toll Party to oppose the expansion of toll roads in Texas, calling them "Lexus highways," and legislators have introduced bills to postpone building more new toll roads. Governor Rick Perry wants to build the Trans-Texas Corridor, a 300-mile toll road parallel to the often-congested I-35 between Dallas and San Antonio. It would be operated by Cintra, a Spanish company, which will pay Texas $1.2 billion up front for developing the corridor at a cost of $6 billion.

Complaints are being made about foreign robber barons taking over Texan roads.

But there is much evidence in favor of tolls and peak pricing techniques in the United States and around the world as a better way of financing roads and highways, and keeping traffic flowing smoothly and safely. As Robert W. Poole, Jr., the nation's foremost authority of market-based transportation solutions, concludes, HOT lanes, toll concessions, and peak pricing strategies produce such important benefits that "they should rapidly become an important part of our transportation system."[6]

Chapter 13

Patient Power

The New Consumer-Driven Medical Plan

In health care today, fundamental principles of the marketplace do not apply. Prices are not determined by supply and demand. . . .
— "America's Economic Outlaw:
The U.S. Health Care System" *New York Times*
(October 26, 1993)

Our health care is a hodgepodge of limited free market, all types of government intervention and regulations, and it is increasingly failing. . . . But Health Savings Accounts (HSAs) are the solution that could solve the entire health care problem.
—John Mackey, CEO, Whole Foods Market

As health care became a national issue, the *New York Times* ran a cover story contending that America's health care system "operates with almost total disregard for basic economic principles" and therefore deserves special treatment by government. "Prices are not determined by supply and demand or by competition among producers. Comparison shopping is impossible. Greater productivity does not lower costs," the reporter claimed. Health care costs are rising rapidly in the United States, and now represent 15 percent of national income, the highest of any nation.

But are medical services really that different from soap, cars, or baseball tickets?

Let's go back to Economics 101 to analyze the health care debate. We shall see that, contrary to the *Times's* statement, supply and demand are working all too well in the health care industry. The fact is that medical costs are rising rapidly and many people are failing to get decent coverage precisely because the economic principles outlined in Chapter 1 are not allowed to function as they should. The level of competition, incentives, and accountability is not as high as it should be in a free economy.

Why is the cost of health care rising so rapidly? In general, supply isn't keeping up with demand. There are several reasons: first, increased demand from "free" or low-cost Medicare and Medicaid, which today accounts for 65 percent of all medical expenses; second, restrictions by the American Medical Association on the number of students admitted to medical school and limitations on what services nurses, paramedics, nurse practitioners, and physicians' assistants are permitted to perform; and third, the third-party pay system, which separates the user from the payer.

The biggest failure facing the health care market is accountability. The natural relationship between beneficiaries and payers has been delinked to a large extent. The user principle states that those who benefit from a service should pay for it. If you buy one loaf of bread, you pay $1. If you buy two loaves, you pay $2. But in the health care industry today, if you go to the doctor, someone else pays, either your business, the insurance company, or the government.

When people don't pay directly for the services or products they are using, there is a tendency to overuse the benefits and less incentive to keep costs down. The connection is obvious: If you use a doctor's services, you should pay for them. If you use more, you should pay more. And if you use less, you shouldn't have to pay the same amount as someone who uses more.

Unfortunately, the link between payers and beneficiaries is breaking down. In more and more cases, Medicare patients are not paying the bill, taxpayers are. Customers of medical services and doctor visits are not footing the bill; the company's insurance company is. A major source of trouble is the pervasive use of employer-paid medical insurance to pay for even routine doctor visits. When employees know that someone else—the insurance company—is going to foot the bill, there is less incentive to shop around and to limit the number of visits to the doctor or the hospital's emergency room. Fortunately, the insurance companies do attempt to maintain some form of cost control on hospitals and doctor services, but the current system is less than optimal. Unfortunately, the system is in trouble because insurance companies do not reimburse doctors the same amount for identical procedures. Insurance companies decide what they will pay, depending on a variety of factors, including how the paperwork is filled out. When doctors are underpaid by insurance companies, they seek alternatives.

Doctors are fighting back, either by limiting the number of Medicare patients they will see each day, or refusing to deal with insurance companies altogether. Many general practitioners now accept patients who pay the doctor directly, and have to get reimbursed by their insurance companies.

Is Universal Health Care the Solution?

Many influential pundits and politicians advocate adopting what most other countries have: universal health care and a single-payer system. In essence, this policy would mean that everyone would carry health insurance under a single plan run by the federal government. It's called "single payer" because the federal government writes the checks for the medical bills. According to supporters, a single-pay universal system would actually reduce costs and red tape.

But universal health care violates the second half of the welfare principle in economics: It offers a taxpayer benefit to people who don't need coverage. Should taxpayers foot the medical bills of Bill Gates, David Rockefeller, or for that matter anyone making more than, say, $100,000? Most people would say no, we shouldn't subsidize the rich.

Yet that is precisely what a universal health care system does—forces everyone to be on the program to pay for it (through their taxes), even those who can afford their own medical health insurance.

How Good Are the British and Canadian Health Care Systems?

Supporters of the single-pay system often look to Britain and Canada for successful alternatives. The British National Health Service (NHS) was instituted by the socialists when they took power after World War II. Under the NHS, patients do not pay directly for medical or hospital services. All costs are paid by the British government. For many years the NHS was regarded as one of the world's best health care systems. But this is no longer the case. With unlimited demand at a zero marginal price, medical services at state hospitals and doctors' offices are now rationed. In some London hospitals, patients routinely wait more than 12 hours to see a physician. (I know this from personal experience, when our family lived in London one summer. When my eight-year-old son injured himself from a fall, we took him to one of the NHS hospitals and waited eight hours before finally giving up and going home.)

Total administrative staff at the NHS has skyrocketed to 3.1 staff for every patient, but this seemingly favorable ratio hasn't helped the shortage problem, because they are part of the bureaucracy and not assigned to the treatment of patients. Since 1948, the number of beds per thousand people has decreased by half. The British newspapers regularly feature stories of bungled operations and patients left untended in hospital hallways.

What about Canada? Some supporters point to Canada as an ideal single-pay plan. The government picks up the entire tab of medical expenses for Canadians. Their system is considered low cost. Canada devotes only 9.5 percent of its national income to health care, compared to 15 percent in the United States.

But the low cost is largely due to a failure to keep up with medical technology and the latest medical devices and procedures. It ranks in the bottom third of developed countries in terms of availability of

Table 13.1   Median Waiting Time for Treatment by Specialist in Canada

Specialty	Average Waiting Time (weeks)
Orthopedics	32.2
Plastic surgery	28.6
Ophthalmology	30.0
Gynecology	15.3
Otolaryngology	16.4
Urology	13.0
Neurosurgery	20.1
General surgery	10.3
Internal medicine	11.1
Cardiovascular	14.1

SOURCE: The Fraser Institute, Vancouver, BC, Canada

technology, such as magnetic resonance imaging (MRI) machines or kidney dialysis machines. As Table 13.1 shows, there are long waiting times for treatment by a specialist in Canada.

Not surprisingly, Canadians who need specialized treatment and surgery go south to the United States, where waiting time is minimal and the latest medical technology is available, that is, if you are willing to pay for treatment yourself.

In short, whenever you hear a candidate or political leader say, "We need universal health care," you can be sure that person doesn't understand sound economics.

The Market Solution: Lower Costs, Higher Quality, and No Waiting

To show how health care could work if market principles were followed, consider two examples: laser eye surgery and cosmetic surgery. Most health care products and services have become more expensive, but not laser eye surgery. Lasik surgery has been performed more than three million times in the past decade, and it has gotten better over time. The Lasik process has the highest patient satisfaction of any surgery. In 1998, the average price of laser eye surgery was about $2,200 per eye, and results were mixed. Today the average has fallen to $1,350 per eye, a decline of 38 percent, and customer satisfaction has increased. Why has laser eye surgery become cheaper and better, while other forms of health care have become more expensive? It's simple. Laser eye surgery is not covered by third-party private insurance, Medicare, or Medicaid. Thus ophthalmologists have an incentive to improve technology and reduce costs in order to compete for patients. Laser eye surgery is one of the few health procedures in a true free market of price competition and consumer choice.

Cosmetic surgery is another example where choice and competition have delivered lower prices and higher quality over time. Patients pay out of their own pockets for elective surgery, and therefore weigh the costs and benefits of each procedure. They also choose their doctor based on quality and price, not on whether the doctor is in the network or not. Consequently, inflation-adjusted prices have fallen every year from 1992 to 2001.[1]

Who's to Blame?

The author of the *Times's* article blames private enterprise for America's health care problems, but the real cause is the government's failure to let the market operate fully. Even employer-paid medical insurance is, in a way, a government creation. High corporate taxes encourage businesses to offer a wide variety of fringe benefits, which are tax-deductible to corporations and tax-free income to employees. Businesses chose to offer these benefits primarily to cut taxes.

Contrast the health care industry with the veterinarian industry. Animal treatment centers do not suffer from the problems facing the medical industry (spiraling costs, bureaucracy, long waits at medical facilities) largely because most veterinarian services are paid for directly by the pet owners. The dental industry used to be another good example, because for years most dental services were paid for directly by patients, and costs were contained. Unfortunately, over time, more businesses and insurance companies are offering dental insurance with low deductibles. Not surprisingly, dental bills are rising rapidly because of the third-payer system.

How to Resolve the Health Care Problem

What should be done to improve the situation? Imitating national health programs in Canada and Europe won't do because they violate market principles. (If you want to know the weaknesses in each country's health care system, analyze each according to market principles.) Hillary Clinton's health care plan, briefly introduced in 1993, wouldn't work either. The Clinton plan made the cost of medical services vary according to recipient's income, not supply and demand; beneficiaries wouldn't pay directly for medical services; and a new federal agency would impose cost controls on drugs and other medically related services. The result would be shortages, bureaucracy, higher costs, reduced services, and less research and development. Fortunately, the plan was aborted.

Introducing Health Savings Accounts (HSAs): The Whole Foods Story

Health Savings Accounts (HSAs) are a practical solution to the medical crisis. Congress enacted Health Savings Accounts in 2003 as part of the Medicare reform package. Earlier, they were called Medical Savings Accounts. They were signed into law by President Clinton in 1996.

HSAs are tax-deferred accounts that allow you to save money for medical expenses.

To show you how an HSA works, and why it has been so successful, let me use an example from one of the most successful companies, Whole Foods Market, the world's fastest growing natural food chain and ranked as number 5 in the Fortune Top 100 Best Companies to Work For. Until 2003, Whole Foods Market had a generous cafeteria plan in health insurance. The plan was costly, with no incentives to economize. Whole Foods faced a $7 million deficit in 2003, and was forced to raise premiums by nearly 35 percent. Employees (known as team players) were not happy with Whole Foods' medical plan.

Whole Foods was one of the first companies to try a health savings account for its employees. To emphasize a positive approach to health care, the company actually calls them "Personal Wellness Accounts."[2]

The company pays 100 percent of insurance premiums for all full-time workers, who are automatically enrolled. However, there is a high deductible of $3,500: $1,000 in medical costs, $500 deductible for prescription drugs, and $2,000 in co-pays. To cover this deductible, each team member is given a MasterCard debit card which they can access for "health and wellness" expenses. (The company tracks carefully MasterCard expenses to make sure they are used only for medical-related items.)

If employees don't use all of the deductible, the remaining funds are transferred to an HSA, which builds up tax-free until withdrawn. Under the new law, HSAs are portable, so workers can take the account with them if they move to another company. Thus, HSAs create an incentive for workers to become smart health care consumers because they can keep any money that is left over. They have two options for handling unspent HSA funds:

- They can save money (tax-free) for future medical expenses in interest-bearing accounts that accrue tax-free.
- They can withdraw money from the HSA at the end of the year, as long as they maintain a minimum balance.

Nonmedical withdrawals would be fully taxed and subject to a 15 percent tax penalty. "Some of our team members are going to have $8,000, $9,000, and even $10,000 tucked away in their accounts," states CEO John Mackey. "They don't have to worry about going bankrupt due to medical problems."

The results have been phenomenal. The employee turnover rate has plummeted to around 20 percent. Company medical costs have come under control. Approximately 74 percent spend less than $500 on their HSA, and 45 percent of employees don't use their HSA at all. Why not? Because they have an incentive to remain healthy, and they don't run to the doctor every time they cough.

Whole Foods Market employees have an incentive to shop around for the best deal in medical services. The high deductible reduces premiums while covering employees for catastrophic illnesses or injuries. They are encouraged to eat healthy foods and to exercise. By reducing the number of visits to doctors and hospitals, they can save money in their HSA. John Mackey calls it "an empowered model."[3]

According to Forrester Research, by 2010, 24 percent of the health insurance market will include consumer-driven health plans (HSAs). It is the future of American health care.

Here are some ways that applied economics can improve the quality and reduce the cost of health care:

1. Increase the supply of doctors by opening the doors to more students entering medical school.
2. Increase the variety of medical care. Nurse practitioners and physicians' assistants should be given more authority to open clinics and offer general care for basic health needs like ear infections, gashes, and the flu.
3. Allow the market to determine prices, not the insurance companies.
4. Tort reform: Limit malpractice awards to reduce malpractice insurance.
5. Full disclosure: Make it easier to know if a doctor has been sued or found guilty of malpractice.

The solution to the health care crisis is to minimize government intervention, not expand it. Private insurance would be able to solve the problem on its own through flexible deductibles and copayment arrangements. This would encourage competition and comparison shopping to control costs, stimulate further medical advances, and encourage preventive care and exercise. The United States would then be reassured of its position as the nation with the world's best health care system.

Chapter 14

Back to Basics

Competition Enters the Classroom

Were the students . . . left free to choose what college they liked best, such liberty might perhaps contribute to excite some emulation among different colleges.

—Adam Smith[1]

A competitive private educational market serving parents who are free to choose the school they believe best for each child will demonstrate how it can revolutionize schooling.

—Milton Friedman[2]

The consummate diplomat Adam Smith always avoided insulting his readers. But he made an exception in the most famous putdown in *The Wealth of Nations*. Referring to "sham-lectures" at his alma mater, the prestigious Oxford University, he declared with obvious disdain, "In the University of Oxford, the greater part of the public professors have, for these many years, given up altogether even the pretence of teaching.... It must be too unpleasant to him [the Oxford professor] to observe that the greater part of his students desert his lectures; or perhaps attend upon them with plain enough marks of neglect, contempt, and derision."[3]

Why was Adam Smith so agitated? In eighteenth-century Britain, teachers and tutors at most schools were paid directly by students (or their parents) and therefore had to compete among themselves to maintain the interest of their pupils and parents. But Oxford was so richly endowed that professors were largely paid by the college. As a result, a student was not allowed to choose the college he liked best, and classes were developed for the benefit of the instructors, not the students. Without incentives, the quality of education at Oxford deteriorated.

Adam Smith opposed all forms of monopoly, which he felt would create a political system characterized by high cost, waste, bureaucracy, and privilege. The invisible hand of natural liberty only functions successfully under conditions of competition and justice. He applied his theory of competitive enterprise to a wide variety of markets—commerce, religion, and even education. He felt that students would enjoy a better education if they could choose among schools and teachers at all levels of training.

Poor Education in the Public Schools

What can Adam Smith teach us today? We have the freedom to choose the college and university level, but what about primary and secondary education? In most countries, including the United States, lower-level public education is provided by a government monopoly. Though real spending per pupil has more than doubled since 1970, American students continue to rank the lowest in academic test scores (reading, mathematics, and science) of members of OECD countries, dropout rates are high, and scores on the SATs have fallen and remain relatively flat. Even simple literacy has declined, and interest in reading books has gradually fallen in the United States as youth spend more time watching television and playing video games. Moreover, there is a troubling racial gap in American education, with black and Hispanic students, whether their families are affluent or low income, falling behind whites and Asians.[4]

Milton Friedman's Idea of School Choice

Milton Friedman, a modern-day Adam Smith, first applied the economic principles of choice and competition to primary and secondary schools in Chapter 6 of his famous book, *Capitalism and Freedom* (1962). He criticized our government educational system as a rigid, uniform, expensive, and highly centralized quasi-monopoly where the program benefits the teachers and administrators more than it does the students and parents. His solution? Give parents each year a fixed amount of funds, known as "vouchers," redeemable at any public or private school of their choice. "The injection of competition would do much to promote a healthy variety of schools. It would do much, also, to introduce flexibility into school systems. Not least of its benefits would be to make the salaries of school teachers responsive to market forces."[5] As Herbert J. Walberg, a Chicago-trained economist who has taught at Harvard and Stanford, states, "competition often brings out the best in people and organizations and provides benchmarks against which to measure all schools' performance; vouchers allow and encourage parents to more actively participate in their children's schooling, which in turn is positively related to student learning."[6]

The idea of school choice—whether through vouchers, tax credits, or charter schools—has gradually gained momentum although the battle has been long and drawn out. Public-spirited citizens and parents are demanding change, including minority groups who feel that their children are being short-changed in government schools. At the same time, the public school systems have become more centralized and unionized, with teachers unions and administrations that are well organized and well financed in opposition to any form of radical change. While some states, including Florida, Ohio, and Wisconsin, have experimented with some form of school vouchers and charter schools, benefiting from a Supreme Court ruling in 2002 affirming the legality of the Cleveland voucher program, statewide voucher systems have been blocked in states such as California, Michigan, and Colorado due to the adamant and effective opposition of teachers unions and educational administrators.

Numerous studies have been conducted by economists examining the benefits of competition and choice in education. In the debate between private and public schools, the consensus is that private schools paid for directly by parents tend to be "more efficient, more academically effective, better physically maintained, and more responsive to parental curriculum demands" than either voucher-funded private schools or government-run schools.[7] Although public voucher programs in the United States have been relatively small in scope, initial findings are overall positive, especially among minorities. Studies of voucher programs in Washington, DC, Cleveland, and Milwaukee show that they reduced racial segregation.[8] The United States has more experience with charter schools. More than 4,000 charter schools enroll more than one million students. Despite heavy regulations and poor funding, charter schools perform well, especially among poor and Hispanic students, and are heavily oversubscribed.

More complete studies have been made in Sweden, the Netherlands, the Czech Republic, and Chile, where school choice was introduced years ago. The Dutch voucher system is the oldest, starting in 1917, and the private sector now accounts for 76 percent of all students. The Netherlands reports high parent satisfaction and high performance in international test score comparisons. Similar results have occurred in Sweden, where the government funds 85 percent of schools of choice (public or private). Despite government regulations, Sweden has witnessed improved student test scores and greater parental satisfaction. Chile introduced a universal voucher program in 1982, at the same time it created a private pension system (see Chapter 5). All students can choose a public, private, or religious institution, including Catholic schools. The conclusion is that "students in private subsidized [that is, voucher] schools outperformed those in public schools." What about the risk that public schools might close because of a massive exodus of students to private schools? The Chilean government doesn't allow it. They receive extra funding to keep them open.[9] Walberg concludes, "While acknowledging and discussing some notable exceptions, the consensus of the high-quality international research overwhelmingly favors competition and parental choice in education over the monopoly systems that dominate the United States and many other industrialized countries."[10]

For Milton Friedman, the battle for school choice has been "both rewarding and frustrating." But he hasn't given up, even beyond the grave (he died in 2006). He and his wife established the Milton and Rose D. Friedman Foundation with the sole mission of promoting support for school choice. Go to www.friedmanfoundation.org for more information.

Chapter 15

Chicago Gun Show

According to the economic approach, criminals, like everyone else, respond to incentives.

—GARY BECKER[1]

Chicago economists believe that economics is all-powerful and can be used to analyze almost anything.

—STUDENT AT UNIVERSITY OF CHICAGO[2]

The Chicago Boys are at it again. This time the economists at the University of Chicago are making headlines in today's hotly disputed debate about the death penalty and gun control. Milton Friedman set the general standard a generation ago by insisting on rigorous empirical work to support sound (though often unpopular) economic theory and policy. More recently, Gary Becker has extended Chicago-style economic analysis into contemporary social problems such as education, marriage, discrimination, professional sports, and crime.

Underlying Becker's analysis is a basic economic concept, the law of demand: If the price of a commodity goes up, people use less of it. In the case of criminal activity, if the cost and risk of committing a crime rises, fewer crimes will be committed. This is often referred to as the market's incentive principle. Becker has showed that increasing the cost of crime through stiffer jail sentences, quicker trials, and higher conviction rates effectively reduces the number of criminals who rob, steal, or rape.[3]

Does the Death Penalty Deter Crime?

New studies indicate that the reinstitution of the death penalty in many states has led to a 38 percent drop in murder rates. New research by economists, including some at the University of Chicago, conclude that each execution deters as many as three to eighteen potential murders.[4]

A 2003 paper by Lawrence Katz, Steven D. Levitt, and Ellen Shustorovich published in the *American Law and Economics Review* demonstrated "a strong and robust negative relationship" between deaths in prison (from executions or other causes) and the crime rate in society: "30–100 violent crimes and a similar number of property crimes" were deterred per prison death.[5]

A recent *New York Times* cover story summarized a dozen studies on the relationship between capital punishment and crime. "The studies, performed by economists in the past decade, compare the number of executions in different jurisdictions with homicide rates over time—while trying to eliminate the effects of crime rates, conviction rates and other factors—and say that murder rates tend to fall as executions rise."[6]

The studies by economists appear to have shifted sentiment in favor of capital punishment. Two law professors, Cass R. Sunstein (Chicago) and Adrian Vermeule (Harvard), wrote in the *Stanford Law Review* that "the recent evidence of a deterrent effect from capital punishment seems impressive, especially in light of its 'apparent power and unanimity . . . Capital punishment may well save lives.'" The evidence caused Professor Sunstein, in particular, to change his mind. "I did shift from being against the death penalty to thinking that if it has a significant deterrent effect it's probably justified."[7]

Still, the evidence seems to indicate that half-hearted execution programs aren't effective in fighting crime. According to Emory economics and law professor Joanna M. Shepherd, capital punishment is only a deterrent in states that executed at least nine people between 1977 and 1996.

Gun Control and Crime

Economists have also entered the controversial field of gun control. In the late 1990s, John R. Lott, Jr., the John M. Olin Law and Economics Fellow at Chicago, made the case that a well-armed citizenry discourages violent crime. Lott analyzed the FBI's massive yearly crime statistics for all 3,054 U.S. counties covering 18 years, and state police documents on illegal gun use. His surprising conclusions, published in his recent book, *More Guns, Less Crime,* find that:

- States now experiencing the largest drop in crime are also the ones with the fastest-growing rates of gun ownership.
- The Brady five-day waiting period, gun buy-back programs, and background checks have had little or no impact on crime reduction.
- States that have recently allowed concealed weapon permits have witnessed significant reductions in violent crime.
- Guns are used on average five times more frequently in self-defense than in committing a crime.[8]

According to Lott, recent legislative efforts to restrict gun ownership may actually keep many law-abiding citizens from protecting themselves from attack, an example of Adam Smith's law of unintended consequences.

Lott also argued that state laws permitting concealed handguns deter crime. "When guns are concealed, criminals are unable to tell whether the victim is armed before striking, which raises the risk to criminals."[9] He produced a variety of statistics and graphs to support his case. For example, Figure 15.1 compares the average number of violent crimes in states before and after the adoption of a concealed-handgun law.

Lott's crime figures bring to mind Frederic Bastiat's brilliant essay "What Is Seen and What Is Not Seen." In 1850, this great French journalist

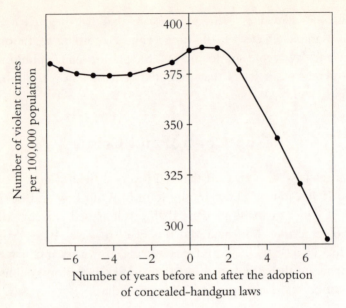

Figure 15.1   The Effect of Concealed Handgun Laws on Violent Crime
SOURCE: John R. Lott, Jr. *More Guns, Less Crime.* Reprinted by permission of the University of Chicago Press.

wrote, "In the economic sphere, . . . a law produces not only one effect, but a series of effects. Of these effects, the first . . . is seen. The other effects emerge only subsequently; they are not seen."[10]

According to Lott, Bastiat's principle applies in crime statistics. "Many defensive uses [of guns] are never reported to the police."[11] Lott gives two reasons. First, in many cases of self-defense, a handgun is simply brandished, the assailant backs off, and no one is harmed, so nothing is reported. Second, in states that have stringent gun laws, citizens who use a gun for protection fail to report the incident for fear of being arrested by the police for illegal use of a weapon. Thus, Lott confirms (through extensive surveys) the initial work of Gary Kleck, professor of criminal justice at Florida State University, who found that guns are used far more frequently in self-defense than in committing crimes. Kleck, by the way, used to have a strong antigun bias until he uncovered this revealing statistic.

Lott's hypothesis has been heavily criticized by other economists who dispute his interpretation of crime statistics. They argue that other factors have been more influential in reducing crime during the 1990s, including a strong economy, the waning crack cocaine epidemic, and even abortion (the latter an argument of Chicago economist Steven Levitt). However, one thing all studies by economists agree on: Right-to-carry laws do not increase violent crime, and a large number of studies make the case that they reduce violent crime.

All this confirms a long-standing legal principle in America: People should have the constitutional right to own a gun for self-protection.

Chapter 16

Economists Catch Auction Fever

Auction theory is one of economics' success stories.
—PAUL KLEMPERER, OXFORD UNIVERSITY

Economist Paul Milgrom's ideas were critical to helping the FCC design its multi-billion dollar spectrum auctions. His thoughtful economic reasoning and attention to practical detail made the auctions successful.
—REED HUNDT, FORMER CHAIR, FEDERAL
COMMUNICATIONS COMMISSION (FCC)

On August 19, 2004, Google, the world's most popular Internet search engine, took its company public, issuing 19.6 million shares at $85 per share. What was unorthodox about the Google Initial Public Offering (IPO) was its method of going public: a sealed-bid public auction open to anyone who cared to bid. Using this controversial method, Google let the investing public, not the Wall Street investment bankers, decide the clearing price.

This controversial, egalitarian move did not sit well with the Wall Street financiers. In a traditional public offering, investment bankers underwrite the process and set a predetermined opening price under the expected market value. By creating a hot issue, brokerage firms can allocate shares to their most favored customers. This system favors company officers, insiders, institutional investors, and high-net worth individuals. Once the stock goes public, the insiders and privileged customers lucky enough to purchase advance shares could double or triple their money by flipping the stock as soon as the general public begins bidding the price up in the secondary market.

Google was not the first company to use an IPO auction, but it was a shock to Wall Street, given Google's size, with a market capitalization exceeding General Motors. Google's young owners didn't need the cash and weren't beholden to Wall Street financiers. They wanted an IPO that would compensate its loyal employees, and still provide a way for the general investing public to participate—a form of democratic capitalism.

Google chose an auction design known as the "uniform-price Dutch auction," the same the U.S. Treasury uses to manage its debt. This is how the Dutch auction worked for Google: The company solicited nonrestrictive bids from any investor who specified the number of shares desired and a price the investor was willing to pay for them. On the day of the IPO, the company allocated shares to bidders in descending price order until the available shares (19.6 million) were exhausted. The price specified in the last bid filled—known as the "market-clearing price"—was the price that all winning bidders paid for their stock ($85 a share).

Theoretically, a Dutch auction discourages the likelihood of a rapid run-up in the IPO stock price on opening day, because the market-clearing price should represent the collective wisdom of the general public and a price where supply equals demand. Nevertheless, when the stock went public on August 19, 2004, the stock did pop 18 percent to close at $100 a share. It rose for two reasons: Many of the brokerage firms handling the Google IPO had restricted the number of bids an investor could place, and Google had retained the option to set the price lower than the market-clearing price if they wished. But this run-up was far lower than the first-day bounce that most technology stocks experienced in the late 1990s (100 to 200 percent).

The Economists behind the Google IPO Auction

The success of the Google IPO can be attributed to several economists specializing in auction design, among them Stanford economist Paul Milgrom, who built his reputation by helping to design the Federal Communications Commission spectrum auctions. The FCC auctions have since been copied and adapted for dozens of auctions in electricity markets and other industries involving more than $100 billion worldwide.

Google's IPO auction is a prime example of how technically advanced auction trading has become. The recent success of auctions in a wide variety of new markets can be attributed to top economists who specialize in game theory. In addition to taking Google public, these expert consultants have applied their techniques to engineer successful auctions of baseball tickets and hotel rooms online; products and collectibles on eBay; T-bills and other government securities; foreign exchange; livestock, fish, timber, oil fields, and other commodities; foreclosures on commercial and residential real estate; cap-and-trade pollution permits; radio bandwidth and mobile phone licenses; and assets, businesses, and lands that governments seek to privatize. These days, when governments decide to auction off state-owned resources, they routinely hire economists for advice on how to design the auction. At the same time, bidders also hire economists to figure out how to beat the system. The result is a highly informed marketplace where both the buyer and seller feel satisfied.

William Vickrey, Father of Auction Theory

Most auction experts acknowledge that the new world of auction design began with a paper published in an obscure journal in 1961 by William Vickrey, professor of economics at Columbia University.[1] In his seminal paper, Vickrey recommended what is now called a Dutch-style "second-price sealed bid auction" as a preferable way to maximize value for both sellers and bidders in auctions that involve a large inventory of assets. Thirty-five years later, Vickrey was awarded the Nobel Prize in Economics for his pioneering work in auction theory. (As luck would have it, he died only a week after receiving the prize.) Professor Vickrey's work has been refined and extended by dozens of economists over the past few decades. It is a powerful theory, leading to several important insights that have had a significant impact on auction design.

To understand the Vickrey auction, as the Dutch-style second-price sealed bid is called, we need to introduce some basic information about auctions. The most popular way to sell individual items is the "going, going, gone" auction, such as is done by such English art houses as Sotheby's and Christie's. Under the English system, bidders start at a low price, above the reserve price set by the owner, and bid the price up until only one bidder remains. The final bidder wins the prize at the final price he bid.

The English Auction and the Winner's Curse

There are several potential drawbacks to the English auction, however. First, in an open outcry bidding war you may suffer from auction fever and, in the presence of competing bidders, make too aggressive a bid. Economists call it the "Winner's Curse." Remember the famed auction of Jacqueline Kennedy's estate? Emotional bidders, anxious to own a piece of Camelot, paid as much as three times the expected prices. Or the baseball fan who paid more than $2 million for Barry Bond's 73rd home run ball in 2001, only to see its value plunge to under $100,000 a few years later. Other examples include a stock in an IPO that subsequently falls in half in the secondary market; an auction for the cell phone market in a small market that turns out to be too expensive; an oil field worth far less than what the oil producer paid; or a building contractor who outbids all his competitors but ends up losing money because he underestimated his costs.

Paul Klemperer, an Oxford University economist who specializes in the economics of auctions, illustrates the winner's curse to his students by auctioning off a jar filled with an undisclosed number of pennies. The students estimate the jar's contents and then bid a little below their estimate to leave a profit. Every time, though, the hapless winner of the jar is the student who overestimates the number of pennies by the greatest amount, and therefore overpays by the most. As we shall see, there are ways to avoid the winner's curse.

Second, the auction might suffer from collusion between bidders to keep the price artificially low, resulting in a low bid for the seller. This is especially true in the case of business-to-business auctions, where a small number of big companies bid on a radio, mobile phone, or tele-communications license, or a major mineral lease. Businesses don't even need to break the law. If only a few companies are competing for a customer's business, they could tacitly agree beforehand that it's in their mutual interest to charge the same high price and share the business. If one supplier defects from the group by dropping its price, its rivals could punish it by dropping their own prices.

For example, in 1995 the U.S. government auctioned off the Los Angeles license for mobile-phone broadband. GTE and Bell Atlantic were ineligible to bid, and MCI failed to enter this auction. Pacific Telephone, the giant provider of local telephone service in the L. A. area, was allowed to compete and intimidated its smaller rivals. The result was that the bidding stopped at a very low price, yielding only $26 per capita for the license. In contrast, the auction for the Chicago market excluded the main local telephone provider. As a result, the auction between several small companies was robust, and the rights sold for $31 per capita, even though Chicago was considered far less valuable than Los Angeles in terms of per capita income. In another example, in 1999 Germany sold 10 blocks of radio spectrum, and only two telecommuni- cations companies, Mannesman and T-Mobile, made a bid. Because each adopted a live-and-let-live philosophy, the auction closed after just two rounds, with each bidder acquiring half of the blocks for the same low price.[2]

Vickrey and other game theorists have created new ways to maximize revenues for sellers while improving satisfaction of buyers in auctions. In a Vickrey auction, bidders enter sealed bids. The highest bidder wins—but pays the second-highest bid price plus a small fee. It may seem illogical, but it actually makes good sense. Sellers are assured that buyers will place realistic bids, and buyers don't have to worry about being outbid at the last minute as in other types of auctions.

How a Vickrey Auction Works

Before attending a live auction, potential buyers usually do some homework. They will read the list of items to be auctioned, examine the items if possible, and do some research to determine what a fair price would be. Added to that price is the desirability factor, the potential buyer's gotta-have-it feeling. Wise shoppers arrive at the auction with a predetermined maximum price, and drop out of the bidding as that price is surpassed by other bidders. Sometimes auction fever hits, and a price will escalate beyond the buyers' predetermined limits, but most of the time the person with the highest predetermined price goes home with the item. However, the highest bidder seldom actually pays the maximum price he or she was willing to pay. Why not? Because, in a live auction, bidders always know the previous price. When the penultimate bidder drops out, the final bidder only has to offer slightly more than the next highest bidder's drop-out price. Consequently, if bidders remain calm and don't surpass their predetermined maximum, they always go home paying less than they were willing to pay.

A sealed-bid auction is a different matter. Collusion is more difficult. The price does not gradually escalate as potential buyers enter and exit the bidding. Hopeful buyers must make a single bid, in advance, carefully calculating not only how much they are willing to spend, but also how much competitors are likely to bid. But what if their calculations are wrong? What if they write down $10,000, while everyone else is bidding in the hundreds of dollars? In a live auction they would have stopped at $1,000, but now they are stuck paying 10 times what the item is worth. Investors are usually more wary of paying too much than of losing the deal, so if they can't see what others are willing to spend, they are more likely to underbid than overbid, and sellers make less. To allay the buyers' fears of grossly overbidding, the seller promises to give the winning bidder a price slightly over that of the second-highest bidder. This policy actually encourages bidders to bid more, because they know they won't be stuck if they go way over the second-highest bidder. In short, if the buyer wins the prize, he gets a price always under his offer. And by using the Vickrey method, the seller gets more participation in the auction.

Stamp Auctions and the Threat of Cheating

The second-price sealed bid rule (the Vickrey method) is relatively uncommon, but it was used as early as the 1870s in the auction of some items such as stamps and autographs that were sold through mailed-in sealed bids based on a catalog listing. It is standard procedure in the markets for paper collectibles, from Civil War soldiers' letters to postage stamps. The first stamp auctions took place from 1870 to 1882, most of them in New York City, and by 1890 the sealed-bid second-highest price rule was in effect. Stamps that were sold at live auctions continued to use the English auction, but mail-order auctions switched to the second-highest bid, plus one minimum bid increment. In 1897, the pioneering stamp dealer, William P. Brown of New York, became the first stamp dealer to offer such an auction, and the idea quickly spread. The Toledo Stamp Company explained its auction format in the following 1907 mail auction sale catalog:

> To those who have never bid on Auction Sales before we wish to say that this is one of the best ways to add to your collection of stamps that you would not be able to purchase at the price otherwise. You say just how much you wish to pay for a lot, and if no one has overbid you, you get the stamps. If your bid is too high we buy for you at a small advance over the next highest bid, so you are protected in any case.

The only downside of second-price auctions is the fear that the auctioneer will cheat. Once you submit your maximum price, what's to keep the auctioneer from opening up your sealed bid and pretending that another was received just under your maximum amount? This fear has discouraged many stamp collectors from sending in such bids to small, little-known stamp dealers. A stamp dealer in Connecticut confesses:

> After some time in the business, I ran an auction with some high mail bids from an elderly gentleman who'd been a good customer of ours and obviously trusted us. My wife, who ran the business with me, stormed into my office the day after the sale, upset that I'd used his full bid on every lot, even when it was considerably higher than the second-highest bid. She threw

his invoice on my desk and said, "I thought we weren't going to do this crap!" I glanced at the paperwork and without even thinking about it, said, "I don't like having to do this, honey, but you know our bank loan is due tomorrow." Looking back, I learned the mind is amazingly creative when it comes to rationalizing bad behavior. After some thought, she said, "Okay, I'll do this, but only if you agree to change the rules in our next auction to read, 'All lots are sold to the highest mail bidder at one advance over the second highest bid, *unless we need the money.'*" With that one sentence she stripped me of all my rationalizations and excuses. She held a mirror up to my conduct and I hated what I saw. I had no choice but to recalculate all our invoices for that sale to conform with our rules. That's when I decided to leave the business of running auctions."[3]

The U.S. Treasury Department Saves Millions

Fortunately, investors probably do not need to be concerned about such moral ethics when bidding through major corporations such as eBay and Google, or the U.S. government, all of which have adopted a Dutch-style Vickrey auction when selling large quantities of uniform goods and securities. A Dutch auction is the opposite of an English auction, where prices start low and move higher. In a Dutch auction, the auctioneer calls out a high price, then keeps lowering it until there is a buyer. For example, when the U.S. Treasury sells debt instruments, the government accepts lower and lower bids until the entire amount of debt is sold. Then everyone who bid higher prices pays the lowest price accepted.

The Treasury adoption of a uniform-pricing Dutch auction to sell Treasury bills and other government securities is another case of academic influence. In 1959, Chicago economist Milton Friedman testified before the Joint Economic Committee, chaired by former Chicago economist Senator Paul Douglas, suggesting the best way to sell government securities. He criticized the then standard practice of the Treasury charging the highest bids and suggested that the government could earn more money by using a uniform-pricing Dutch auction because it would increase demand. Nothing was done about Friedman's proposal until 1972, when George Shultz (also from Chicago) became secretary of the treasury. Friedman persuaded his friend Shultz to experiment with Dutch auctions for some issues of long-term Treasuries. Two economists at the Treasury evaluated the performance of comparable bond issues sold by Dutch auction and by the standard procedure. "The results were unambiguous," concluded Friedman. "The Treasury got a better deal under the Dutch auctions."[4] But the experiments ended in 1974, when Bill Simon became secretary. Simon had been a bond trader on Wall Street who vigorously opposed this new way to raise funds for the government.

In 1991, Salomon Brothers was accused of manipulating a Treasury securities auction, and soon after, the Treasury modified its method of auctioning securities in favor of a uniform-pricing competitive bidding under rules that are very similar to a Dutch-style Vickrey auction. The Treasury Web site states:

> A Single-Price Auction, also known as the Dutch Auction process, allows each successful competitive bidder and each noncompetitive bidder to be awarded securities at the price equivalent to the highest accepted rate or yield. This type of auction is now used for all T-Bills, Notes, and Bonds [and Inflation-Indexed Securities or TIPS]. In the past it applied only to the 2-year and 5-year note auctions. The Federal government holds the auctions for these securities. When the size of a pending auction is announced, retail customers have an opportunity to participate by submitting noncompetitive tenders or bids. These orders are less than $1 million in size for Treasury bills and $5 million or less for Treasury notes and coupon bonds. The remaining participants in the auction are institutional dealers who submit competitive bids to the Treasury. Institutional dealer prices will vary according to the competitive level of their bid. After all competitive bids are submitted by dealers, retail customers will receive an average price from the auction as determined from all the accepted competitive bids.[5]

The FCC and Cellular Licenses

In the 1980s, the Federal Communications Commission (FCC) began conducting lotteries to assign cellular licenses in cities across the United States. But in the early 1990s, the government realized that it was losing millions of dollars in potential revenues. Since 1994, the FCC has conducted competitive-bidding auctions of licenses for cellular and radio spectrum. These auctions are conducted electronically and are accessible over the Internet. Thus, qualified bidders can place bids from the convenience of their home or office. Further, anyone with access to a computer with a web browser can follow the progress of an auction and view the results of each round. The FCC has found that spectrum auctions more effectively assign licenses than either comparative hearings or lotteries.

Who is behind these changes? Economists who specialize in auction design. They have been pushing for auctions for years. Ronald Coase, another Chicago economist, was among the first to advocate auctioning radio licenses in 1959. One of the premier designers is Paul Milgrom of Stanford University. As Nobel Prize winner Joseph Stiglitz says of Professor Milgrom, "One of the recent revolutions in economics is an understanding that markets do not automatically work well. Design matters, and the Federal Communications Commission spectrum auction design that Milgrom pioneered kicked off a new era of market design using economic theory to make real markets work better."[6]

Oxford Professor Paul Klemperer has been instrumental in designing the British government's first auction of licenses for third-generation mobile-phone services. He writes:

February 2000 was a stressful month for me: the UK 3G auction was about to begin. For over two years I had been working with the UK government to design the world's first auction of spectrum for "third generation" (3G) mobile-phone services. A lot was at stake. If our auction worked well, it would allocate the spectrum efficiently and raise a lot of money, but many previous auctions had been embarrassing flops that had failed to generate the sums expected. This time the politicians were hoping for billions of dollars. . . .

The tension only mounted over the seven weeks the auction ran. The auction started well. Day after day the prices climbed, but we continued to worry about what we might have missed, and what could still go wrong. As prices kept rising through 150 rounds of bidding, and records started falling, nerves gave way to astonishment. Still, it was an enormous relief when the gavel finally came down on five bids totalling over 34 billion dollars—our auction had raised more money than any previous auction in history.[7]

Business isn't the only place where auctions are gaining popularity. Individuals are buying and selling everything from used DVDs to baseball cards on eBay, Yahoo, Amazon, and other Web sites. E-commerce is big business. eBay alone has 10 million customers and a market value of $21 billion.

The founders of eBay have learned from William Vickrey and other economists. This premier online trader uses second-price auction rules, where the highest bidder has to pay only the second-highest bid plus an extra fee. Thus, eBay's second-price rule helps to avoid the winner's curse. Another benefit is that bidders can study past auctions of similar items. They can also find out more about the trustworthiness of sellers by reading customer feedback about them. And if they are still uncertain, bidders often watch the behavior of fellow bidders.

The site's official guide urges users to bid their maximum offer, and relax. They won't actually pay that price unless someone else bids that high. As others join in, the site automatically and incrementally outbids the next-highest offer, keeping the maximum bid hidden until the bidding climbs to meet it. If someone outbids your maximum, that's okay— the item is clearly worth more to that person than it is to you. But Ken Steiglitz, author of *Snipers, Shills and Sharks: eBay and Human Behavior,* says that this strategy is "disconcertingly naive." An early offer attracts competition, he says. Studies show that the more bids an item gets, the more likely it is that other bids will follow. So even if no one else tops your maximum bid, the second-highest bid could rise significantly. Mr. Steiglitz's advice: "Bid late. The first few weeks of an auction mean nothing. It's all about what happens in those last few seconds." eBay has a "hard close" rule—after a set time, no further bidding is allowed. That encourages a frenzy of bidding before the electronic gavel comes down.[8]

In conclusion, the improvement in auction design by economists has benefited everyone—the buyers who are less likely to overpay; the sellers, who are more likely to get a better price for their goods; and the auction houses, who are getting more traffic.

Chapter 17

If You Build It Privately
. . . They Will Come

The Economics of Sports Stadiums

Government provides certain indispensable public services without which community life would be unthinkable and which by their nature cannot appropriately be left to private enterprise.

—PAUL A. SAMUELSON

I f you take a course in public finance, you will invariably encounter the "public goods" argument for government: Some services simply can't be produced sufficiently by the private sector, such as schools, courts, prisons, roads, welfare, and lighthouses.

The lighthouse example has been highlighted as a standard public good in Paul Samuelson's famous textbook since 1964. "Its beam helps everyone in sight. A businessman could not build it for a profit, since he cannot claim a price for each user."[1] In other words, since one cannot prevent the light from being seen by all ships, regardless of whether the ship has paid for this valuable service, no one would pay without being forced through government taxation or harbor fee.

But that may not be the case. Chicago economist Ronald H. Coase revealed that numerous lighthouses in England were built and owned by private individuals and companies prior to the nineteenth century. They earned profits by charging tolls on ships docking at nearby ports. Trinity House was a prime example of a privately owned operation granted a charter in 1514 to operate lighthouses and charge ships a toll for their use. The cost of the lighthouse was simply bundled into the port-docking fee.

Samuelson went on to recommend that lighthouses be financed out of general revenues. According to Coase, however, such a financing system has never been tried in Britain: "the service [at Trinity House] continued to be financed by tolls levied on ships."[2]

What's even more amazing, Coase wrote his trailblazing article in 1974, but Samuelson continued to use the lighthouse as an example of an ideal public good that only the government could supply. After I publicly chided Samuelson for his failure to acknowledge Coase's revelation,[3] Samuelson finally admitted the existence of private lighthouses "in an earlier age," in a footnote in the 16th edition of his textbook, but insisted that private lighthouses still encountered a free rider problem.[4]

Private Solutions for Public Services

The lighthouse isn't the only example of a public good that can be provided for by private enterprise. A privately run toll road operates in southern California. Wackenhut Corrections manages state prisons for profit. Catholic schools provide a better education than public schools. The Mormon Church offers a better welfare plan than the USDA food stamp program. Habitat for Humanity builds houses for responsible poor people.

And now, for the first time in 38 years, there is a privately built major league baseball stadium—AT&T Park, new home of the San Francisco Giants. After Bay Area voters rejected four separate ballot initiatives to raise government funds to replace the windy and poorly attended Candlestick Park, Peter Magowan, a Safeway and Merrill Lynch heir, teamed with local investors to buy the club and, with the help of a $155 million Chase Securities loan, built the new stadium for $345 million. The owners also secured huge sponsorships from Pacific Bell, Safeway, Coca-Cola, and Charles Schwab.

So far the private ballpark has been a resounding success, selling a league-leading 30,000 season tickets for the 41,000-seat stadium. The team's 81 home games are nearly sold out. Other team owners, whose stadiums are heavily subsidized, were skeptical, but a dozen team owners have visited the new operation to study what they've done. They include George Steinbrenner, who is building a new $1 billion Yankee stadium.[5]

Economists Attack Public Financing

Perhaps private funding of major league sports facilities has been influenced by two recent in-depth studies by professional economists attacking publicly subsidized sports arenas. In *Major League Losers,* Mark Rosentraub of Indiana University (and a big sports fan) studied stadium financing in five cities and meticulously demonstrated that pro sports produce very few jobs or ripple effects in the community. In fact, they take business away from suburban entertainment and food venues, and often leave municipalities with huge losses.[6]

A Brookings Institution study came to similar conclusions. After reviewing major sports facilities in seven cities, Roger G. Noll (Stanford) and Andrew Zimbalist (Smith College) found these municipal arenas were not a source of local economic growth and employment, and the net subsidy exceeded the financial benefit to the community.[7]

These empirical studies confirm a long-standing sound principle of public finance, the accountability principle: Beneficiaries should pay for the services they use. It's amazing how often politicians violate this basic concept. For example, John Henry, a commodities trader worth $300 million and owner of the Marlins baseball team, tried to push through the Florida state legislature a bill to tax cruise-ship passengers to help fund a new Miami ballpark. (Fortunately, then Governor Jeb Bush vetoed the bill.)

The Sports Economist

The accountability principle isn't the only example where economists are applying economics to baseball and other sports. Trade-offs, opportunity costs, and incentives are also important aspects of the game.

J. C. Bradley, associate professor at Kennesaw State University and University of the South, has attached a name to applying economics to sports: He calls it sabernomics. "Saber" comes from the Society for American Baseball Research (SABR). Sabernomics combines analytical and statistical methods and the principles of economics; it tests various theories with multiple regression analysis and other econometric methods. For example, why do pitchers hit more batters in the American League than in the National League? One hypothesis is that the incentives to hit batters changed when the American League adopted the designated hitter (DH) rule in 1973, while the National League continued to play without it. Some economists argued that with the DH, American League pitchers could get away with hitting batters, since the pitcher never had to go to bat and risk retaliation. From 1921 until 1972, there was never much of a difference between the two leagues in terms of hit batters. But starting in 1973, when the DH rule was adopted by the American League only, the hit batter rate was consistently higher in the American League. From 1973 to 2005, the hit batter rate was 15 percent higher in the American League than in the National League. "This is pretty strong evidence that pitchers are responding to the price differences in hit batters in accordance with the law of demand," concludes Professor J. C. Bradley.[8]

Another issue in major league sports is the alleged big-city advantage. Do big-market teams have an inherent advantage over clubs in small markets? Critics complain that cities like New York, Los Angeles, and Chicago have clear advantages over smaller markets like Seattle, Cincinnati, and Tampa. They tend to ignore exceptions to this rule, however. The Yankees, for instance, didn't make the playoffs for 13 years between 1981 and 1995. Still, the evidence is clear. According to studies of wins per season compared to population size of markets, there is a definite advantage, albeit marginal, of big-market teams.[9] Leagues use a variety of methods to keep the big cities from dominating, such as (1) reverse order drafts where the worst teams get the best new players first; (2) luxury tax, requiring teams who have payrolls exceeding a set amount pay a certain percentage (as high as 40 percent) above that amount to the league; and (3) revenue sharing, giving low-revenue teams more cash. Interestingly, a former Federal Reserve governor Edward "Ned" Gramlich, a long-time baseball fan, was the staff director for the Economic Study Committee on Major League Baseball, a blue-ribbon panel set up to find ways to bolster financially troubled teams. In 1992, the committee recommended a program for richer teams to channel some of their profits to poorer teams. Baseball adopted such a revenue-sharing plan following a strike in 1994.

However, some economists are critical of revenue sharing because it creates a disincentive for winning. "Tying revenues to winning creates a strong incentive for management to put winning teams on the field. A small-market owner who receives a share of big-market earnings may prefer to live off this wealth transfer rather than put together a good team."[10]

Chapter 18

Who Is
Henry Spearman?

Economics of the Mystery Novel

So if there is a real model for Spearman, his identity remains a mystery, at least to me.

—HERBERT STEIN, FOREWORD,
MURDER AT THE MARGIN

Now for something light. During the past summer, I took a break from writing and decided to read three murder mystery novels, all authored by Marshall Jevons, a pen name for William Breit and Kenneth G. Elzinga, professors of economics at Trinity University in San Antonio and the University of Virginia, respectively.

131

Elementary Economics, My Dear Watson

What makes these mysteries fascinating is the ingenious way the writers incorporate basic principles of economics to solve the murders. Marginal utility, the law of demand, consumer surplus, opportunity cost, profit maximization, game theory, and Adam Smith's invisible hand all play a part in advancing the stories and ultimately catching the culprits. As Henry Spearman, the detective-hero, says to the local police investigator in *Murder at the Margin,* "Elementary, my dear Vincent. Elementary economics, that is!"

Let me give you an example from each novel, without revealing the entire plot. *In Murder at the Margin* (Princeton University Press, 1978; paperback, 1993), Spearman is able to dismiss Mrs. Forte as a suspect in the killing of her husband because "a woman usually would be financially far better off by divorcing her husband than by killing him." Mrs. Forte's alimony payments over her expected lifetime would far exceed the death benefits from his insurance policy. Clearly, someone else must have killed Mr. Forte.

In the second novel, *Fatal Equilibrium* (MIT Press, 1985; Ballantine Books paperback, 1986), Spearman uncovers a fraud in the research of a fellow Harvard professor. In reviewing the professor's book on prices of various commodities on a remote island, Spearman discovers a statistic that violates the law of utility maximization. The sleuth quickly concludes that his colleague made up the figures . . . and therefore engaged in murder to hide his fictitious research.

In the third novel, *A Deadly Indifference* (Carroll & Graf, 1995), Spearman is led to suspect an individual who purchases an automobile even though another car in better condition is available at the same price. Obviously, Spearman reasons, the suspect values something in the first car to justify the monetary difference. That something leads to the murderer.

Defending the Free Market

Another likeable feature is the free-market bias running through the mystery series. Henry Spearman consistently defends economic liberty and attacks socialist thinking. He supports free trade, economic inequality, imperfect competition, and private property rights. The economist takes on collectivists of all shades—anthropologists, sociologists, environmentalists, social democrats, Keynesians, and Marxoids.

Who Is This Free-Market Economist?

Who is Henry Spearman, this remarkable proponent of free markets? Spearman is described as a short, balding, stubborn, frowsy professor, former president of the American Economic Association, and a "child of impecunious Jewish immigrants." Breit and Elzinga admit that they originally had Milton Friedman in mind, except that instead of the University of Chicago, Spearman comes from Harvard. "There is no such thing as a free lunch," Spearman declares in *Murder on the Margin* (p. 90). And like Friedman, Spearman is old-fashioned, using a pencil and paper, rather than a computer, to solve problems. Yet the focus of the amateur sleuth is decidedly microeconomic in nature, not monetary policy or macrotheorizing.

Austrian economists will be happy to find a great deal of Ludwig von Mises in Henry Spearman as well. (I thank Auburn economist Roger Garrison for this observation.) The detective-economist defends Say's Law, the financial markets, advertising, competition, commodity money, even methodological dualism. "Economics is different from chemistry," Spearman declares. "The methods are different. What goes on in one place doesn't necessarily go in another" (*Fatal Equilibrium,* p. 111). In *A Deadly Indifference,* the august professor delivers an unpopular speech before the Cambridge faculty in the mid-1960s, forecasting the collapse of Communism because it "is inconsistent with all that we know about the motivations of human action" (p. 36). Like Mises, who predicted the impossiblility of socialist economic calculation, Spearman is ridiculed for his extreme position.

More Like Becker?

However, having read all three novels, my feeling is that Henry Spearman is more like Gary Becker than anyone else. Becker, Chicago professor and Nobel laureate, applies economics to marriage, crime, and other nontraditional areas.[1] So does Spearman, "pushing his economics into criminology." He declares, "Love, hate, benevolence, malevolence or any emotion which involves others can be subject to economic analysis" (*Murder at the Margin,* p. 61).

Spearman, like Becker, also favors Alfred Marshall's definition of economics as the "study of man in the ordinary business of life." "Spearman took this definition seriously even though it was considered a bit old-fashioned to some of his younger colleagues who saw economics as a solving of abstract puzzles unrelated to real events" (*Murder at the Margin,* p. 113). The authors write that Spearman is trained in statistics and corroborates his "high logical standards" with "empirical evidence" (*Fatal Equilibrium,* p. 103). Gary Becker's faithful application of microeconomic principles to solving problems is consistent with Henry Spearman's *modus operandi.* He may not look like Spearman, but he acts like him.

Breit and Elzinga are to be congratulated for developing a creative, clever way to expound the principles of free-market economics. The response has been gratifying. Many professors make *Murder at the Margin* and the other novels required reading in their classes. I recommend you put them on your summer reading list.

Now if only Breit and Elzinga will put their creative minds together to come up with a Broadway play called *The Mysterious Case of the Invisible Hand!*

Part Four

SOLVING INTERNATIONAL PROBLEMS

Economists are active in analyzing and solving global issues, including extreme poverty in Africa, Asia, and Latin America; pollution and environmental degradation; overpopulation; income and wealth inequality; and creating an economic freedom index.

Chapter 19

Eco-nomics Debate

Angry Planet or Beautiful World?

The bright promise of a new millennium is now clouded by unprecedented threats to humanity's future.

—Worldwatch Institute, 2002[1]

We know that the environment is not in good shape. . . . My claim is that things are improving.

—Bjorn Lomborg[2]

Bjorn Lomborg, a Danish professor of statistics, was an environmental activist and member of Greenpeace for years. He accepted at face value the Malthusian views, expressed by Paul Ehrlich, Lester Brown, and groups such as the Worldwatch Institute, Greenpeace, and the Sierra Club, that the world was running out of renewable resources, clean water, and forestland; that the earth was becoming more polluted; and that population growth was exploding.

Then along came Julian Simon, an American economist from the University of Maryland, who challenged Lomborg's thinking. Simon had published several books and papers filled with data supporting his view that life was actually getting better, that air in the developed world was becoming less polluted, that fewer people were starving, and that the population growth was slowing.[3]

Simon made two devastating arguments against the pessimists: First, natural resources are virtually unlimited in the long run because higher prices, reflecting scarcity, encourage the discovery of additional reserves and the use of substitutes. Entrepreneurs and inventors are always developing new technologies and cost-cutting techniques that allow more resources to be discovered and developed. Second, a large and growing population leads to a higher standard of living because it increases the stock of useful knowledge and trained workers.

Lomborg decided to test Simon's statistics. In the fall of 1997, he and a group of students examined Simon's data. Their conclusion: Simon was right. Lomborg reversed course and in 2001 published his findings in *The Skeptical Environmentalist,* which has created a furor within the environmentalist community. His book has created such an impact that *Time* magazine voted Lomborg one of the 100 most influential people in the world.

Now Lomborg joins Simon in refuting most of the claims of the perma-bear environmentalists. Lomborg reports that global forests have increased since World War II; the world's population growth rate peaked in 1964 and has since declined; only 0.7 percent of species has disappeared in the past 50 years; fewer people in the world are denied access to water; incidence of infectious disease is still on the decline worldwide; the number of extremely poor/starving people is also declining; air pollution is lessening in many parts of the world.

Economists have also debunked the popular myth that economic development is responsible for environmental degradation. The truth is largely the opposite. As Lomborg states, "environmental development often stems from economic development—only when we get sufficiently rich can we afford the relative luxury of caring about the environment."[4]

What about Global Warming?

But what about global warming, the overriding concern that our capitalistic lifestyle is changing the climate and could do permanent damage to our ecosystem? The evidence is clear that temperatures have been rising in the past century, but the questions remain: How much of the temperature increase is due to global carbon dioxide emissions and what is the best course of action? Economic analysis shows it will be far more expensive to cut CO_2 emissions radically than to pay the costs of adapting to global warming.[5]

In his most recent book, *Cool It,* Lomborg argues that many of the elaborate and expensive actions now being considered to stop global warming will cost hundreds of billions of dollars, are often based on emotional rather than strictly scientific assumptions, and may very well have little impact on the world's temperature for hundreds of years. "It's a bad deal," he concludes. Unfortunately, the debate is often emotional and shrill. In several chapters, Lomborg recounts what self-proclaimed climatologists have said about anyone who questions their orthodoxy, thus demonstrating the illiberal, antidemocratic tone of the current debate. Lomborg himself takes a less emotional stance, explaining in detail why the tone of hysteria is inappropriate to addressing the problems we face. He begins by dispatching the myth of the endangered polar bears. Lomborg discusses the issue in detail, first citing sources from Al Gore to the World Wildlife Fund, then demonstrating that polar bear populations have actually increased fivefold since the 1960s.

Lomborg believes firmly that climate change is real, but his approach, grounded in data and economic analyses, leads him to a different solution. Rather than starting with the most radical procedures for long-term change, Lomborg argues that we should first focus our resources on more immediate concerns, such as fighting malaria and HIV/AIDS and assuring and maintaining a safe, fresh water supply—which can be addressed at a fraction of the cost and save millions of lives within our lifetime.[6]

The Polluted State: Tragedy of the Commons

Economists have also emphasized "government failure" in the debate about the environment. Recent studies reveal that less-developed countries, including the former Soviet Union, have had more pollution, lower health standards, and more environmental hazards than industrialized nations. Economists Terry Anderson and Donald Leal point to several examples of government mismanagement: National parks such as Yellowstone are in major disrepair, the U.S. Park Service is notoriously wasteful (it built a $330,000 outhouse), the Canadian government destroyed the cod industry, and the government of Brazil and Indonesia forced migrants to burn once-pristine rain forests in order to plant crops.[7]

Economics has provided workable solutions to pollution and environmental degradation. One problem is what is known as the "tragedy of the commons." In a 1968 issue of *Science,* Garrett Hardin, emeritus professor of biological sciences at the University of California at Santa Barbara, wrote a seminal article arguing that a resource tends to be overexploited when owned by the public and not by private individuals. For example, if no one owns a piece of grazing land, each herdsman has an incentive to add another animal to the herd until the land is overgrazed. Similarly, if no one owns a forest, no one has an incentive to plant new trees to replace those that are harvested. As a result, "Freedom in a common brings ruin to all."[8]

Hence, the lack of property rights and market prices creates a "tragedy of the commons"—unnecessary pollution, extinction of animals, destruction of forests, strip mining, and more. At first government favored regulation as a solution, but economists have encouraged the establishment of clearly specified property rights and accompanying price signals in water, fishing, and forestland, so that owners can preserve and renew these resources in a balanced way.

Cap-and-Trade, or Carbon Tax?

In the 1990s, economists played a major role in the passage of the 1990 Clean Air Act, which established "emissions trading" for the first time. The Clean Air Act established the first "cap-and-trade" system to reduce emissions of sulfur dioxide (SO_2), the primary cause of acid rain. Cap-and-trade draws on the power of the marketplace to reduce greenhouse gases and other emissions in a cost-effective and flexible manner. Essentially, emissions trading creates a financial incentive to reduce polluting.

Here's how it works. First a government environmental agency establishes a limit ("cap") on the amount of pollution permitted by a designated group, such as power plants or mining companies. The emissions allowed under the new cap are then divided up into individual permits—usually equal to one ton of pollution—that represents the right to emit that amount. Companies are then free to buy and sell permits ("trade") on an exchange. Companies with lower emission costs can sell their permits to companies with higher costs.

How does this encourage a reduction in overall pollution? Both the buyer and seller of emissions permits benefit from lowering their costs of polluting. If Plant A is a low polluter, below the cap, it can sell its permits to Plant B, a high polluter. By reducing its emissions, Plant A can sell more permits. And Plant B, by cutting its emissions, can buy fewer permits and therefore save money. Both win by cutting back on pollution.

Thus, cap-and-trade exerts constant pressure on polluters and creates a financial incentive for companies to adopt or create new pollution-saving technology that meets or exceeds their emission targets in an innovative and cost-effective way. This system has proven to be an environmental and economic success—reducing SO_2 emissions at a fraction of the expected costs. Moreover, environmental groups have gotten into the business by purchasing and retiring pollution credits, thereby doing their part to reduce overall emissions and raise the price of the remaining credits according to the law of demand. Some corporations have also retired their pollution credits by donating them to a nonprofit environmental group taking advantage of a tax deduction.

The European Union and other regions have also designed their own cap-and-trade systems for CO_2 emissions. As a result, a healthy competition has sprung up in Europe around the trading of emissions credits. The European Exchange ECX has skyrocketed in value, causing shares of Climate Exchange, Plc, the Isle of Man–based parent company of ECX, to surge on the London Stock Exchange. Total volume for emissions contracts on the ECX has jumped from 94.3 million metric tons in 2005 to over 600 million metric tons in 2007.

Some environmental groups and economists have criticized cap-and-trade as too volatile and uncertain in meeting the goals of lower pollution. The United States has had tradable permits for SO_2 since the mid-1990s, and their price can vary by more than 40 percent a year.

Extreme price volatility might also deter people from investing in green technology. In addition, cap-and-trade provides no revenue to the government, which could use the cash to reduce other inefficient taxes. Critics favor a carbon tax imposed directly on companies. Even then, there are problems. Can policymakers have sufficient knowledge to set an optimal tax? Austrian economist Friedrich Hayek warned that it is difficult if not impossible for a central authority to know the optimal level of emissions and the optimal tax rate.

In sum, free-market environmentalism has come a long way in showing how to replace the regulatory fist of command with a greener invisible hand. Many free-market think tanks, such as the Property and Environment Research Center (PERC) and the Competitive Enterprise Institute, have challenged the supremacy of the Sierra Club and Greenpeace.[9] Earth Day will never be the same.

Chapter 20

The Population Bomb

Economists Enter the Malthusian Debate

Overpopulation is the most serious threat to human happiness and progress in this very critical period in the history of the world.

—JULIAN HUXLEY (1962)[1]

In 1968, the Sierra Club published an alarmist book, *The Population Bomb,* by a young Stanford biologist, Paul R. Ehrlich. Ehrlich described a scary scenario, warning that "at this late date nothing can prevent a substantial increase in the world death rate.... In the 1970s the world will undergo famines—hundreds of millions of people are going to starve to death." What could bring about this disaster? Ehrlich spoke in Malthusian tones: "We must take action to reverse the deterioration of our environment before population pressure permanently ruins our planet. The birth rate must be brought into balance with the death rate or mankind will breed itself into oblivion."[2]

143

Ehrlich and the Sierra Club raised awareness of an issue that has attracted the attention of governments, foundations, and wealthy do-gooders everywhere: population control, especially in countries with high birth rates. Ehrlich and friends argued that uncontrolled population was a menace, using up too many precious resources, destroying the wilderness, cutting down too many trees, and polluting the environment. In developing countries, Ehrlich took a page from the nineteenth-century political economist Thomas Robert Malthus—the first political economist to raise the issue of overpopulation—when he identified a "population-food crisis," in which "each year food production in underdeveloped countries falls a bit further behind burgeoning population growth, and people go to bed a little bit hungrier. . . . Mass starvation now seems inevitable."[3]

The First Population Alarmist: Reverend Malthus

Thomas Robert Malthus (1766–1834) was a British minister who, in 1798, at the age of thirty-two, published an anonymous work entitled *Essay on Population*. In it, he contended that earth's resources could not keep up with the demands of an ever-growing population. His brooding tract forever changed the landscape of economics and politics, and quickly cut short the positive outlook of Adam Smith, J. B. Say, Benjamin Franklin, and other thinkers of the Enlightenment. Malthus asserted that pressures on limited resources would always keep the overwhelming majority of human beings close to the edge of subsistence.

Malthus has had a powerful impact on modern-day thinking. He is considered the founder of demography and population studies. He is acknowledged to be the mentor of social engineers who advocate strict population control and limits to economic growth. His essay on population underlines the gloomy and fatalistic outlook of many scientists and social reformers who forecast poverty, crime, famine, war, and environmental degradation due to population pressures on resources. He even inspired Charles Darwin's theory of organic evolution, describing how limited resources facing unlimited demands create the power of natural selection and survival of the fittest. Ultimately the fatalistic pessimism of Malthus (and his friend David Ricardo) gave economics its reputation as a "dismal science."

Malthus's doomsday thesis is that "the power of population is indefinitely greater than the power of the earth to produce subsistence for man," and therefore the majority of humans were doomed to live a Hobbesian existence.[4] His book identified two basic "laws of nature:" first, that population tends to increase geometrically (1, 2, 4, 8, 16, 32 . . .), and second, food production (resources) tends to increase only arithmetically (1, 2, 3, 4, 5 . . .). The means of supporting human life were "limited by the scarcity of land" and the "constant tendency to diminish" the availability of resources, a reference to the law of diminishing returns. The result would be an inevitable crisis of "misery and vice" whereby the earth's resources would not satisfy the demands of a growing population.[5]

Is Malthus right about the first "law of nature," that human population grows geometrically? Indeed, since Malthus wrote his essay, the world's population has skyrocketed from fewer than 1 billion people to over 6 billion. However, in looking more deeply at the sharp rise in world population since 1800, we see that the cause is not Malthusian in nature. The increase has been due to two factors unforeseen by Malthus. First, there has been a sharp drop in the infant mortality rate due to the elimination of many life-threatening diseases and illnesses through medical technology. Second, there has been a steady rise in the average life span of individuals, due to improvements in sanitation, health care, and nutrition; higher living standards; medical breakthroughs; and a decline in the accident rate. As a result, more people are living into their adult lives, and more adults are living longer.

Moreover, there is a good chance that world population will soon top out, due especially to the sharp slowdown in the birthrate in the past 50 years, both in industrial and developing countries. This is largely due to the wealth effect: Wealthier people tend to have fewer children (contrary to what Malthus predicted). Over the past 50 years, the birthrate in developed countries has fallen from 2.8 to 1.9, and in developing countries from 6.2 to 3.9. The trend is unmistakable. Women are having fewer children and in some more developed countries, especially Europe, the birthrate is far below replacement. Europe today isn't worried about Malthusian overpopulation. Far from it—they are more worried about the depopulation of Europe and their growing dependence on immigration.

Malthus's Sins of Omission

What about Malthus's second "law of nature," that resources are limited and restricted by the law of diminishing returns? Here again, history has not supported Malthus. The law of diminishing returns only applies if we assume "all other things being equal," that technology and the quantity of other resources are fixed. But no input is fixed in the long run—neither land, labor, nor capital. The economic importance of land has in fact dwindled in the modern world, due to intensive farming techniques and the green revolution. Malthus ignored the technological advances in agriculture, the constant discovery of new minerals and other resources in the earth, and the role of prices in determining how fast or slow resources are used up. In short, he failed to recognize human ingenuity.[6]

Malthus proved to be spectacularly wrong about food production, the advent of farming technology, the use of fertilizers, and the vast expansion of irrigation. The amounts of cultivated land and food production have risen dramatically. Most famines can be blamed on ill-advised government policies, not nature.

The story of Thomas Malthus is instructive in developing an understanding of the dynamics of a growing economy and a rising population. Granted, Malthus recognized that government intervention is typically counterproductive in alleviating poverty and controlling population growth, and thus he joined Adam Smith in adopting a laissez-faire policy (he was vilified by critics for opposing poverty programs, birth control, and even vaccines). But he ultimately abandoned his mentor by disavowing faith in Mother Earth and the free market's ability to match the supply of resources with the growing demands of a rising population. Essentially, he failed to comprehend the role of prices and property rights as an incentive to ration scarce resources and a problem-solving mechanism. Worse, he misunderstood the dynamics of a growing entrepreneurial economy—how a larger population creates its own seeds of prosperity through the creation of new ideas and new technology.

Chapter 21

A Private-Sector Solution to Extreme Poverty

The able-bodied poor don't want or need charity. . . . All they need is financial capital.

—MUHAMMAD YUNUS

Prior to teaching at New York University, economist William Easterly spent the bulk of his adult life working for the World Bank, living in the Third World, and helping poor countries develop into rich countries. In his highly acclaimed book, *The Elusive Quest for Growth,* he warns how difficult it is to create the right atmosphere for sustained growth and escape the vicious cycle of poverty. But above all, Easterly lectures his former employer, the World Bank, about the impossibility of foreign aid and most other development policies pursued by government to help poor countries. While he admits that "there are no magic elixirs," it is clear that "incentives matter" and "government can kill growth."[1]

For years economists have protested the waste and abuse of foreign aid programs, International Monetary Fund loans, and World Bank projects.[2] Lord Peter Bauer was in the forefront as a dissenter against government development programs. During the second half of the twentieth century, he argued forcefully that government assistance in developing nations only retards economic growth.[3] In a follow-up book, Easterly labels the IMF and the World Bank as "bloated aid bureaucracies that are accountable to no one." In conclusion, he declares, "After fifty years and more than $2.3 trillion in aid from the West, there is shockingly little to show for it."[4]

But if IMF lending, foreign aid, and the World Bank are abolished, what should be done to alleviate poverty, especially among the billion people on earth who live on $2 a day or less? Bauer and other classical liberals advocate establishing property rights, the rule of law, and a stable monetary policy; reducing trade barriers; increasing foreign investment; and encouraging free markets and limited government domestically. But is this enough?

Private-Sector Microlending

Not to be ignored is the burgeoning private-sector success story known as "microlending," the lending of extremely small amounts of money to self-employed entrepreneurs in the Third World by independent banks and institutions. The most famous of these microlenders is the Grameen Bank, founded in 1983 by Muhammad Yunus in Bangladesh, the world's poorest country. In less than three decades, Yunus and his Grameen Bank have done more to alleviate extreme poverty than the entire $2.3 trillion in wasted foreign aid programs.

As we mentioned at the beginning of this book, Yunus was a professional economist who taught for years at Chittagong University in Bangladesh. After years of teaching about poverty and economic growth, he finally decided to do something about it. In 1976, during visits to the poorest households in the village of Jobra near the university, Yunus discovered that very small loans could make a disproportionate difference to a poor person. These desperately poor women made bamboo furniture and had to take out usurious loans in order to buy bamboo. They then sold these items to the moneylenders to repay them. With only a profit of BDT 0.50 (US$ 0.02), the women were unable to support their families. Yunus's first loan to them was the equivalent of $27 each, taken from his own pocket, which he lent to 42 women in the village of Jobra. It turned out to be the beginning of a worldwide industry.

Only an economist would devise such a plan to help alleviate poverty. For centuries, do-gooders and socialites gave away billions and created tax-exempt foundations to help the poor, but people like Professor Yunus, trained in the principles of accountability, incentives, profit and loss, thrift, and education, know that a genuine loan program from a for-profit bank can really work.

When I say "small loans," I mean shockingly minuscule. The Grameen Bank lends only $30 to $200 per borrower. Applicants don't have to read or write to qualify. No collateral or credit check is required. Amazingly, the Grameen Bank has made these microloans to millions of poverty-stricken people in Bangladesh, $3 billion so far. These loans are not an interest-free handout. The Grameen Bank is a for-profit private-sector self-help bank that charges 18 percent interest rates. The default rate? Less than 2 percent. This remarkable record is due to the requirement that borrowers must join small support groups. If anyone in the group defaults, no one else can borrow more. Consequently, it is social pressure, not the collection agency, that keeps the loans current.

The Grameen Bank lends to entrepreneurs, overwhelmingly female, who need only a few dollars to buy supplies and tools. Borrowers might want to make bamboo chairs, sell goat's milk, or drive rickshaws. By avoiding the outrageous rates charged by other moneylenders (often 20 percent per month), these people are finally able to break the cycle of poverty. Their small businesses grow, and some use their profits to build new homes or repair existing ones (often using a $300 Grameen house loan). Thousands of Grameen borrowers now own land, homes, and even cell phones. They are sending their children to school. And they are no longer starving. Yunus has plans to issue private stock and eventually go public with his antipoverty program.

His bank has been so successful that other microlending institutions have sprung up throughout the world. The concept has gained credence everywhere, to the point that the World Bank, other government agencies, and even for-profit Western banks have gotten into the million-dollar microloans businesses.

Saying No to the World Bank

But Yunus won't have anything to do with the World Bank. In his autobiography, *Banker to the Poor* (highly recommended), Yunus decries the World Bank: "We at the Grameen Bank have never wanted or accepted World Bank funding because we do not like the way the bank conducts business." Nor does he much like foreign aid: "Most rich nations use their foreign aid budgets mainly to employ their own people and to sell their own goods, with poverty reduction as an afterthought. . . . Aid-funded projects create massive bureaucracies, which quickly become corrupt and inefficient, incurring huge losses. . . . Aid money still goes to expand government spending, often acting against the interests of the market economy. . . . Foreign aid becomes a kind of charity for the powerful while the poor get poorer."[5] Peter Bauer couldn't have said it better.

From Marxism to Marketism

Yunus's statements are all the more amazing given that he grew up under the influence of Marxist economics. But after earning a Ph.D. in economics at Vanderbilt University, and seeing firsthand "how the market [in the United States] liberates the individual," he rejected socialism. "I do believe in the power of the global free-market economy and in using capitalist tools. . . . I also believe that providing unemployment benefits is not the best way to address poverty." Believing that "all human beings are potential entrepreneurs," Yunus is convinced that poverty can be eradicated by lending poor people the capital they need to engage in profitable businesses, not by giving them a government handout or forcing population control.

His former Marxist colleagues call it a capitalist conspiracy. "What you are really doing," a communist professor told him, "is giving little bits of opium to the poor people. . . . Their revolutionary zeal cools down. Therefore, Grameen is the enemy of the revolution."[6]

Precisely. He is an enemy to the violent overthrow of the capitalist society. There's no better example of a program that encourages "peace through commerce." And for that Muhammad Yunus well deserves the Nobel Peace Prize he won in 2006.

Chapter 22

Poverty and Wealth: India versus Hong Kong

The government of India regulates nearly everything, so there's very little progress; whereas in Hong Kong the government keeps its hands off . . . and the standard of living has multiplied.

—John Templeton[1]

The mutual fund magnate John Templeton traveled around the world during the 1930s, noting in particular the extreme poverty in two Asian nations under British control: India and Hong Kong. Forty years later, in the 1970s, Templeton returned. Once again he witnessed the incredible poverty in India, which was now politically independent. But Hong Kong had changed tremendously. "The standard of living in Hong Kong had multiplied more than tenfold in forty years, while the standard of living in Calcutta has improved hardly at all."[2]

Today neither country is under British rule, but the contrast is even more clear. Hong Kong enjoys the greatest concentration of wealth in the world. India, even after considerable progress recently, suffers the greatest concentration of poverty in the world.[3]

In the early 1980s, development economist P. T. Bauer wrote a famous little essay in which he pondered, "How would you rate the economic prospects of an Asian country which has very little land (and only eroded hillsides at that), and which is indeed the most densely populated country in the world; whose population has grown rapidly, both through natural increase and large-scale immigration; which imports all of its oil and raw materials, and even most of its water; whose government is not engaged in development planning and operates no exchange controls or restrictions on capital exports and imports; and which is the only remaining Western colony of any significance?"[4]

Indeed, the prospects for Hong Kong were dismal. Yet by manufacturing cheap products for export to the faraway West, it managed to become the powerhouse of Southeast Asia. Today its citizens' incomes rival the Japanese, despite its teeming 7 million people crowded into 400 square miles. What broke the vicious cycle of poverty? According to Bauer, Hong Kong's economic miracle did not depend on having money, natural resources, foreign aid, or even formal education, but rather on the "industry, enterprise, thrift and ability . . . of highly motivated people."[5] Hong Kong's "overpopulation" turned out to be an asset, not a liability.

Equally important, Britain did not interfere in private decision making. It adopted a laissez-faire economic policy, except in the area of subsidized housing and education. Communist China has continued this largely noninterventionist approach since it took over in 1997, and as a result, Hong Kong continues to flourish with a stable currency, free port, and low taxes. Its maximum income tax rate is 18 percent, and it imposes no capital-gains tax. In its economic freedom index, the Fraser Institute has always ranked Hong Kong number one in the world.[6]

From Tragic India . . .

India is an entirely different story. Its population of 1 billion remains relatively poor. Yet, unlike Hong Kong, India has valuable natural resources, including forests, fish, oil, iron ore, coal, and agricultural products, among others. It has achieved self-sufficiency in food since its independence in 1947, but deep poverty persists.

Many pundits blame India's anticapitalist culture, its fatalistic caste system, its overpopulation problem, and its hot and humid climate (it reached a humid 117 degrees when we visited the Taj Mahal in June a few years ago). But Milton Friedman identified the real culprit when he wrote, "The correct explanation is . . . not to be found in its religious or social attitudes, or in the quality of its people, but rather in the economic policy that India has adopted."[7]

Indeed, in the decade after independence, Nehru and other Indian leaders were heavily influenced by Harold Laski of the London School of Economics and his fellow Fabians, who advocated central planning along Soviet lines. India adopted five-year plans, nationalized heavy industries, and imposed import-substitution laws. Worse, they perpetuated the British civil-service tradition of exercising controls over foreign exchange and requiring licenses to start businesses.

Even today, India is a bureaucratic nightmare.[8] Parth Shah, an economist and head of the Centre for Civil Society (www.ccsindia. org),[9] describes how he recently returned to India and toiled to find an apartment in New Delhi (thanks to rent controls), then spent half a day standing in line to pay his first telephone bill and another half a day to pay his electricity bill. "Corruption has become the standard among those who are in public service at every level," reports Gita Mehta, a well-known Indian writer.[10] India has ranked around number 100 over the years on the Fraser Institute's index of economic freedom.

. . . To New India

Yet there is hope. In 1991, facing default on its foreign debt, India abandoned four decades of economic isolation and planning, and freed the nation's entrepreneurs. It sold off many of its state companies, cut tariffs and taxes, and eliminated most price and exchange controls. As a result, India became one of the world's fastest-growing economies since the mid-1990s, averaging nearly 10 percent growth per year. Most important, while the rich have gotten richer, poverty rates have fallen sharply in India.

Can India ever catch up to Hong Kong? As the world's most populous country, it seems impossible. But India could make great strides by cutting its government deficits; slashing tariffs and taxes further; privatizing more state enterprises; eliminating red tape in business; and restoring honesty in government. International business is also playing a major role as India has become a major outsourcing of service jobs. It's a tall order but the only way to achieve what Adam Smith called "universal opulence which extends itself to the lowest ranks of the people."[11]

Chapter 23

How Real Is the Asian Economic Miracle?

Singapore grew through a mobilization of resources that would have done Stalin proud.
> —Paul Krugman, "The Myth of Asia's Miracle"
> *Foreign Affairs* (November/December, 1994)

If there is one formula for our success, it is that we were constantly studying how to make things work, or how to make them work better.
> —Lee Kuan Yew, former prime minister, Singapore[1]

The postwar Asian economic miracle has come as a great shock to many political pundits. In recent textbooks, few historians have described the wonders of Japanese prosperity and the secrets of the Four Tigers (Hong Kong, Singapore, Korea, and Taiwan) or the newly industrialized economies (Indonesia, Malaysia, and Thailand). Even the Chinese economic miracle has only recently been highlighted.

A desperate, starving, shattered Japan of 1945 was one of the poorest countries on earth. There were no skyscrapers, no wealthy banks, no automobile and electronics industries. Yet within a single human life span, Japan has become an economic superpower, ranking second behind the United States among the world's richest nations.

Hong Kong has faced gigantic problems: 6 million people jammed into 400 square miles, with no oil or other natural resources, most of its water and food imported, and its trading partners thousands of miles away. Yet this small British colony has broken the vicious cycle of poverty to become the second-most prosperous country in the Pacific Basin.

Since 1965, the 23 economies of East Asia have grown faster than all other regions of the world. The high-performing Asian economies have experienced extremely rapid growth and rising incomes. The proportion of Asians living in absolute poverty has dropped sharply. Life expectancy has increased from 56 years in 1960 to 71 years in 1990.[2]

The Cause of the Miracle

Why have American historians ignored until recently these economic success stories? Perhaps because the Asian development model does not fit neatly into the Keynesian framework and policy prescriptions, which favor high levels of consumption, debt, and government spending. In almost all of the rapidly growing economies in East Asia, the degree of government taxation and central planning has been relatively low, savings rates excessively high by Keynesian standards, government budgets normally in surplus, and the welfare state relatively small. As the World Bank concluded in its 1993 study, "the rapid growth in each economy was primarily due to the application of a set of common, market-friendly economic policies, leading to both higher accumulation and better allocation of resources."[3]

Krugman's Challenge

Now along comes Professor Paul Krugman to throw water on the whole idea of an Asian miracle. Krugman, who teaches at Princeton University, is the darling of the establishment media and is referred to repeatedly as a brilliant *wunderkind,* a future Nobel Prize winner, and according to *The*

Economist, "the most celebrated economist of his generation." According to Krugman, there is nothing miraculous about Asian economic growth. It is *déjà vu,* a repeat of the incredible growth rates of the Soviet Union in a bygone era (1920–1990). Krugman sees "surprising similarities" between East Asia and the former Soviet Union. Both engaged in an "extraordinary mobilization of resources." In the case of the Soviet Union, Krugman notes, "Stalinist planners had moved millions of workers from farms to cities, pushed millions of women into the labor force and millions of men into longer hours, pursued massive programs of education, and above all plowed an ever-growing proportion of the country's industrial output back into the construction of new factories."[4]

According to Krugman, East Asian leaders have been just as authoritarian, pushing more of the population to work, upgrading educational standards, and making an awesome investment in physical capital. In short, East Asia is just like the Soviet Union, "growth achieved purely through mobilization of resources."

Moreover, like the Soviet Union, growth in East Asia is likely to diminish, due to limits on labor and capital. Krugman states, "it is likely that growth in East Asia will continue to outpace growth in the West for the next decade and beyond. But it will not do so at the pace of recent years."[5] Asia, in other words, is subject to the law of diminishing returns.

The Tyranny of Numbers

I have serious reservations about Krugman's ivory-tower analysis of the Asian miracle. First, his comparison to the Soviet Union is attention-getting, but fundamentally flawed. The Soviet Union was primarily a command economy; the Asian nations (with the exception of China) are relatively free economies. The Stalinists engaged in grim industrialization and militarization at the expense of the Soviet standard of living. In this sense, Soviet growth statistics were largely fictitious. As Soviet expert Marshall Goldman stated in the early 1980s, "This system keeps producing steel and basic machine tools, when what is wanted is food, consumer goods, and more modern technology."[6]

On the other hand, the Asians mobilized resources by producing an increasingly sophisticated range of products demanded by international markets, and thereby increased dramatically their own standard of living.

Singapore's Economic Miracle

Let's look more closely at Singapore. Was it a Soviet-style command economy, as Paul Krugman alleges? Lee Kuan Yew's autobiographical account of Singapore is revealing in this regard. Lee became president of the tiny, poverty-stricken British colony after it was granted independence in 1965. In one generation, he oversaw its transformation into an Asian giant with the world's number-one airline, best airport, busiest port of trade, and the world's fourth-largest per capita real income.

How did this economic miracle happen?

First, Lee offered real leadership. He was a seminal figure in Asia who accomplished extraordinary things. He built an army from scratch, won over the unions, and destroyed the communists after the British left a vacuum. Despite strong opposition, he insisted on making English one of four official spoken languages, knowing it was fast becoming the language of international business. Singapore, like other Southeast Asian countries, was known for its nepotism, favoritism, and covert corruption; Lee cleaned up the courts, police, and immigration and customs offices. Today Singapore is ranked as the least corrupt country in Asia. Singapore was also dirty, so Lee began a "clean and green" campaign. Rivers, canals, and drains were cleaned up and millions of trees, palms, and shrubs were planted.

The Lee government tore down dilapidated shacks and replaced them with high-rise apartments. He imposed law and order by demanding severe sentences for murder and other crimes. Today Singapore ranks number one in the world for security. To reduce traffic congestion, a huge problem in Asian cities, Singapore built an underground subway system, and imposed an electronic road-pricing program. Every vehicle has a "smart card" on its windshield, and the toll amount varies with the road used and the time of day. During rush hour, the price goes up. "Since the amount people pay now depends upon how much they use the roads, the optimum number of cars can be owned with the minimum of congestion."[7] We discussed this sound transportation system earlier in Chapter 12.

Lee rejected Soviet-style central planning and domestic heavy industry, although he did target certain industries for development. He focused on a two-pronged plan to advance Singapore: First, his government encouraged domestic industry to leap over their close neighbors and link up with the developed world of America, Europe, and Japan, by attracting their manufacturers to produce in Singapore. Second, Lee created a First World oasis in the Third World by establishing top standards in security, health, education, communications, and transportation, and a government offering a stable currency, low taxes, and free trade. Singapore would become a base camp for multinational corporations from around the world. And, after years of effort, it worked.

Under Lee's brilliant leadership, Singapore has advanced far beyond anyone's dreams. Yet we cannot ignore his mistakes—his paternalistic strong-arm tactics, his interventionist targeting of industries, his forced saving programs, his denial of a free press, and his excessive punishments for certain crimes. Lee stepped down as prime minister in 1990, but has continued to function as "Minister Mentor" under his son Lee Hsien Loong, who became the nation's third prime minister in 2004. Singapore remains one of the fastest-growing nations in Asia.

The Lessons of Asia

Since writing his negative assessment of Asia in 1994, Krugman has been proven wrong. So far there's no evidence of diminishing returns hitting Asia. If anything, with the growth in China, we've witnessed increasing returns. Ultimately, Krugman misses the bigger picture. The real question is: Why have so few developing countries outside the Asian region been able to produce their own miracles? And what can industrial nations such as the United States and Europe learn from the Asian miracle?

The answer is clear. The Asian economies have grown rapidly for a number of reasons. First, they are largely market-friendly, avoiding wage-price controls and excessive regulation of business. Second, they encourage macroeconomic stability by avoiding high levels of inflation and budget deficits, limit government activism, and discourage social welfare schemes. Third, they offer stable and secure financial and legal systems (the 1997 Asian currency crisis being an exception). Fourth, they promote high levels of saving and capital investment rather than high-consumption spending. Fifth, many East Asian nations offer tax holidays for export-oriented businesses and impose few (if any) taxes on investments. Sixth, they are open to global technology and foreign capital.

Granted, many Asian countries limit civil liberties, engage in industrial planning, restrict imports, and artificially undervalue their currencies, but overall the degree of government intervention is relatively low, or has been reduced sharply as in China.

Many developing countries in Latin America and Africa are adopting free-market reforms and creating their own miracles. The industrial nations could regain their traditional growth rates by adopting a large dose of supply-side economics, cutting taxes on business and investment, privatizing Social Security, promoting better education and training, streamlining regulations on business and employment, and eliminating the federal deficit. As Ludwig von Mises concludes, "it is one of the foremost tasks of good government to remove all obstacles that hinder the accumulation and investment in new capital."[8]

Chapter 24

Whatever Happened
to the Egyptians?

*Governments are generally reluctant to admit mistakes and to change
mistaken policies until much harm has been done.*
                                        —P. T. BAUER AND B. S. YAMEY[1]

In *Whatever Happened to the Egyptians?* (American University in Cairo
Press, 2001), a popular book in Egypt, author Galan Amin raises a
good question. Thousands of years ago Egypt was the birthplace of
one of the world's greatest civilizations, with remarkable advances in
architecture, astronomy, mathematics, and economics. The pharaohs ruled
Egypt for centuries.

But today Egypt is a fallen nation. On our arrival a few years ago
at the port of Alexandria, once the city of dreams, we saw garbage and
dust scattered profusely on the public highways. Arriving in Cairo to

see the ancient pyramids, we saw filthy canals, undrinkable water, dire poverty, noisy traffic, teeming millions, incessant vendors, and more dust.

I picked up a copy of a book on what it's like for a Westerner to live in Cairo. Author Claire Francy lists so many shortages that she urges foreign residents to bring the following with them: answering machine, major appliances, computers, modems, printers, telephones, fax machines, cosmetics, flashlights, pantyhose, wines, books in English, clothes, and shoes. Yes, shoes. "In a city with nearly as many shoe stores as feet, it is almost impossible to find decent shoes."[2] Oh, the joys of import-substitution laws![3]

And yet Egypt has tremendous resources: oil, cotton, some of the best fertile land in the world along the Nile Valley, a first-rate irrigation system, the Suez Canal, and a huge labor force (nearly 70 million and growing rapidly). Yet true unemployment is 20 percent, and underemployment is endemic. Egypt suffers from a huge brain drain, with 2.5 million Egyptians working abroad. The nation has illiteracy rates of 66 percent among women and 37 percent among men. It imports half of its food. After Israel, this Arab-African nation is the highest recipient of U.S. foreign aid in the world.

Islamic Economics

What's the cause of this economic collapse? A few blame the Islamic religion for their troubles. Over 90 percent of Egyptians are Sunni Muslims who, critics say, pray too much (five times a day), are overly generous to the poor (and thus support a socialistic welfare state), bear too many children (Egypt has one of the highest birthrates in the world), and suffer an excessive financial burden (in the practice of providing housing for their children as a marital dowry). Egyptians are constantly celebrating holidays, among them the month-long Ramadan consisting of daytime fasting and nighttime feasting, when business activity becomes erratic.

But religion is not the true cause of Egypt's struggles. The real culprit is socialist interventionism in the economy. As one unnamed economist states, "The Egyptian economy bears the legacy of economic policies dating from the 1950s which were motivated by concern for equity and assistance to the poor. These policies were characterized by price regulation, subsidization of consumer goods, a dominant public sector and state control."[4] When Gamal Abdel Nasser gained power in 1954, he established a "democratic socialist state," nationalized everything under the sun (including the local beer company), and dramatically increased government control of the economy. Moreover, under a Napoleonic code, Egypt suffers from a regulatory nightmare of paperwork and bureaucracy.

One of the most harmful policies in Egypt has been import-substitution laws—the use of tariffs, quotas, subsidies, and restrictions to protect and promote local production of all kinds of consumer goods, from shoes to toothpaste to automobiles. This form of protectionism has been popular in Third World countries ever since development economists such as Gunnar Myrdal and Paul Rosenstein-Rodan claimed that import restrictions would stimulate domestic industry and employment. In Egypt, for example, the U.S. government spent roughly $200 million to help Egypt create a domestic cement industry, even though cement could be obtained more cheaply abroad.

Such policies have proven counterproductive. Today Cairo is covered with dust caused by the local cement factories. Egypt's import-substitution laws have created shoddy workmanship and above-market prices in shoes, appliances, and consumer products. Today most economists have changed their minds about import-substitution laws, admitting that they stifle growth. They point to the rapid expansion of East Asian nations, which eschewed import substitution and have concentrated instead on producing inexpensive exports.[5]

Fortunately, Nasser's successor, Anwar el-Sadat, began a program of reducing the role of government. After his tragic assassination in 1981, Hosni Mubarak accelerated market policies of privatization and foreign investment, and eliminated price and exchange controls. The local beer company is now in private hands. Yet even today, 36 percent of the labor force is employed by the government, and the economy continues to suffer from overregulation and controls.

Egypt has made some progress since 1990, when the Fraser Institute ranked it 88th in the Institute's economic freedom report. Today it is ranked 80th.[6] Clearly the Egyptian leaders have a long way to go to fulfill the Koran's promise of "wealth and children" as the "adornments of this present life."

Chapter 25

The Irish
Economic Miracle

Can We Grow Faster?

It would not be foolish to contemplate the possibility of a far greater progress still.

—JOHN MAYNARD KEYNES[1]

In 1930, at the beginning of the Great Depression, John Maynard Keynes wrote an optimistic essay titled "Economic Possibilities for our Grandchildren." After lambasting his disciples who predicted never-ending depression and permanent stagnation, Keynes foresaw a bright future. Through technological improvements and capital accumulation, mankind could virtually solve its economic problem within the next hundred years, he said. Goods and services would become so abundant and cheap that leisure would be the biggest challenge. According to Keynes, capital could become so inexpensive that interest rates might fall to zero.

Interest rates have not fallen to zero, but our standard of living has advanced remarkably since the Great Depression. In fact, we have probably already fulfilled Keynes's prediction that "the standard of living in progressive countries one hundred years hence will be between four and eight times as high as to-day."[2]

Outlook by Top Economists

Today's economists don't appear to be as optimistic as Keynes, even as we enter another year of a dynamic, full-employment economy. I asked several well-known economists for recommendations that would give us sustained (long-term, not short-term) economic growth rates of 6, 7, or maybe even 10 percent a year, eventually fulfilling Keynes's economic nirvana.

"Not possible!" most of them exclaimed. "I think it's impossible to double the long-term growth rate in the U.S.," answered Harvard economist Robert Barro. David Colander of Middlebury College agreed. "The idea of doubling economic growth in ten years sounds very much like a central planning goal of the former Soviet system." He quoted Herbert Stein: "Economic policy is random with respect to the performance of the American economy, but thank God there isn't much of it."

On the other hand, a whole book of essays was recently devoted to charting a course toward higher growth rates. In the foreword to *The Rising Tide,* Dana Mead, CEO of Tenneco and former chairman of the National Association of Manufacturers, rejected the notion that the U.S. economy can't exceed its secular long-term growth pattern of around 3 percent a year. He argued that faster economic growth is achievable without creating shortages, rising labor costs, and higher interest rates. As Jack Kemp stated, "We can raise the ceiling on growth by judicious changes in policy."[3]

Of course, not all the economists in the book agree with Mead and Kemp. The late James Tobin, Yale professor and Nobel laureate, declared, "Although politicians freely promise faster growth, governments have no handy set of tools for effecting it."[4] Apparently he hasn't found the formula to fulfill his mentor Keynes's dream of universal opulence.

Despite their skepticism of substantially higher growth rates, major economists do offer several ways to improve long-term prospects. The late Rudi Dornbusch of MIT recommended privatizing Social Security and education. Harvard economist Robert Barro urged a flat-rate consumption tax, exemption of savings from taxation, deregulation of labor and business, and a 10 percent cut in the size of government. Nobel laureate Robert Mundell warned against inflating the money supply as a growth tool and instead favors slashing capital gains and income tax rates to encourage entrepreneurship and investing. "A lower level of government spending would make more of the surplus of society available for capital formation and growth. A shift in government priorities from consumption and redistribution to social overhead capital, improved education, and investment in scientific and medical research would go far in raising the productivity of capital with a permanent effect on growth."[5]

The Celtic Tiger: The Luck of the Irish

Ireland is an excellent example of potential change in economic growth. For years Ireland was known as the stepchild of Britain, suffering from rigid controls, underdevelopment, stagnation, violence, political instability, and even famine. As late as 1987, the unemployment rate was 17 percent.

But then things suddenly changed. Ireland joined the European Community, including the adoption of the new euro currency. It created a free-trade zone and worked out a deal with the trade unions to offer a flexible, highly skilled labor force. Irish leaders aggressively courted multinational corporations in the United States and Europe by providing a well-educated but relatively cheap labor force and offering substantial tax breaks. Today Ireland has the lowest corporate tax rate in Europe, at 12.5 percent. It recruits immigrants with advanced skills from other countries, especially those of Irish descent. It offers a stable, healthy government and an excellent infrastructure. (Of course, EC subsidies of up to 1.2 billion euro a year didn't hurt, either.)

The results have been exceptional. For the past decade, the Republic of Ireland has grown three times faster than the rest of Europe and twice as fast as the United States. In the last half of the 1990s, real GDP grew at a 10 percent annual rate. Employment growth was even more spectacular, rising 50 percent over the past decade. Unemployment, once 17 percent, is virtually nonexistent. Wages are also on the rise, and today the average income of the Irish worker is on par with the rest of Europe. The only downside is price inflation, which is double the European rate. Ireland used to be considered a place to escape from. Now it's a proud nation to embrace and escape to.

The Future Is Boundless

My own view is that we are selling America short by thinking that super-growth cannot be sustained over the long run. Imagine how our standards of living could advance if we:

- Slash federal spending to its legitimate functions, which undoubtedly means less than 15 percent of GDP.
- Replace the current tax code with a simplified 15 percent flat tax.
- Privatize Social Security, or better yet, let Americans make their own plans for retirement.
- Establish a sound money standard that would discourage malinvestment and the boom–bust business cycle.
- Establish a fair system of justice that would free 90 percent of the lawyers in this country to become productive citizens.
- Stop interfering in foreign military affairs.

Imagine the breakthroughs in medicine, transportation, housing, telecommunications, and science that could take place by adopting this laissez-faire program. It boggles the mind to think that we could double or triple our living standards in a short time. To quote Keynes: "Thus for the first time since his creation man will be faced with . . . how to use his freedom from pressing economic cares, how to occupy his leisure, which science and compound interest will have won for him, to live wisely and agreeably and well."[6]

Chapter 26

The Marginal Tax Revolution

The Laffer Curve Goes Global

*Arthur Laffer and the Reagan economic philosophy of lower taxes, less reg-
ulation and free trade, have never been more in vogue abroad—so much so
that it has become the global economic operating system.*
—STEPHEN MOORE, *WALL STREET JOURNAL*[1]

S upply-side economics[2] has largely been associated with the
tax-cut movement, specifically with efforts to slash high marginal tax rates. Progressive taxation[3] coupled with growing
inflation in the 1960s and 1970s created bracket creep, which moved
middle-class income earners into higher tax brackets. "As tax rates
rise one will get less saving, more consumption, less work, and more

unemployment," Bruce Bartlett observes.[4] Supply-siders advocate a sharp reduction in marginal tax rates on income, capital gains, and other forms of wealth as a way to unleash entrepreneurship, innovation, and risk taking, and to discourage investors and businesspeople from engaging in wasteful tax shelter loopholes.

What has led to the decline in progressive taxation in the United States and the Western economies? In many ways, it is the triumph of supply-side economics, especially the policy of cutting high marginal tax rates, as developed by economists Arthur B. Laffer, Jude Wanniski, Paul Craig Roberts, Bruce Bartlett, and Nobel laureate Robert Mundell.

Consider these supply-side arguments for lower marginal tax rates:

1. *Supply-siders believe in the triumph of entrepreneurship and the efficiency of capitalism.* Cutting taxes, they say, stimulates economic growth by transferring more funds from the public sector, which they view as relatively inefficient and wasteful, to private enterprise, which they consider more productive. Real growth in the economy is seen as more beneficial to the average worker than wealth redistribution schemes. Even John Kenneth Galbraith once admitted: "It is the increase in output in recent decades, not the redistribution of income, which has brought the great material increase, the well-being of the average man."[5]

2. *Cutting taxes increases revenues.* When tax rates are extremely high (at one point exceeding 90 percent), it is easier to cut the marginal tax rate than to reduce the average tax rates. In fact, by closing loopholes designed to circumvent onerous marginal rates, the reduction in marginal rates is offset by higher total revenues. Cutting marginal tax rates is a win-win situation for the politicians. Historically, when marginal rates have been cut, tax revenues have risen.

3. *Cutting marginal tax rates eliminates the need for wasteful and inefficient tax shelters, and reduces black-market activities.* Excessively high rates cause armies of accountants and attorneys to discover new ways to circumvent the tax man. As a result, huge new industries are created in real estate, foundations, and offshore trusts just to avoid confiscatory taxes. Reducing the marginal rate decreases the need for these tax shelters, as many people decide it is more economical simply to pay the tax, and money can be allocated to more profitable ventures.

The tremendous growth of an untaxed underground economy is one indicator of excessive taxation and bloated, overregulated government. Some economists estimate that half of Italy's economy goes unreported. Growth in the underground economy should be a danger sign that taxation is excessive. Unfortunately, too often it is taken as a sign that government needs to get tough and crack down more on those who aren't paying their fair share by increasing the penalties and hiring more IRS agents to catch tax evaders. However, many economists suggest that imposing a reasonable tax rate would make evasion less attractive and would result in increased voluntary compliance. After studying the underground economy, economist Dan Bawley concluded, "If the IRS were to make every effort to collect every cent due to it, America would be much closer to being a police state."[6]

4. *Taxes distort incentives.* Economists William Baumol and Alan Blinder ask, "What would happen if we tried to achieve perfect equality by putting a 100 percent income tax on all workers and then divided the receipts equally among the population? No one would have any incentive to work, to invest, to take risks, or to do anything else to earn money, because the rewards for all such activities would disappear."[7]

Supply-side economist Paul Craig Roberts argues that high progressive taxes are a strong disincentive to work, to invest, and to save. "Supply-side economics brought a new perspective to fiscal policy. Instead of stressing the effect on spending, supply-siders showed that tax rates directly affected the supply of goods and services. Lower tax rates mean better incentives to work, to save, to take risks, and to invest. As people respond to higher after-tax rewards, or greater profitability, incomes rise and the tax base grows, thus feeding back some of the lost revenues to the Treasury. The saving rate also grows, providing more financing for government and private borrowing."[8]

Introducing the Laffer Curve

Supply-siders refer to the Laffer curve to support their contention that cutting marginal tax rates can stimulate economic growth and, under the right circumstances, increase tax revenues. The Laffer curve (Figure 26.1) shows a theoretical relationship between the tax level and revenues. It

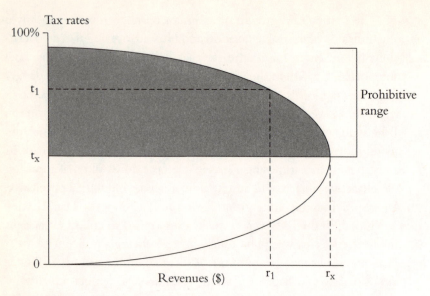

Figure 26.1   Laffer Curve: A Tax Cut Can Increase Tax Revenues
SOURCE: Arthur B. Laffer and Associates

was invented by Arthur B. Laffer, a former economics professor at the University of Chicago and University of Southern California, who drew the famous curve on a napkin at a Washington, DC, restaurant in the late 1970s to prove his point that tax cuts could potentially increase tax revenues.

According to the Laffer curve, an increase in tax rates will generate more revenues as long as the rates aren't too high. But once the tax rate exceeds X, further increases in tax rates will actually shrink revenues because higher tax rates discourage work effort and encourage tax avoidance and even illegal evasion. In Figure 26.1, if tax rates have reached a prohibitive range, a tax cut (t_1 to t_x) could increase revenues (from r_1 to r_x). Supply-siders point to capital gains tax cuts in 1978 and 1996 in the United States, when tax cuts actually increased revenues to the U.S. Treasury from capital gains.

Keynesians and other critics of the Laffer curve dispute where we stand on the Laffer curve. For example, they point out that when taxes were cut under President Reagan in 1981, the deficit got worse, not better. Conversely, in 1994, when President Clinton pushed through Congress an increase in the federal income tax rate to 39.6 percent, supply-siders warned that the tax increase would reduce revenues, but revenues actually rose during an expansionary boom. There are many variables at work in the marketplace.

Supply-side economics has been closely associated with the Republican administrations of Ronald Reagan and George W. Bush, who advocated a sharp reduction in marginal tax rates on personal and corporate income, capital gains, and dividends. Many other nations around the world have adopted supply-side tax cuts to stimulate economic activity. A tax cutting competition has developed in Europe, after Ireland cut its corporate tax rate to 12.5 percent. Other countries have followed, including the United Kingdom, Germany, and Austria. The latest is France under President Nicolas Sarkozy, who plans to cut the country's business income tax by five percentage points.

The Flat Tax Movement

In the preface to his study on the underground economy, Dan Bawley recommends that "the free society substantially reduce and simplify taxation rates." That seems to be the direction many countries are taking. Supply-siders advocate a single low tax rate with a limited number of personal exemptions as the ideal tax system. The movement to eliminate the current complex, loophole-ridden, wasteful tax system in the United States and replace it with a simple one-rate flat tax is closely linked to the supply-side revolution. Following the publication of *Low Tax, Simple Tax, Flat Tax* by Robert E. Hall and Alvin Rabushka (1983), the movement to set one simple low income tax rate has gained support, especially in former Communist countries.

For example, in the early 1990s, post-Soviet Estonia was facing 1,000 percent annualized inflation rates and an economy weakening by 30 percent over two years. Under Estonian Prime Minister Mart Laar, the small nation adopted a single tax rate for individuals and a zero corporate tax rate on reinvested profits, along with a deregulated economy. The results have been spectacular so far, with real GDP growth rates of 8 percent a year.

Other Eastern European countries have followed suit: Russia adopted a 13 percent flat income tax in 2001; Ukraine chose the same flat rate in 2004; Slovakia introduced a 19 percent rate in 2004; Romania 16 percent in 2005; Albania plans to set a 10 percent rate in 2008. Greece and Croatia plan similar flat rates. The flat tax movement is clearly spreading. What could be more fair and easy to calculate than everyone paying the same rate?

Hong Kong has also enjoyed a flat 16 percent tax on individual income for many decades, and no tax on capital gains. Singapore has recently cut its tax rate to compete with Hong Kong. Other tax havens have adopted a zero income tax system, while compensating with other taxes on imports and corporate fees. However, so far no major industrial nation has adopted a flat tax system, although several nations have reduced the number of brackets. At last count, 14 nations have adopted a flat income tax, 10 of them in former Iron Curtain countries.

In the United States, Steve Forbes, editor of *Forbes* magazine and author of *The Flat Tax Revolution* (2005), ran for president in 1996 and 2000 on a platform endorsing a 17 percent flat tax. His plan didn't get very far. Clearly, there is more support for a flat tax outside the United States.

Chapter 27

The Debate over Economic Inequality

The Rich Get Richer, and the Poor Get . . .

The modern market economy accords wealth and distribution income in a highly unequal, socially adverse and also functionally damaging fashion.
—JOHN KENNETH GALBRAITH[1]

After you adjust for inflation, the wages of the typical American worker have risen less than 1 percent since 2000.
—THE ECONOMIST (JUNE 15, 2006)

The allegation is appearing everywhere: Real average wages are stagnating, and the distribution of wealth and income in the United States is becoming more unequal. In its cover story,

"The Rich, the Poor and the Growing Gap Between Them," *The Economist* concludes, "Every measure shows that, over the past quarter century, those at the top have done better than those in the middle, who in turn have outpaced those at the bottom."[2]

Inequality of income is substantially greater in the United States compared to other countries, as measured by the Gini ratio. The Gini ratio is defined as a number between 0 and 1: The numerator is the area between the Lorenz curve (see Figure 27.1) of the distribution and the uniform distribution line; the denominator is the area under the uniform distribution line. Thus, a low Gini coefficient indicates more equal income or wealth distribution, while a high Gini coefficient indicates more unequal distribution.

The Lorenz curve measures the percentage of a nation's total income as earned by various income classes. Typically, it is divided into five income

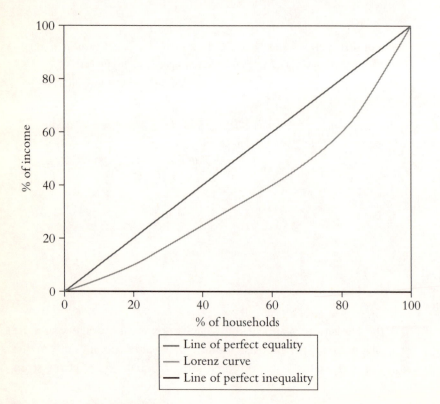

Figure 27.1 The Lorenz Curve

groups. In the United States, the highest fifth (the highest income earners) usually earn 40 percent of the nation's income, while the lowest fifth (the lowest-income earners) earn around 5 percent. Using the Lorenz curve, U.S. income appears to be seriously maldistributed, now the extreme case among the major industrial countries.

Critics of market capitalism are often misled by conventional measures of economic well-being, in particular the Lorenz curve and the Gini ratio. However, the Lorenz curve establishes an unfair and misleading guide for measuring social welfare. Suppose, for example, that an ideal line of perfect equality is achieved on the Lorenz curve, that is, the highest fifth (top 20 percent of income earners) only receive 20 percent of the nation's income, while the bottom fifth (lower 20 percent) increase their share to 20 percent. What would this ideal mean? Everyone—the teacher, the lawyer, the plumber, the actor—earns the same amount of income![3]

Since few economists think equal wages for everyone is an ideal situation, why do they think moving toward perfect equality on the Lorenz curve is appropriate? Moreover, the Lorenz curve is unable to account for an increase in a country's standard of living over time. It merely measures distribution of income, when in actuality each individual's personal standard of living may be increasing year to year.

To measure changes in social welfare, economists often rely on a second measure—average real income. This, too, has its shortcomings. A single statistic may mask improvements in an individual's standard of living over time. For example, average real income shows hardly any change since the mid-1970s. Yet other measures of well-being, such as consumer expenditures and the quantity, quality, and variety of goods and services, show remarkable advancement over the past 35 years. Consumer spending rose a dramatic 50 percent per person in real terms during this period. As Ohio University professor Richard Vedder asks, "How many Americans in 1975 had VCRs, microwaves, CD players, and home computers?"

The Work of Stanley Lebergott

Stanley Lebergott, professor emeritus of economics at Wesleyan University, has probably conducted more work in this area than anyone else. Instead of relying on general measures such as average real income, he uses a more commonsense approach—looking at individual consumer markets in food, clothing, housing, fuel, housework, transportation, health, recreation, and religion. His work is fascinating.

For example, he developed the measurements that appear in Table 27.1 to demonstrate changes in living standards from 1900 to 1970.

In another work, *Pursuing Happiness,* Lebergott demonstrates repeatedly how American consumers have sought to make an uncertain and often cruel world into a pleasanter and more convenient place. Medicines and medical facilities, artificial lighting, refrigeration, transportation, communication, entertainment, finished clothing—all have advanced living conditions.

Regarding women's work, Lebergott notes that weekly hours for household and family chores fell from 70 in 1900 to 30 by 1981. The 1900 housewife had to load her stove with tons of wood or coal each year and fill her lamps with coal oil or kerosene. Central heating also reduced the housewife's tasks. She no longer had to wash the carbonized kerosene, oil, coal, or wood from clothes, curtains, and walls, nor sweep floors and vacuum rugs as persistently. Automated and mechanical equipment reduced her labor further. . . . By 1950, over 95 percent of U.S. families had the facilities [of] central heating, hot water, gas, electric light, baths, and vacuum cleaners.[4]

Regarding water, Lebergott comments, "The average urban resident consumed about 20 gallons of water per day in 1900. Rural families had virtually no piped water; 55 percent did not even have privies. . . .

Table 27.1   Living Standards, 1900–1970

Percentage of homes with	Among all families in 1900	Among poor families in 1970
Flush toilets	15	99
Running water	24	92
Central heating	1	58
One (or fewer) Occupants per room	48	96
Electricity	3	99
Refrigeration	18	99
Automobiles	1	41

SOURCE: Stanley Lebergott, *The American Economy* (Princeton University Press, 1976), p. 8.

By 1990, American families devoted two days' worth of their annual income to get about 100 sanitary gallons every day, piped into the home."⁵

Everything Is Cheap and Getting Cheaper

In their book, *The Myths of Rich and Poor,* W. Michael Cox, an economist at the Federal Reserve Bank of Dallas, and Richard Alm, a business writer for the *Dallas Morning News,* did an exhaustive study of the cost of basic goods and services in the United States. They conclude that the real prices of housing, food, gasoline, electricity, telephone service, home appliances, clothing, and other everyday necessities have fallen significantly. Examples: In 1919, it took two hours, 37 minutes of work to buy a three-pound chicken. Today, it's down to 14 minutes. In 1915, a three-minute long-distance telephone call from New York to San Francisco cost $20.70. Today, it's less than 50 cents, equal to two minutes of work at the average wage. In 1908, a Model T cost $850, equivalent to more than two years' wages for an average factory worker. Today, the average worker toils only about eight months to buy a Ford Taurus.

Many products have fallen dramatically in price (real, if not nominal) over the past 25 years, including computers, radios, stereos and color televisions, telephones, microwave ovens, gasoline, soft drinks, and most airline tickets. Cox and Alm do point to two exceptions: medical care and higher education. But even in these two cases, they argue that the medical care is better than it used to be, and that the higher costs of an education result in higher lifetime income. Cox and Alm summarize, "As we enter the 21st century, Americans take for granted our ability to afford the trappings of the world's most envied middle-class lifestyle. It's the result of the decline of real prices in a dynamic economy, played out over and over."⁶

More and more Americans have benefited from an increase in the quantity, quality, and variety of goods and services because of the nature of the free-enterprise system: Competition reduces costs, encourages new products and improved processes, and promotes quality improvements. In the labor market, increased productivity leads to higher wages, which allows workers to buy better, cheaper products.

Benefits to the Poor and Unskilled

Recent work by economic historians confirm Lebergott's findings over longer periods. Karl Marx and David Ricardo predicted that, under capitalism, landlords and capitalists would gain at the expense of workers. But they could not have been more wrong. Gregory Clark, chair of the economics department at University of California, Davis, has summarized the findings of numerous economic historians on the distribution of income since the Industrial Revolution. Amazingly, he concludes that return on land and capital has fallen in relation to wages as a percentage of GDP. He comes to the shocking declaration, "unskilled male wages in England have risen more since the Industrial Revolution than skilled wages, and this result holds for all advanced economies. The wage premium for skilled building workers has declined from about 100 percent in the thirteenth century to 25 percent today. . . . Thus the payment per unit of unskilled labor rose farther as a result of the Industrial Revolution than the payment for land, the payment for capital, or even the pay per unit of skilled labor."[7]

Moreover, according to Clark, the gap between men's and women's wages has been narrowing. "In the reindustrialized era women's wages averaged less than half of men's. . . . Now unskilled female workers in the United Kingdom earn 80 percent of the male unskilled hourly wage."[8]

Clark also looks at other factors besides income, including life expectancy, health, number of surviving children, and literacy. He notes that the rich are still on average taller than the poor, and have a longer life expectancy, but the differences have narrowed. He concludes "the differences between rich and poor have probably narrowed since the Industrial Revolution."[9]

Today the Poor Are Gaining

This kind of historical perspective is refreshing and eye-opening. The increase in the standard of living as measured by the quantity, quality, and variety of goods and services has increased dramatically and profoundly in the nineteenth and twentieth centuries, for people of all incomes. In many ways, the poor have advanced the most and are now

capable of living in decent housing, owning an automobile, and enjoy-
ing many of the pleasures previously afforded by the wealthy. Cheap
airline services allow them to travel extensively. Television gives them
the chance to see sports events and musical shows previously limited to the
rich and the middle class. Compared to yesteryear, every house today is
a castle, every man is a king. As Gregory Clark concludes, "The envious
have inherited the earth."[10]

Chapter 28

One Graph Says It All

The Development of the Economic Freedom Index

To talk about economic freedom is easy; to measure it, to make fine distinctions, assign numbers to its attributes, and combine them into one overall magnitude— that is a much more difficult task.

—MILTON FRIEDMAN[1]

What is the best way to produce and distribute goods and services to the greatest number of people and secure a prosperous economy? Should we opt for central planning, laissez faire, or somewhere in between?

Of all the various freedoms we enjoy, economic freedom remains the most controversial. Globalization, free trade, income inequality, monopoly power, immigration, price gouging, commercial fraud and deception—all these aspects of the laissez-faire capitalism are subjects of fierce debates.

Adam Smith, the eighteenth-century Scottish professor of moral philosophy, is considered the father of modern economics. His magnum opus, *The Wealth of Nations,* was published appropriately in 1776 as a declaration of economic independence. He called his program of unfettered capitalism a "system of natural liberty," which consisted of three parts: maximum freedom, competition, and justice. He declared:

> Every man, as long as he does not violate the laws of *justice,* is left perfectly *free* to pursue his own interest his own way, and to bring both his industry and capital into *competition* with those of any other man, or order of men[2] (emphasis added).

Smith even went so far as to declare economic freedom a sacred right:

> To prohibit a great people . . . from making all that they can of every part of their own produce, or from employing their stock and industry in a way that they judge most advantageous to themselves, is a manifest violation of the most sacred rights of mankind.[3]

Using the symbol of the "invisible hand," Adam Smith argued that his model of enlightened self-interest would benefit all society. "He is led by an invisible hand . . . By pursuing his own interest he frequently promotes that of the society."[4] Most importantly, economic freedom would benefit mankind; it would lead to economic growth and "universal opulence which extends itself to the lowest ranks of the people."[5] In other words, giving people their economic freedom would lead to higher standards of living for everyone, both rich and poor.

Economic Freedom: A Cost or a Benefit?

Adam Smith's libertarian doctrine of laissez-faire—granting the liberty to do as you please as long as you don't hurt others—is a relatively new concept. Monarchies and dictatorships have been taken for granted for most of history. After Smith's groundbreaking work was published, the idea of civil and economic liberty began to be hotly debated. In particular, after the Great Depression and World War II in the twentieth century, laissez-faire capitalism became an unwelcome phrase in the halls of government and on college campuses. Governments in America and abroad nationalized industry after industry, raised taxes, inflated the money supply, imposed price and exchange controls, created the welfare state, and engaged in all kinds of interventionist mischief in an attempt to control the economy and prevent another depression. In academia, Keynesianism and Marxism became all the rage, and many free-market economists had a hard time obtaining full-time positions on college campuses.

The big-government economy was viewed by the establishment as an automatic stabilizer and growth stimulator. Starting in the late 1950s, many top economists argued that central planning, the welfare state, and industrial policy would lead to *higher* growth rates, contradicting Adam Smith. Incredibly, as late as 1985, Paul Samuelson (MIT) and William D. Nordhaus (Yale) still declared, "The planned Soviet economy since 1928 . . . has outpaced the long-term growth of the major market economies."[6] Mancur Olson, a Swedish economist, also stated, "In the 1950s, there was, if anything, a faint tendency for the countries with larger welfare states to grow faster."[7]

Henry C. Wallich, a Yale economics professor and former member of the Federal Reserve Board, wrote a book arguing that freedom leads to lower economic growth, greater income inequality, and less competition. In *The Cost of Freedom,* he boldly declared, "But the free market is not primarily a device to procure growth. It is a device to secure the most efficient use of resources." Furthermore, he stated, "The ultimate value of a free economy is not production, but freedom, and freedom comes not at a profit, but at a cost."[8] And he was considered a conservative economist!

The New Enlightenment

Starting in the inflationary 1970s, the attitudes of the establishment gradually shifted. In recent years defenders of Adam Smith's philosophy have gained ground and, since the collapse of the Berlin Wall and Soviet central planning in the early 1990s, have claimed victory over the dark forces of Marxism and socialism. Today, governments around the world are denationalizing, privatizing, cutting taxes, controlling inflation, and engaging in all kinds of market reforms. Market-friendly economists can now be found in most economics departments, and almost all of the most recent Nobel Prize winners in economics have been pro–free market.

Furthermore, new evidence demonstrates forcefully that economic freedom comes as a benefit, not a cost. Looking at the data of the 1980s, Mancur Olson concluded, "It appears that the countries with larger public sectors [government control] have tended to grow more slowly than those with smaller public sectors."[9] Contrast that with his statement about the 1950s.

The Creation of the Economic Freedom Index

In the 1980s, Michael Walker, president of the Fraser Institute in Canada, brought together a group of free-market economists to see if they could find empirical evidence of the Adam Smith hypothesis, that more economic freedom leads to higher economic growth. Inspired by Milton Friedman and led by Alvin Rabushka of the Hoover Institution, these experts eventually constructed an "Economic Freedom of the World Index" for individual countries over time, based on five areas of economic freedom—taxation, public spending, money and credit, economic regulation of business and labor, and foreign trade.[10]

In the early 1990s, James Gwartney, professor of economics at Florida State University, became involved in the project and now is the lead economist in constructing the annual Economic Freedom of the World Index for the Fraser Institute. Since 1996, Gwartney has been assisted by co-author Robert Lawson, economics professor at Capital University. According to Gwartney and Lawson, the key ingredients of economic freedom are "personal choice, voluntary exchange, freedom to compete, and protection of person and property."[11]

Under Gwartney and Lawson's guidance, the index has become more complex. Initially, the index was based on 17 quantifiable components, such as government expenditures as a share of GDP. However, they soon discovered that important legal and regulatory elements were omitted from the index. To correct this deficiency, new components were added to the index during 1997–2000. It now contains 38 components that are divided into five areas:

1. Size of government expenditures and tax policy.
2. Legal structure and security of property rights.
3. Access to sound money.
4. Freedom to trade internationally.
5. Regulation of credit, labor, and business.

Using this criteria, the Economic Freedom Index objectively seeks to rank with a single number the level of economic freedom in over 100 countries on an annual basis. The Fraser Institute also ranks states and provinces in North America. In 2007, they published for the first time a world map of economic freedom, ranking each country by various colors.

Heritage/*Wall Street Journal* Study

Since 1995, every January the Heritage Foundation has also published its own annual Index of Economic Freedom. The index is copublished by the *Wall Street Journal,* accompanied by a world map ranking countries with different colors. Authors of the study have varied over the years, including Gerald P. O'Driscoll, Jr., Edwin J. Feulner (president of the Heritage Foundation), and Mary Anastasia O'Grady.

Heritage defines economic freedom as "the absence of government coercion or constraint on the production, distribution, or consumption of goods and services beyond the extent necessary for citizens to protect and maintain liberty itself."[12] The authors use 50 variables in 10 broad categories to construct a rating for 157 countries:

1. Trade policy (now called trade freedom).
2. Fiscal burden of government (fiscal freedom).
3. Government intervention in the economy (freedom from government).
4. Monetary policy (monetary freedom).
5. Capital flows and foreign investment (investment freedom).
6. Banking and finance (financial freedom).
7. Wages and prices (labor freedom).
8. Property rights.

9. Regulation (business freedom).
10. Informal market activity (freedom from corruption).

In the Heritage formula, all 10 factors are weighted equally in determining an overall economic freedom score running from 0 to 100 percent, with 100 indicating the highest degree of economic freedom and 0 the lowest.

The countries are divided into five categories:

Free—countries with an average overall score of 80–100.
Mostly free—countries scoring 70–79.9.
Moderately free—countries scoring 60–69.9.
Mostly unfree—countries scoring 50–59.9.
Repressed—countries scoring 0–49.9.

Economic Freedom and Growth

Both the Fraser and Heritage studies reach similar conclusions, as documented in Figures 28.1 and 28.2.

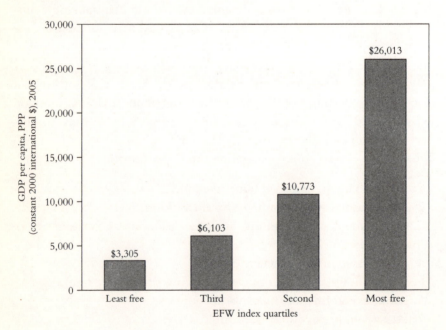

Figure 28.1   Economic Freedom and per Capita Real Income
SOURCE: Fraser Institute (2006).

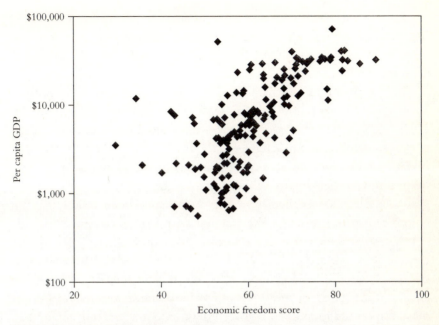

Figure 28.2   Per Capita GDP and Economic Freedom
SOURCE: Heritage Foundation (2007).

Both think tanks conclude that the greater the degree of freedom, the higher the standard of living (as measured by per capita real GDP growth). Nations with the highest level of freedom (e.g., United States, New Zealand, Hong Kong) grew faster than nations with moderate degrees of freedom (e.g., United Kingdom, Canada, Germany) and even more rapidly than nations with little economic freedom (e.g., Venezuela, Iran, Congo).

When Milton Friedman first saw this graph, he exclaimed, "The actual correlation between the Economic Freedom Index and the rate of economic growth is most impressive. No qualitative verbal description can match the power of that graph."[13]

The Fraser studies also find that (a) low-income nations with high levels of economic freedom tend to grow faster than low-income nations with low levels of freedom, and (b) a legal structure that secures property rights and enforces contracts and rule of law is essential if a country is going to grow and achieve a high level of income. Overall, Gwartney and Lawson conclude: "This research has found that economic freedom is positively correlated with per-capita income, economic growth, greater life expectancy, lower child mortality, the development of democratic institutions, civil and political freedoms, and other desirable social and economic outcomes."[14]

But what about the data that seemed to demonstrate a positive correlation between big government and economic growth in the 1950s and later? In the case of the Soviet Union, Gwartney and others generally agree that the data were faulty and misleading. In the case of Europe, perhaps the economic stimulus of rebuilding after the war overshadowed the growth of the welfare state. In other words, Europe grew in spite of, not because of, government. Once rebuilding was complete by the late 1950s, the weight of government began to be felt.

Several years ago I asked Professor Gwartney what surprised him the most in preparing the Economic Freedom Index. "It turns out," he said, "that the legal system—the rule of law, security of property rights, an independent judiciary, and an impartial court system—is the most important function of government, and the central element of both economic freedom and a civil society. It is far more statistically significant than the other variables." Gwartney pointed to a number of countries that lack a decent legal system, and as a result suffer from corruption, insecure property rights, poorly enforced contracts, and an inconsistent regulatory environment, particularly in Latin America, Africa, and the Middle East. Gwartney and Lawson wrote, "The enormous benefits of the market network—gains from trade, specialization, expansion of the market, and mass production techniques—cannot be achieved without a sound legal system."[15]

Ending Political Corruption: The Virtue of Being Rich

Economists are taking an increasing interest in comparative legal systems and ways to apply economic analysis to the problem of high-level corruption, payoffs, and the role of international organizations. Traditionally political analysts viewed corruption as a political and cultural issue outside the purview of the World Bank and economic institutions. But recent studies demonstrate that economic factors play a major role in the level of corruption, especially in developing countries. Corruption can be at many levels: bribery of high-level officials; favoritism and nepotism; kickbacks and under-the-table commissions for lucrative state projects, misdirected foreign aid and loans that end up in Swiss bank accounts; below-market sales of valuable commodities, payoffs to avoid regulations, customs duties, and taxes; cronyism in concession awards; and influence peddling. Susan Rose-Ackerman, a Yale economist and legal authority on corruption, states, "Bribes represent illegal user fees, taxes, or access charges paid to public agents. These payments influence economic decisions ranging from the size and character of public investment projects to the level of compliance with business regulations."[16]

Jakob Svensson, an economist at Stockholm University, has done extensive research on political corruption and the rule of law. As Figure 28.3 demonstrates, Svensson found that socialist and recently socialist economies show higher levels of corruption than others.

According to Svensson and other economists, corruption tends to decline as countries become more prosperous. Among factors he has

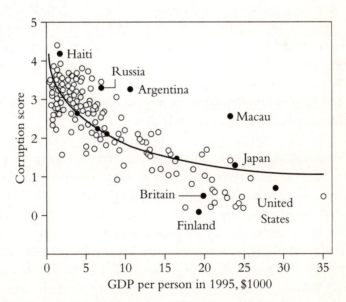

Figure 28.3   Corruption Index versus National Income (GDP per person, 1995)
SOURCE: *The Economist,* December 23, 2006, p. 116.

tested, Svensson found that educational level, openness to imports, freedom of the press, and number of days to start a business all showed clear correlations between these variables and overall level of corruption.[17]

But political analysts aren't sure which comes first: the rule of law or prosperity. Does prosperity come about by the state cracking down on corruption, or does higher income naturally lead to lower levels of corruption? Certainly when citizens achieve a higher level of ownership in assets and property, they have a greater incentive to preserve those assets by demanding a better judicial and legislative system. Many Asian countries have grown rapidly at a time when cronyism and political corruption were common. As *The Economist* reports, "Although most economists agree that corruption slows development, a corrupt country is nevertheless capable of rapid growth. Countries may be corrupt because they are poor, and not the other way around."[18]

Critique of the Economic Freedom Indexes

Some economists have been critical of the Fraser and Heritage efforts to measure economic freedom and link it to growth and other statistics. Their objections include the difficulty of accurately measuring economic freedom and comparing different countries. What items should be included, and how much weight should be given to each? Is Saudi Arabia more free than China? Why does Heritage give high scores of economic freedom to notorious welfare states such as Sweden and Denmark? Why should Singapore get such a high rating given its level of industrial policy and forced savings plans? Is a high level of "informal [black] markets" a sign of economic freedom or the lack of it?

Keynesians and Marxists also raise the issue of how objective the indexes and studies are, given that the economic freedom indexes are constructed by free-market economists. Despite statements by Milton Friedman and James Gwartney that they are objective empiricists, one always wonders to what extent subjective opinions affect their methodology. Certainly the endorsement and copublishing of the Heritage freedom index by the *Wall Street Journal* give it credibility. In addition, the Fraser Institute offers an open forum to encourage debate on the index. Their Web site references peer-refereed papers on economic freedom issues (go to http://www.freetheworld.com/papers.html).

Whether one agrees or not with the findings of the economic freedom indexes published by the Fraser Institute or the Heritage Foundation, the indexes are gaining notoriety. According to Ed Feulner, president of the Heritage Foundation, political leaders are anxious to see how they rank each year, and there is evidence that they make decisions such as cutting taxes and lowering tariffs in a bid to increase their ranking in the Economic Freedom Index.

Chapter 29

Amazing Graph

Economists Enter
Sacred Ground

Both liberal and strict religious groups are more dynamic when they have to
compete for members on a level playing field.

—GARY BECKER[1]

R eligion is another area where economic research has recently
made its mark. Laurence R. Iannaccone (George Mason University)
is one of a handful of economists who specialize in religion
and economics.[2] They even have founded their own organization, the
Association for the Study of Religion, Economics, and Culture, which
holds an annual meeting to discuss recent scholarship.

In the late 1980s Iannaccone tested Adam Smith's hypothesis that freedom of religion would lead to a higher level of attendance in church services. Smith believed that competition benefits religious groups because they are motivated to satisfy the needs of their members.[3] In testing this theory, Iannaccone compared attendance at church and the degree of religious monopoly in various Protestant and Catholic countries between 1968 and 1976. His test produced a striking result: Church attendance varied inversely with church concentration in Protestant nations. Church attendance among Protestants was high in freely competitive nations, such as the United States, and low in countries monopolized by a single Protestant denomination, such as Finland. In short, the more religious freedom a nation enjoys, the more religious people are (as measured by church attendance).[4]

Soon after Iannaccone's study was completed, two sociologists applied market principles to the history of American religion and came to the same conclusion: Religion thrives in a free-market environment. Roger Finke (Purdue) and Rodney Stark (University of Washington) found the United States to be almost a perfect experiment in what they termed an unregulated, free-market, religious economy. By the start of the American revolution, religious persecution had largely ended, and tolerance gradually gave way to religious freedom. The largest denominations sought to become a tax-supported state religion, and even formed cartels aimed at preventing competition, but all efforts failed. Most states followed Virginia's lead in opposing any state church.

Finke and Stark came to the following remarkable findings using their explicit market model in studying religion in America.

First, fierce competition and the constant evolution of new religions in America have resulted in a steady rise in church participation over the past two centuries. Amazingly, America shifted from a nation in which most people took no part in organized religion to a nation in which nearly two-thirds of American adults do.[5] (See Figure 29.1 below.)

The Impossible Dream of One Faith

The socioeconomists found, second, that it is impossible for one faith to dominate the nation in an environment of relentless competition. In colonial times, the Congregationalists and Episcopalians dominated. But they could not cope with the fierce competition from the

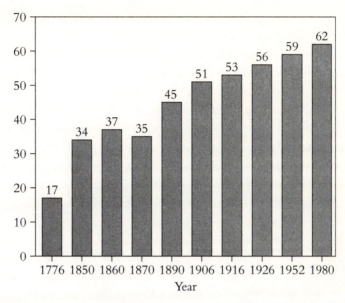

Figure 29.1   Rates of Religious Adherence: 1776–1980
SOURCE: Finke and Stark, *The Churching of America,* p. 16.

Methodists, Catholics, and Baptists during the frequent revival periods of American history. Just as no corporate monopoly lasts forever, so also does it seem impossible for a mainstream religion to stay on top for long. Finke and Stark conclude that no religion, no matter how successful in the short run, can convert the whole world. Christians just don't seem to be content with one church, just as consumers can't agree on one car model or one type of tennis shoes. Over time, all markets—whether for automobiles, shoes, or religions—tend to show an increase in quantity, quality, and variety. As Finke and Stark demonstrate, despite the constant call for all Christian groups to be as one, unification efforts have repeatedly failed. The conventional wisdom that "all churches are alike" is inaccurate. Diversity is the lifeblood of religious life in America.

Third, Finke and Stark discovered that mainstream churches which compromised their principles and eliminated their "strong doctrines" invariably experienced widespread defection and ultimate failure, while churches that maintained high doctrinal standards, such as the Catholic Church, prospered. In other words, the market rewards the quality of religious worship. "We argue repeatedly that religious organizations can thrive only to the extent that they have a theology that can comfort souls and motivate sacrifice."[6]

Fourth, the scholars refuted the popular belief that urban communities are less religious than those in country life. Debunking the preachers' myth that city life is "wicked and secular," Finke and Stark provide evidence that church attendance rates are higher in cities than in rural areas.[7]

In sum, we can see that the principles of economics are universal. Incentives, competition, quality, and choice apply not only to the material world, but to the spiritual realm as well. Perhaps peace and prosperity could be established in the Middle East by applying the principles of competition, choice, and free markets in business and in religion.

Chapter 30

Peace on Earth, Good Will toward Men

The Case for Religious Competition

A great multitude of religious sects . . . might in time [become] free of every mixture of absurdity, imposture, or fanaticism.

—ADAM SMITH[1]

Closed economies are breeding grounds for intolerance, fanaticism, and violence.

—GERALD P. O'DRISCOLL,
JR., *WALL STREET JOURNAL*

History is replete with religious wars between Protestants and Catholics and Muslims and Jews. Today's hostilities in the Middle East have a religious origin. Is it possible to have peace on earth, good will toward men among countries and religious faiths?

According to Leonard Read, founder of the Foundation for Economic Education, true freedom means practicing the Golden Rule and preserving the God-given rights of the individual as declared in the Declaration of Independence. "Everyone is completely free to act creatively as his abilities and ambitions permit; no restraint in this respect—none whatsoever."[2]

What do economists have to say about military and religious conflict? The latest edition of the *Index of Economic Freedom,* published by the Heritage Foundation and the *Wall Street Journal,* shows that many parts of the world are "mostly unfree" or "repressed," as judged by the level of corruption, taxation, protectionism, inflation, black markets, and government interventionism. Of the 157 nations surveyed, over half (81) receive a negative grade. Most telling, the area of the world with the highest concentration of "repressed" freedom is the Middle East, particularly Saudi Arabia, Iran, Iraq, Libya, and Afghanistan.[3] Judging from recent events, the Middle East confirms Read's thesis. Most of the Arab world continues to suffer from economic dislocation, political turmoil, and military conflict. "When the wicked rule, the people mourn" (Proverbs 29:2). Economic journalist Henry Hazlitt summed it up well: "It is socialist governments, notwithstanding their denunciations of imperialist capitalism, that have been the greatest source of modern wars."[4]

Commerce and Trade Break Down Barriers

The Middle East is also known for dictatorships and religious intolerance. It seems that economic repression goes hand in hand with political and religious repression, just as economic freedom leads to political and religious freedom.[5] Montesquieu, Adam Smith, and other classical-liberal thinkers made the case that liberalized trade and the spirit of capitalism break down cultural, religious, and social monotheism, while destroying fanaticism and intolerance. Montesquieu saw many virtues in *doux commerce,* stating that the pursuit of profit-making serves as a countervailing bridle against the violent passions of war and abusive political power. "Commerce cures destructive prejudices," Montesquieu declared. "It polishes and softens barbarous mores. . . . The natural effect of commerce is to lead to peace."[6] Adam Smith seconded Montesquieu and taught that the commercial society moderates the passions and prevents a descent into a Hobbesian jungle.

Business encourages people to become educated, industrious, and self-disciplined. As economist Albert Hirschman observes, "The spirit of commerce brings with it the spirit of frugality, of economy, of moderation, of work, of wisdom, of tranquility, of order, and of regularity."[7] Businesspeople are ultimately practical—they are by nature compromisers and tolerant of other viewpoints. In fact, the purpose of business is to fulfill the needs of others by developing and producing something someone else wants—for a price of course. John Maynard Keynes once said, "It is better that a man should tyrannise over his bank balance than over his fellow-citizen."[8]

Economists Gerald P. O'Driscoll, Jr., and Sara J. Fitzgerald conclude, "The fact is that allies and trading partners are more likely to resolve differences than to resort to armed conflict." They cite a seminal study in which Solomon W. Polachek analyzed 30 pairs of countries from 1958 to 1967 and found that higher levels of trade dampen conflict. "Trade agreements dampen conflict because such hostilities threaten the very economic benefits that states expect to achieve and are achieving from the agreements. The free exchange of goods builds wealth and prosperity for all concerned."[9]

The Case for Religious Competition

What about religious freedom? The Middle East is also infamous for its lack of religious freedom and diversity. A few Protestant Christians live and worship there, but proselytizing is prohibited, even in Israel. Egyptians are divided into only two Muslim sects; there are virtually no Jews in the country, and no Christian missionaries. Islamic fundamentalists hate the West's idea (as expressed originally by John Locke) of a free religious society where churches compete for members. According to Andrew Sullivan, America has achieved "one of the most vibrantly religious civil societies on earth," and America "is living, tangible rebuke to everything they [Taliban and bin Laden] believe in."[10]

Adam Smith contends that a state religion breeds fanaticism, intolerance, and persecution. Numerous examples of holy wars waged by state-supported Christianity, Islam, and other religions demonstrate Smith's thesis. But Smith goes further. He argues that creating a free, competitive environment in religions would be beneficial. Natural liberty, he said, favors "a great multitude of religious sects," which would generate interest in religion and encourage higher attendance at church. "In little religious sects, the morals of common people have been almost remarkably regular and orderly: generally much more so than in the established church."[11] According to Smith, religious competition would reduce zeal and fanaticism and promote tolerance, moderation, and rational religion.

In short, a good dose of open markets and competition in all walks of life could go a long way toward bringing peace, prosperity, and good will in this dangerous part of the world. Until that happens, they will shout "'peace, peace,' when there is no peace" (Jeremiah 8:11).

Part Five

PREDICTING THE FUTURE

In this final section of *EconoPower*, I look at how the economics profession has improved its ability to forecast the stock market, inflation, and the economy. Economists used to be the butt of many jokes, but with several high-profile cases of accurate predictions, the media is no longer laughing.

Chapter 31

New Yale
Forecasting Model

Has the Irving Fisher Curse Been Lifted?

*People in much of the world are still overconfident that the stock market,
and in many places the housing market, will do extremely well, and this
overconfidence can lead to instability.*

—ROBERT SHILLER (2005)[1]

Yale professor Irving Fisher (1867–1947) is the father of monetary
economics and is considered by many economists (for example,
James Tobin and Milton Friedman) to be the greatest American
economist who ever lived. Born in 1867 in New York, the son of a cler-
gyman, Fisher excelled in mathematics and graduated first in his class at
Yale University. Under the influence of Social Darwinist William Graham

Sumner, he developed an interest in economics, devoting the rest of his life to the study of money, prices, and the economy. After obtaining his Ph.D. from Yale, he married, had children, and settled down to living the life of a professor and author. He authored dozens of books on monetary economics, healthy living (having survived tuberculosis), and investing in the stock market. In 1918 he was elected president of the American Economic Association, and later helped found the Econometric Society.

A creative mind, he invented a card index system (today's Rolodex), which he sold for Remington Rand stock. At the height of the Wall Street bull market, his Remington "A" stock was valued at $10 million. In addition to teaching economics at Yale, Fisher became a financial advisor and became known as the "Oracle on Wall Street," and was quoted frequently in the financial media.

Fisher was an incurable New Era optimist who believed that the Roaring Twenties would usher in a new and better world. He was a promoter extraordinaire of the bull market on Wall Street. With the Federal Reserve in control of the monetary system, Fisher was convinced that the business cycle had been abolished, and with stable prices in the 1920s, he was unconcerned about the "orgy of speculation" on Wall Street, even though stocks had tripled on average in only seven years leading up to 1929.

When Boston financial advisor Roger Babson warned investors of an impending crash in early September 1929, Fisher dismissed this dire prediction with his now infamous statement, "stock prices have reached what looks like a permanently high plateau."[2] His monetary theories completely failed him, and both his reputation and financial status were destroyed in the 1930s. He never recovered, and died a broken man in 1947.

Yale University has never quite lived down Fisher's famous forecast, and economists' forecasts have always been viewed with suspicion. As Paul Samuelson once commented in humor, "Economists have predicted seven of the past three recessions."

Interestingly, in 1988, three econometricians from Harvard and Yale reviewed the monetary model and data that Irving Fisher used to forecast the economy and, using modern-time series analysis, ran the most sophisticated regression analysis and econometric techniques to see if they could predict the crash and depression. They came to the remarkable conclusion that Fisher "would be justified in appearing optimistic about the economy on the eve of and in the months following the Crash." Why? Not because Fisher's model was defective, but because the 1929 stock market crash and the Great Depression was "unforecastable!"[3]

Reading this paper by three top econometricians was not especially comforting in light of recent fears of growing macroeconomic instability due to stock market and real estate bubbles that might unleash havoc around the financial world.

A New Macro Model at Yale

But as I headed up to Yale University in the fall of 2006, I felt a sense of optimism about the future of economic forecasting—that maybe things weren't as bad as I thought. There I met Robert Shiller, professor of economics, who had written a bestseller entitled *Irrational Exuberance,* which was published in 2000 at the height of the bull market in technology stocks. In fact, the book was released in March, 2000, the very top of the Nasdaq market. In this prescient work, Shiller predicted that "the present stock market displays the classic features of a *speculative bubble,*" and warned that the future outlook for stocks was "likely to be rather poor—and perhaps even dangerous."[4] He was absolutely right, not only about the direction of the markets, but the timing.

Looking back, I first thought his forecasting model was more coincidence than science, but then in late 2005 he came out with the second edition of *Irrational Exuberance.* In the new edition, he added a chapter on U.S. real estate, where he pointed clearly to an unprecedented and unsustainable "rocket-taking-off" effect in home values starting in 1997. "We are increasingly feeling worried and vulnerable," he declared, warning investors that a similar "market bubble" could be a "dangerous" investment. Within a year, real estate prices in the hottest markets (especially Florida, California, and Nevada) peaked out, culminating in falling prices, higher inventories, and a collapse in the subprime mortgage lending in 2007.

When I interviewed Professor Shiller, my first question was, "Given your incredible success in predicting the tops in stocks and real estate, and David Swensen's spectacular returns managing the Yale endowment fund, has the Irving Fisher curse finally been lifted from Yale University?" He was hopeful. "Well, I suppose so," he responded with a grin.

In one way Shiller is like Fisher. In addition to being a full-time professor, Shiller is a businessman-economist and entrepreneur. He recently founded a company called MacroMarkets LLC, which helps create new marketplaces, including Exchange Traded Funds (ETFs), to expand risk management. He helped create a futures and options market on the Chicago Mercantile Exchange for U.S. residential real estate (at the top of the market!). For more information on his company, go to www.macromarkets.com.

On a more serious note, how is Shiller's forecasting model distinct from the econometric models of the past that have failed to anticipate changes in the trends in stocks, bonds, and real estate? His book, *Irrational Exuberance,* is a study in human behavior and the psychology of speculation in financial markets. "Behavioral and financial economics are gaining a lot of momentum and is the most exciting thing that's happening in economics now. But it tends to be in the business school," he told me.

He works with other behavioral economists, such as Richard Thaler at Chicago and Karl Case at Wellesley College, and organizes behavioral finance workshops at the National Bureau of Economic Research to examine market bubbles in stocks, bonds, real estate, and commodities, and how markets become overvalued or undervalued from historical trends due to influences of the media, government policy, and "animal spirits," Keynes's phrase for herd instinct. "Ultimately, we learn how to forecast by looking at past episodes," Shiller remarks.[5] When markets move outside the normal long-term trend, on either side, it does not mean for sure that recent movements in prices are unsustainable and must return to the long-term direction, but it is time to be cautious. "My approach in behavioral economics is to look for insights, and not just the data. One must look at the broadest possible picture to see what's going on. One must use your intuitive faculties, and recognize patterns," he explained.

According to Shiller, an astute observer can do well in the financial markets. "It is a competitive business, and most money managers can't beat the market. But there is a reward to sound, intelligent research.

Successful investing requires inspiration, a special effort of commitment of time and energy, and attention and focus. One of the reasons investors make mistakes is because they don't pay enough attention. People are capable of extraordinary brilliance, but they don't often know where to apply it. They end up following the herd and not thinking independently. It's not just a matter of smarts. It's a matter of being able to sustain interest."

Chapter 32

Forecasting Elections

Economists Do It Better!

It is the competition of profit-seeking entrepreneurs that does not tolerate the preservation of false prices. . . .

—LUDWIG VON MISES[1]

In the spring of 1988, three economists at the University of Iowa—Forrest Nelson, Robert Forsythe, and George Newmann—were having lunch together and the subject of the Michigan Democratic Primary came up. The polls had shown Michael Dukakis ahead in the primary, but Jesse Jackson turned out to be the surprise winner the night before. "How could the pollsters be so wrong?" asked one of the economists. "If traders on the COMEX in Chicago set the November price of corn that badly, they would be out of a job!" said another. It was the last comment that got the economists thinking. Could there be a futures market in political races where traders might do a better job of forecasting elections than the pollsters?

Thus began the Iowa Electronic Markets (IEM) program. Since 1988, the economics faculty at the Henry B. Tippie College of Business at the University of Iowa, steeped in statistics and economic analysis more than political science, has offered its own version of predicting elections. IEM offers futures contracts on the outcome of presidential and congressional elections, and occasionally important senate races. Traders bet money (up to $500 per person) on who is going to win the presidential race and whether Republicans or Democrats will control Capitol Hill.

Which Forecasts Better: Gallup or IEM?

What have been the results? So far the evidence is clear that IEM traders as a whole do a much better job than professional pollsters in predicting election outcomes, and at far less expense. Summarizing the evidence from 49 IEM election markets between 1988 and 2000, financial economists from Iowa concluded that (a) election-eve prediction errors by IEM traders averaged less than 2 percent, (b) polling proved to be more volatile during the election campaign, and (c), approximately 70 percent of the time, IEM traders bettered the pollsters in predicting the percentage outcome of each election during the campaign period. "The market [IEM] appears to forecast the election outcomes more closely than polls months in advance," they state.[2] And this despite the fact that IEM traders differ greatly from a representative sample of voters.

The three Iowa professors recently updated the statistics and found that the IEM has improved its ability to predict elections compared to the professional pollsters. They conclude: "We compared market predictions to 964 polls over the five presidential elections since 1988. The market is closer to the eventual outcome 74 percent of the time. Further, the market significantly outperforms the polls in every election when forecasting more than 100 days in advance."[3]

Who Won in 2000: Bush or Gore?

The IEM has run markets in five U.S. presidential elections. The political futures markets predicted with great accuracy the election of George H. W. Bush in 1988, Bill Clinton in 1992 and 1996, and

George W. Bush's reelection in 2004. What about 2000? Here the Iowa futures market predicted an extremely close race. According to the futures market, George W. Bush and Al Gore were neck-and-neck from May until September, when Gore opened a slight lead. Through the debates, Gore's lead evaporated, and Bush barely pulled ahead. But two days before the election, the lead switched to Gore. Then, finally, on election eve, it barely switched back to Bush. In contrast, the polls showed Bush with large leads from April through mid-August, a relatively large Gore surge (the traditional convention bounce) until mid-September, and a relatively large Bush resurgence into the election night. "Thus, through the election, the IEM showed a close race in absolute terms and a closer race than the polls did."[4]

However, the IEM traders still predicted a slight victory in the popular vote for Bush on election night, when in fact Gore won by 0.2 percent while still losing the electoral college by one vote. Thus, interestingly, traders who paid approximately $510 on election eve betting that Bush would win, lost their entire investment, while those who paid approximately $480 betting that Gore would win, earned $1,000 payoff. The winner-take-all market for president was based on plurality of votes, not electoral college votes. For both Republican and Democratic traders, the 2000 presidential election was a bittersweet experience.

Like the futures markets in Chicago and New York, IEM speculators can still be on the wrong side of the trade, and the overall market consensus can, like the pollsters, still make mistakes. Another prediction error occurred in the 2006 congressional elections. The IEM traders predicted that the Democrats would win the House (accurate) and that the Republicans would retain the Senate (inaccurate). The best we can say is that the futures markets in politics do tend to minimize errors— they are right most of the time. But so are the polls.

Why Speculators Outperform Pollsters

The more interesting question is: Why are futures traders better forecasters of elections than professional pollsters? Is it luck, or do they have some economic advantages? Economists give two basic reasons. First, traders appear to have a stronger profit motive in predicting the outcome of an election. Because they are putting their own money at risk, they tend to be more confident in their predictions, and willing to spend the time and effort to investigate more deeply the potential strength and weaknesses of candidates. Admittedly, Gallup and other professional pollsters also have a financial interest in making accurate forecasts of elections, but they are at a decided disadvantage. The establishment media poll potential voters with the question, "If the election were held today, who would you vote for?" To be more accurate, they should be asking voters, "Who would you bet to win the election in November?" Consequently, the public has less of a vested interest in taking the question seriously. Their answers can be fickle, and sometimes they may even lie. As a result, published polls vary significantly over time and between polling surveys. Sometimes the polls are downright wrong, the most famous being the Truman-Dewey presidential election of 1948.

Second, the market aggregates the diverse information of traders in a more dynamic, efficient manner. The Austrian economist F. A. Hayek suggested this point years ago when he noted that markets have a dual role. They allocate resources to their most productive use, and, through the discovery process, they rapidly provide information about the value of these resources.[5]

Traditional methods of predicting elections, such as polling, have some difficulty in estimating the dynamic forces at work during an election, while IEM traders incorporate polls, marketing surveys, economic data, charismatic appeal, and other information to improve their predictive power. Individual voters have little incentive to become experts on the outcome of an election—they tend to vote their conscience or vested interest—while the speculator needs to take into account as much relevant information as possible to be successful in the marketplace.

Who is likely to win control of the House and the Senate or the Presidency in November? Check out www.biz.uiowa.edu/iem. You can watch the results whether you bet or not.

Chapter 33

What Drives the
Economy and Stocks

Consumer Spending or Business Investment?

Though not one in a thousand recognizes it, it is business, not consumers, that is the heart of the economy. When businesses produce profitably, they create income-paying jobs and then consumers spend. Profitable firms also purchase new equipment because they need to modernize and update all their tools, structures and software.
— LARRY KUDLOW, *KUDLOW AND COMPANY*, CNBC-TV

We hear it all the time on the news:

"What the consumer does is the most important thing."
"If the consumer stops spending, we're in big trouble."
"If the consumer doesn't spend the tax cut, it won't help the recovery."

217

"The Consumer Expectations Index is down this month. . . . This is bad news for the economy and the stock market."

During the most recent 2001–2003 global recession, most reporters focused on consumer spending. In 2001, the French government, fearful that their citizens were not buying enough, increased government spending by 6 percent. Slowing retail sales in Europe "will spoil the party," warned *The Economist* magazine. In Japan, economic analysts contended that Japanese consumers were saving too much, and the only way to jump-start the giant Asian economy was to get Japanese consumers to stop saving and start spending.

"What the consumer does is the No. 1 issue for the economic outlook," stated Edward McKelvey, senior economist at Goldman Sachs. In the United States, pundits on CNN and CNBC frequently warned in 2001, "If the Bush tax rebates are saved, and not spent, they will do nothing for the economic recovery."

Yet the reality is that consumer spending is the effect, not the cause, of a productive, healthy economy. Renewed business spending on capital goods, tax cuts, lower interest rates, and productivity are more significant than a spurt in consumer spending. In a business cycle turnaround, production and investment come first, followed by retail spending.

The Importance of Say's Law

This truth prevails in the marketplace: It's supply—not demand—that drives the economy. Productivity and saving are the keys to economic growth. This principle was discovered and developed by the brilliant French economist Jean-Baptiste Say in the early nineteenth century and is known as Say's Law.[1]

Say used an agricultural example in his textbook to prove Say's Law. Suppose a farming community has a good harvest. "The greater the crop, the larger are the purchases of the growers." On the other hand, what happens if there is a shortfall or famine? "A bad harvest, on the contrary, hurts the sale of commodities at large."

To use a modern example, look at Seattle. When Bill Gates created Microsoft, many employees became wealthy, even millionaires, and Seattle's economy boomed. Consumer spending rose rapidly. But what happened when the federal government sued Microsoft in the late

1990s, and Microsoft stock fell? The boom ended in Seattle for a while, and consumer spending slowed down. It is clear in the business cycle that business spending drives the economy; consumer spending follows.

What the Leading Economic Indicators Are Telling Us

Let's examine how important consumer spending and the investment sector are when it comes to the leading economic indicators. Here we see that both sectors influence economic performance, but the business sector appears to play a stronger role. If we look at the Index of Leading Economic Indicators in nine major countries, which is published monthly by the Conference Board (www.conferenceboard.org), here are the results:

- Of the nine leading indicators of Germany compiled by the Conference Board, two are linked to consumer spending: the consumer confidence index and the consumer price index for services. The rest are connected to earlier-stage production, such as inventory changes, new purchases of capital equipment, and new construction orders.
- Among France's 10 leading indicators, 2 are consumer related, and the remainder are tied to commercial measures such as stock prices, productivity, building permits, the yield spread, and new industrial orders.
- The UK's leading indicators are linked to export volume, new orders in engineering industries, inventories, housing starts, and money supply. The Consumer Confidence Index is the lone consumer indicator.
- None of Japan's leading indicators are consumer related: overtime worked in manufacturing, business conditions survey, labor productivity, real operating profits, and new orders for machinery and construction.
- Mexico's six indicators include a monthly survey of inventories, industrial construction, stock prices, interest rates, and the cost of crude oil. Retail sales is a coincident indicator in Mexico.
- In the United States, the Conference Board highlights the Consumer Confidence Index, while the other nine indicators are only remotely related to final use, such as manufacturers' new orders for consumer goods and materials, building permits, average weekly manufacturing hours, stock prices, and new orders for nondefense capital goods.

What about the Consumer Confidence Index?

But what about the Consumer Confidence Index that the media high-lights every month? Isn't it a leading economic indicator? Indeed it is, but surprisingly the Consumer Confidence Index appears to be more about business conditions than consumer attitudes. Here are the questions consumers are asked to determine their "expectations":

1. Are current business conditions good, bad, or normal?
2. Do you expect business conditions to be good, bad or normal over the next six months?
3. Are jobs currently plentiful, not so plentiful, or hard to get?
4. Do you expect jobs to be more plentiful, not so plentiful, or hard to get over the next six months?
5. Do you plan to buy a new/used automobile/home/major appliance [Note: These are all durable consumer goods, not unlike durable capital goods] within the next six months?
6. Are you planning a U.S. or foreign vacation within the next six months?

In other words, the much-touted "consumer" confidence index is more a forecast on the outlook for business, employment, and durable goods than retail sales and consumer spending. It does not ask any questions about current consumption patterns other than durable goods. It asks nothing about food, clothing, entertainment, and other short-term buying, because these expenditures seldom change from month to month.

Why Doesn't the Conference Board Include Corporate Profits as a Leading Indicator?

It should also be pointed out that corporate profits have been one of the best forecasters of recessions. In fact, corporate profits are usually the first indicator of a coming boom or bust. They tend to peak a year before a recession officially begins. Yet oddly enough, the U.S. Leading Economic Indicators Index put out by the Conference Board does not include corporate profits in its list of 10 indicators. Why? It's because corporate profits are released quarterly, and the U.S. Leading Economic Indicators Index comes out monthly. Consequently, they don't use corporate profits as an indicator, even though it's better than most of the other business cycle statistics! This is just one example of the many methodological problems facing the Conference Board's Index of Leading Economic Indicators.

The reality is that business and investment spending are the true leading indicators of the economy and the stock market. If you want to know where the stock market is headed, forget about consumer spending and retail sales figures. Look to manufacturing, capital spending, and productivity gains.

Beware of Keynes's Law

The reason we hear so much about the consumer is because we are still under the influence of Keynesian economics, which teaches us "Keynes's Law," that demand creates supply. . . . Keynes's Law is just the opposite of Say's Law, supply creates demand. According to Keynes, consumer spending drives the economy, and saving is bad when the economy is in a short-term contraction.

One of the reasons for this "consumer spending" myth is how we figure Gross Domestic Product (GDP). Economists note that personal consumption expenditures are the largest sector of GDP, representing approximately 70 percent. This statistic has led the press to make statements like this one from the Associated Press: "Analysts watch consumer spending closely because it represents roughly two-thirds of all economic activity."

But is consumption the largest and most important part of the economy? In fact, it's not. Journalists should know that GDP is not meant to be a complete measure of all activity or spending in the economy. GDP measures only *final* output of goods and services. It deliberately leaves out all intermediate production or goods-in-process, that is, all the sales of products in earlier stages of production, such as steel in car production. Why? Because GDP is meant to measure only finished goods and services—usable products in homes, businesses, and government. To include spending at every stage of production would be double and triple counting. For example, in bread making, it would count both the wheat and the flour in the value of the bread. Yet GDP is only interested in the final usable product—the bread that people consume at home.

Gross Domestic Expenditures (GDE):
A New Measure of Total Economic Activity

Economists are also interested in intermediate production processes, the stages of production that lead to final output. This process begins in the earliest stages of commodity production resource development, such as R&D; then leads to manufacturing and semimanufacturing production; wholesale and distribution channels; and ultimately all the way to final sales at the retail level.

To measure all transactions in the economy, we must add up all sales of goods and services at every stage of production, not just the final stage. There are literally millions of intermediate transactions occurring prior to the sale of finished goods and services to final users. In my book, *The Structure of Production,* I developed a new national statistic to measure total spending in the economy called Gross Domestic Expenditures (GDE).[2]

For example, for 2005, I estimate that GDE—total spending in the economy—amounted to approximately $27 trillion, compared to final output (GDP) of $12.5 trillion for 2005. As a percentage of GDE, personal consumer expenditures amounted to $8.75 trillion, or only 32 percent of total spending in the economy, not 70 percent as previously reported. On the other hand, gross business expenditures—adding together private investment and intermediate business spending—came to $14.6 trillion, or approximately 54 percent of GDE. Thus, we see that business investment is substantially larger than consumer spending in the economy.

U.S. Commerce Department Introduces
New Macro Statistic

In years past, economists determined the value of intermediate production through input-output statistics collected every five years from census and IRS data. In recent years, however, the Bureau of Economic Analysis (BEA) of the U.S. Commerce Department has recognized the need for an annual measure of total spending in the economy and has introduced a new national-income statistic called Gross Output (GO). It seeks to determine the value of output at all stages of production, including services. However, while Gross Output is a step in the right direction, it is not a complete measure of total spending in the economy. It leaves out some wholesale and retail expenditures. Still, Gross Output measures almost twice the size of GDP.[3]

In sum, stimulating consumer spending in the short run will undoubtedly encourage some lines of business activity. If people go on a buying spree at a local grocery store or mall, merchants and their suppliers will see sales and production rise. But the consumer spending binge cannot last when the credit card bills come due, and more spending by consumers is not likely to help construct a bridge, build a hospital, pay for a research program to cure cancer, or provide funds for a new invention or a new production process. Only a higher level of saving will do that. Thus, in nations following Keynesian proconsumption policies, it is not surprising to see luxurious retail stores and malls alongside dilapidated roads and infrastructure. Their consumption/ investment ratio is systematically out of balance. Before he died, management guru Peter Drucker chastised the United States for a "crisis in productivity and capital formation" and "under investing on a massive scale."[4]

Saving, investing, and capital formation are the principal ingredients of economic growth. Countries with the highest growth rates are those that encourage saving and investing, and invest in new production processes, education, technology, infrastructure, and labor-saving devices. Such investing in turn results in better consumer products at lower prices. Such countries do not seek to artificially promote consumption at the expense of saving. Stimulating the economy through excessive consumption or wasteful government programs may provide artificial stimulus in the short run, but cannot lead to genuine prosperity in the long run.

Using our new statistic, GDE, we now see that cutting taxes on businesses and investments will have a dramatically favorable effect, far more than previously thought. When business investment represents over 50 percent of the economy, not 15 percent, reducing investment taxes on interest, dividends, and capital gains can clearly have a multiplying impact on the nation's economy.

In sum, it is capital investment, not consumer spending, that ultimately drives an economy. As Ludwig von Mises declared years ago, "Progressive capital accumulation results in perpetual economic betterment."[5]

Chapter 34

The Midas Metal

A Golden Comeback

A more timeless measure is needed; gold fits the bill perfectly.
> —MARK MOBIUS, TEMPLETON MONEY MANAGER

Gold maintains its purchasing power over long periods of time, for example, half-century intervals.
> —ROY JASTRAM, THE GOLDEN CONSTANT[1]

W hen speaking of the Midas metal, I'm reminded of Mark Twain's refrain, "The reports of my death are greatly exaggerated." During the 1990s, after years of central-bank selling and a bear market in precious metals, the *Financial Times* declared the "Death of Gold." But it wasn't dead, it was hibernating.

What's Missing from This Picture?

During the disinflationary decades of the 1980s and 1990s, I battled with the editors of the *Wall Street Journal* and the *New York Times* about the importance of gold as an indicator of global inflation and geopolitical instability. During this period, gold was relatively moribund, and the establishment press ignored the Midas metal. In the financial pages, the *Times* highlighted oil, not gold, as the best inflation signal. The front page of the *Wall Street Journal* listed a dozen market indicators, including stocks, bonds, currencies, and commodities, including oil, yet omitted gold.

But that all changed in the new millennium. Gold came back to life in 2001, after the terrorists' attacks launched a new inflationary era of big-government spending and easy money. It is now move than $800 an ounce.

Return to the Gold Standard?

Following the Asian financial crisis in 1997–1998, Mark Mobius, the famed Templeton manager of emerging markets, advocated the creation of a new regional currency, the *asian,* convertible to gold, including the issuance of Asian gold coins. "All their M1 money supply and foreign reserves would be converted into asians at the current price of gold. Henceforth asians would be issued only upon deposits of gold or foreign-currency equivalents of gold." Mobius castigated the central banks of Southeast Asia for recklessly depreciating their currencies. As a result, "many businesses and banks throughout the region have become bankrupt, billions of dollars have been lost, and economic development has been threatened." Why gold? "Because gold has always been a store of value in Asia and is respected as the last resort in times of crisis. Asia's history is strewn with fallen currencies. . . . The beauty of gold is that it limits a country's ability to spend to the amount it can earn in addition to its gold holdings."[2]

Not Just Another Commodity

Although Mobius's monetary proposal has not gone anywhere, Asian central bankers, including the Bank of China, have continued to accumulate large amounts of gold. Recent studies give support to Mobius's plan. According to these studies, gold has three unique features: First, gold provides a stable numeraire for the world's monetary system, one that closely matches the "monetarist rule." Second, gold has had an amazing capacity to maintain its purchasing power throughout history, what the late Roy Jastram called "The Golden Constant." And, third, the yellow metal has a curious ability to predict future inflation and interest rates.

Let's start with gold as a stable monetary system. With most commodities, such as wheat or oil, the "carryover" stocks vary significantly with annual production. Not so with gold. Historical data confirm that the aggregate gold stockpile held by individuals and central banks always increases and never declines.[3] Moreover, the annual increase in the world gold stock typically varies between 1.5 and 3 percent, and seldom exceeds 3 percent. In short, the gradual increase in the stock of gold closely resembles the "monetary rule" cherished by Milton Friedman and the monetarists, where the money stock rises at a steady rate.

Compare the stability of the gold supply with the annual changes in the paper money supply held by central banks. The G–8 money-supply index rose as much as 17 percent in the early 1970s and as little as 3 percent in the 1990s and 2000s. Moreover, the central banks' monetary policies were far more volatile than the gold supply. On a worldwide basis, gold proved to be more stable and less inflationary than a fiat money system.

Critics agree that gold is inherently a "hard" currency, but complain that new gold production can't keep up with economic growth. In other words, gold is too much of a hard currency. As noted, the world gold stock rises at a miserly annual growth rate of less than 3 percent and oftentimes under 2 percent, while GDP growth usually exceeds 3 or 4 percent and sometimes 7 or 8 percent in developing nations. The result? Price deflation is inevitable under a pure gold standard. Critics are correct that gold-supply growth is not likely to keep up with real GDP growth. Only during major gold discoveries, such as in California and Australia in the 1850s or South Africa in the 1890s, did world gold supplies grow faster than 4 percent a year. Because of deflationary pressure, the chances of going back on a classical gold standard are remote.

Gold as an Inflation Hedge

What about gold as an inflation hedge? Berkeley professor Roy Jastram and others have demonstrated the relative stability of gold in terms of its purchasing power—its ability to maintain value and purchasing power over goods and services over the long run. But the emphasis must be placed on the long run. In the short run, gold's value depends a great deal on the rate of inflation and therefore often fails to live up to its reputation as an inflation hedge.

The classic study on the purchasing power of gold is *The Golden Constant: The English and American Experience, 1560–1976,* by Roy W. Jastram, late professor of business at the University of California, Berkeley. The book, now out of print, examines gold as an inflation and deflation hedge over a span of 400 years.

Two Amazing Graphs

Jastram's work and updated data by the American Institute for Economic Research in Great Barrington, Massachusetts, tell a powerful story:

1. Gold always returns to its full purchasing power, although it may take a long time to do so.
2. The price of gold became more volatile as the world moved to a fiat money standard beginning in the 1930s. Note how gold has moved up and down sharply as the pound and the dollar have lost purchasing power since going off the gold standard. (See Figures 34.1 and 34.2.)

In my economics classes at Rollins College and Columbia University, I demonstrate the long-term value of gold by holding up a $20 St. Gaudens double-eagle gold coin. Prior to 1933, Americans carried this coin in their pockets as money. Back then, they could buy a tailor-made suit for one double eagle, or $20. Today this same coin—which is worth between $900 and $1,200, depending on its rarity and condition—could buy the same tailor-made suit. Of course, the double-eagle coin has numismatic, or rarity, value. A one-ounce gold-bullion coin, without numismatic value, is worth only around $900 today. Gold has risen substantially in dollar terms but has not done as well as numismatic U.S. coins.

The price of gold bullion was over $800 an ounce in 1980 and steadily declined in value for nearly two decades. Now it is making a comeback. Is gold a good inflation hedge? Indeed, the record shows that when the inflation rate is steady or declining, gold has been a poor hedge. The yellow metal (and mining shares) typically responds best to

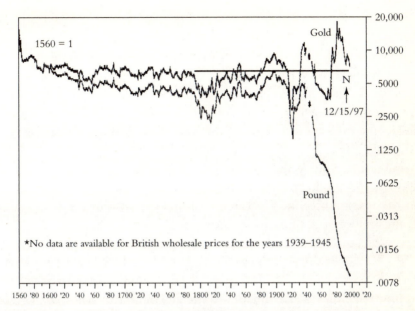

Figure 34.1   Purchasing Power of Gold and British Pound, 1560–2006
SOURCE: American Institute for Economic Research.

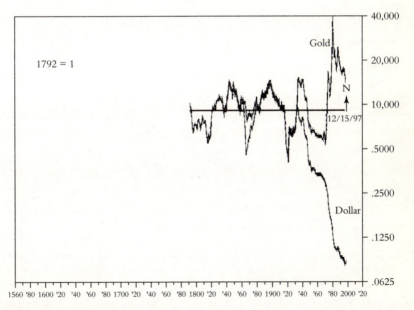

Figure 34.2   Purchasing Power of Gold and U.S. Dollar, 1792–2006
SOURCE: American Institute for Economic Research.

accelerating inflation. Over the long run, the Midas metal has held its own, but should not be deemed an ideal or perfect hedge. In fact, U.S. stocks have proven to be much more profitable than gold as an investment.

The work of Wharton professor Jeremy Siegel demonstrates that U.S. stocks have far outperformed gold over the past two centuries. Like Jastram, Siegel confirms gold's long-term stability. Yet gold can't hold up to the performance of the U.S. stock market. As he demonstrates in *Stocks for the Long Term,* stocks have far outperformed bonds, T-bills, and gold. Why? Because stocks represent higher economic growth and productivity over the long run. Stocks have risen sharply in the twentieth century because of a dramatic rise in the standard of living and America's free-enterprise system.

When price inflation accelerates, industrial stocks tend to do poorly and gold stocks shine. As Siegel states, while stocks are excellent long-term hedges against inflation, they "are not good shorter-term hedges against inflation."[4] Price inflation is the key indicator: When the rate of inflation moves back up, watch out. Stocks will flounder and gold will come back to life. (See Figure 34.3.)

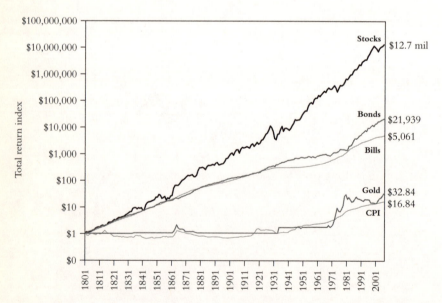

Figure 34.3   Total Nominal Return Indexes for Stocks, Bonds, Bills, and Gold: 1802–2001

What's left for the yellow metal? I see two essential functions for gold: first, a profitable investment when general prices accelerate and, second, an important barometer of future price inflation and interest rates.

Gold as a Profitable Investment

Since the United States went off the gold standard in 1971, gold bullion and gold mining shares have become well-known cyclical investments. Investors should be warned of the volatile nature of gold and mining stocks, with mining shares tending to fluctuate more than gold itself. The gold industry can provide superior profits during an uptrend and heavy losses during a downtrend.

One of the reasons for the high volatility of mining shares is their distance from final consumption. Mining represents the earliest stage of production and is extremely capital intensive and responsive to changes in interest rates.[5] Gold stocks should not be viewed as buy and hold investments, given their inherent volatility.

Gold as a Forecaster

However, gold has the amazing ability to forecast accurately the direction of the general price level. In the mid-1990s, John List (then an economist at the University of Central Florida and now at Chicago) and I developed a forecasting model for inflation. We tested three commodity indexes (Dow Jones Commodity Spot Index, crude oil, and gold) to determine which one best anticipated changes in the Consumer Price Index (CPI) between 1970 and 1992. It turned out that gold proved to be the best indicator of future inflation as measured by the CPI. The lag period is about one year. That is, gold does a good job of predicting the direction of the CPI a year in advance. (All three indexes did a poor job of predicting changes in the CPI on a monthly basis.)

In sum, if you want to know the future of price inflation, watch the gold traders at the New York Mercantile Exchange. If gold enters a sustained rise, expect higher inflation in the future.

Today, the *Wall Street Journal* and CNBC highlight the price of gold. Fed chairmen and G-7 central bankers watch it closely. Referring to the easy-money, low-interest-rate strategy of the Federal Reserve in 2003–2004, the *Wall Street Journal* editorialized, "The Fed was feeding inflationary expectations that hadn't been seen since the late 1970s. The price of gold is one rough proxy for those expectations, and the gold chart suggests the magnitude of its mistake."[6]

Gold is the ultimate indicator.

Chapter 35

Is Another Great Depression Possible?

The American economy is depression-proof.
—Milton Friedman (1954)[1]

I s another Great Depression possible, with collapsing stocks, plunging corporate profits, and skyrocketing unemployment of 25 percent or more? Most economists agree with Milton Friedman who gave a speech on this topic in Sweden in 1954, arguing that government leaders and central bankers now understand the basic inner workings of the economy and have the technical tools to prevent a full-scale collapse. He referred to several institutional changes that make such an event inconceivable, such as federal bank deposit insurance; abandonment of the international gold standard; and the growth in the size of government, including welfare payments, unemployment insurance, and other built-in stabilizers. Most importantly, the Federal Reserve knows not to repeat the mistakes of the past and how to avoid a monetary collapse at all costs (mainly injecting liquidity into the marketplace and banking system).

Certainly, Friedman's prediction of no more depressions has been proven correct so far. We've had numerous contractions and recessions in the economy, and even a few stock market crashes, but we have avoided the big one, a massive Great Depression similar to the 1930s debacle.

Yet, I would like to suggest that even though another Great Depression may not be probable, it is certainly not impossible. We are depression-resistant, but not depression-proof. Before explaining, let's review the significance of the Great Depression, why it occurred, why it lasted as long as it did, and how we got out of the Depression.

The Impact of the Great Depression

The Great Depression of the 1930s may be a dim memory now, but its impact is still being felt in policy and theory. The prolonged Depression created an environment critical of laissez-faire policies and favorable toward ubiquitous state interventionism throughout the Western world. The Depression led to the Welfare State and boundless faith in Big Government. It caused most of the Anglo-American economics profession to question classical free-market economics and to search for radical anticapitalist alternatives, eventually converting to the new economics of Keynesianism and demand-side economics.

Prior to the Great Depression, most Western economists accepted the classical virtues of thrift, limited government, balanced budgets, the gold standard, and Say's Law. While most economists continued to defend free enterprise and free trade on a microeconomic scale, they rejected traditional views on a macroeconomic level in the postwar period, advocating consumption over saving, fiat money over the gold standard, deficit spending over a balanced budget, and active state interventionism over limited government. They bought the Keynesian argument that a free market was inherently unstable and could result in high levels of unemployed labor and resources for indefinite periods. They blamed the Great Depression on laissez-faire capitalism and contended that only massive government spending during World War II saved the capitalist system from defeat. In short, the Depression opened the door to widespread collectivism in the United States and around the world.

Fortunately, free-market economists have gradually punctured holes in these arguments, and the pendulum has slowly shifted toward a reestablishment of classical free-market economics. Three questions needed to be addressed: What caused the Great Depression? Why did it last so long? Did World War II restore prosperity? Economic historian Robert Higgs had dubbed these three arenas of debate the Great Contraction, the Great Duration, and the Great Escape.

The Cause of the Great Contraction

Many free-market economists had attempted to answer the first question, including Benjamin M. Anderson and Murray N. Rothbard,[2] but none had the impact equal to Milton Friedman's empirical studies on money in the early 1960s. His was the first effective effort to destroy the argument that the Great Depression was the handiwork of an inherently unstable capitalistic system. Friedman (and his co-author, Anna J. Schwartz) demonstrated forcefully that it was not free enterprise, but rather government—specifically the Federal Reserve System—that caused the Great Depression. In a single sentence underlined by all who read it, Friedman and Schwartz indicted the Fed: From the cyclical peak in August 1929 to a cyclical trough in March 1933, the stock of money fell by over a third.[3] (This statement was all the more shocking because until Friedman's work, the Fed didn't publish money supply figures, such as M1 and M2!)

Friedman and Schwartz also proved that the gold standard did not cause the Depression, as some Keynesian economists have alleged. During the early 1930s, the U.S. gold stock rose even as the Fed perversely raised the discount rate and allowed the money supply to shrink and banks to collapse.[4]

The Prolonged Slump

Economic activity and employment stagnated throughout the 1930s, causing a paradigm shift from classical economics to Keynesianism.

Friedrich Hayek, the Austrian economist who challenged Keynes in the 1930s, was so disheartened about the state of the free-world economy that he abandoned the study of economics in favor of political philosophy.

Why did the Depression last so long? Many free-market economists have picked up where Murray Rothbard's *America's Great Depression* left off, at the time Franklin Delano Roosevelt took office in 1933. Gene Smiley (Marquette University) attempted an Austrian perspective on the perverse role of fiscal policy in the 1930s. I summarized the causes of stagnation and persistent unemployment, such as the Smoot-Hawley Tariff, tax increases, government regulation and controls, and prolabor legislation.[5]

More recently, Robert Higgs of the Independent Institute has made an in-depth study of the 1930s' malaise and focused on the lack of private investment during this period. According to Higgs, private investment was greatly hampered by New Deal initiatives that destroyed investor and business confidence, the key to recovery.[6] In short, the New Deal prolonged the depression.

What Got Us Out?

In another brilliant study, Higgs attacked the commonly held view that World War II saved us from the Depression and restored the economy to full employment. The war gave only the appearance of recovery, when in reality private consumption and investment declined while Americans fought and died for their country. A return to genuine prosperity—the true Great Escape—did not occur until after the war ended, when most of the wartime controls were abolished and most of the resources used in the military were returned to civilian production.[7] Only after the war did private investment, business confidence, and consumer spending return to form.[8]

In sum, it has been a long and hard-fought war to restore the case for free-market capitalism. Finally, through the path-breaking work of Friedman, Rothbard, Smiley, Higgs, and other scholars, we can now say the battle has been won.

Can It Happen Again?

But what if government officials forget the lessons of the Great Depression? Here are several scenarios:

1. The government could destabilize the economy by promising too much in entitlements, welfare payments, and war spending, threatening bankruptcy and massive inflation.
2. The government could cause economic malaise and permanent recession by imposing excessive regulations, bureaucracy, and taxes on business and trade.
3. A series of unexpected events could trigger a major financial accident— a run on the dollar, a real estate crisis sudden shifts from one class of assets (such as government bonds) to another (such as gold, or a hard currency), a major terrorist attack, or a natural disaster—that could overwhelm the monetary authorities.

As long as the global financial system is built on a volatile, destabilizing inflationary policy coupled with a fragile fractional reserve banking system and laissez-faire global markets, the possibility of financial chaos and a subsequent economic cataclysm should not be discounted. For years governments have been able to respond effectively to a variety of crises, and the markets have recovered. But the most recent financial panic is surely not the last, and one should never underestimate the ability of the global marketplace to react in unpredictable ways.

Chapter 36

Today's Most
Influential Economist?

But half a century later, it is Keynes who has been toppled and _____,
the fierce advocate of free markets, who is preeminent.
— DANIEL YERGIN AND JOSEPH STANISLAW[1]

F ill in the blank. Who is the mysterious economist named above?
Most of my colleagues named Milton Friedman, but in Daniel
Yergin and Joseph Stanislaw's bestseller book and PBS series, the
Chicago economist runs a close second to . . . F. A. Hayek, the Austrian
economist!

Why Hayek? Because, according to Yergin and Stanislaw, Hayek has
done more than any other economist to debunk socialism in its many
forms—Marxism, communism, and industrial planning—and to promote free markets as an alternative system. Hayek's influence perfectly

illustrates John Maynard Keynes's remark that politicians, "madmen in authority," are the "slaves of some defunct economist."[2]

Indeed, Hayek's influence has been ubiquitous. As Yergin and Stanislaw point out, *The Road to Serfdom* greatly affected Margaret Thatcher in reforming Great Britain and raised doubts about industrial planning. Hayek's criticisms of Keynesianism (*A Tiger by the Tail*) called into question deficit spending and the ability of the state to fine-tune the economy. His theory of decentralized knowledge and competition as a discovery process has had an impact on microeconomic theory and experimental economics. His work on the trade cycle and the denationalization of currencies has influenced monetary policy. His co-founding of the Mont Pelerin Society spread the gospel of free markets, property rights, and libertarian thought throughout the globe. And his books have been translated into several languages, including Chinese.[3]

Yergin and Stanislaw's revelation in *The Commanding Heights: The Battle Between Government and the Marketplace That Is Remaking the World* is a monumental victory for market-based economics. It is all the more remarkable given Yergin's background as an establishment journalist and author of *The Prize,* a Pulitzer Prize–winning book about big oil.

Other Austrian Heroes: Drucker and Schumpeter

In the early 1990s, I argued in *Economics on Trial* that the "next economics" would be the Austrian model, with its focus on entrepreneurship, microeconomics, disequilibrium, deregulation, savings, free enterprise, and sound money. But which Austrian economist to choose from? The most best-known Austrian in business circles is the late Peter Drucker, known for his emphasis on entrepreneurship, innovation, and investment capital as well as his denunciations of big government, excessive taxation, and Keynesian economics. For Drucker, the large corporation was the ideal social institution, "the modern free, non-revolutionary way" and superior to big government as an ideal social institution for citizens. Drucker's style of management is Austrian through and through. Time, expectations, new information, and potential change in production processes—all Austrian focal points—are constantly emphasized in his writings and consultations. The manager must be an entrepreneur, not just an administrator. Innovation is essential.

In financial circles, the premier Austrian economist is Joseph Schumpeter, who was born in Austria and taught at Harvard University until his death in 1950. He emphasized entrepreneurship, the dynamics of competitive markets, and the cycle of "creative destruction." In fact, Peter Drucker predicted in an article, "Modern Prophets: Schumpeter or Keynes?" that "it is Schumpeter who will shape the rest of this century, if not for the next thirty or fifty years."[4]

A Tale of Two Cities

Yergin and Stanislaw rightly point to two schools of free-market economics responsible for the shift from government to private enterprise as the solution to world economic problems. "And the eventual victory of this viewpoint was really a tale of two cities—Vienna and Chicago," declare the authors.[5]

In the judgment of many economists, Milton Friedman and the Chicago school have had even a greater influence than Hayek and the Austrians. Yergin acknowledges Friedman as "the world's best-known economist," noting that "the Chicago School loomed very large" in its sway on monetarism at the Federal Reserve and economic policy (under Ronald Reagan). And, of course, all top-ten textbooks in economics have significant sections on Friedman and his theories (monetarism, natural rate of unemployment, welfare reform, privatization). Friedman and the Chicago school have mounted an effective counter-revolution to Keynesianism.

The Great U-Turn

But Keynes's principal rival in the 1930s was Hayek. Teaching at the London School of Economics, Hayek defended the classical model of thrift, balanced budgets, the gold standard, and free markets, while Keynes (Cambridge University) promoted the "new economics" of consumption, deficit spending, easy money, and big government. Keynes won the first battle for the hearts of economists, and his brand of "mixed economy" swept the profession. Hayek fell out of favor and went on to write about law and political science. The task of dethroning Keynes fell to Friedman; he has accomplished it masterfully.

After he won the Nobel Prize in economics in 1974, Hayek and the Austrians have had a rebirth. Equally, Friedman and the Chicago school have come out of obscurity into prominence. Fifty years ago the Keynesian-collectivist consensus expressed the sentiment, "The state is wise, and the market is stupid." Today, the growing consensus is just the opposite: "The market is wise, and the state is stupid."

But it may be too early to break out the champagne and celebrate the triumph of free-enterprise capitalism. Battles have been won, but the war is never over. As Milton Friedman states, "Freedom is a rare and delicate flower."

Chapter 37

Economics for
the 21st Century

Nature has set no limit to the realization of our hopes.
—Marquis de Condorcet

Recently I came across the extraordinary writings of the Marquis de Condorcet (1743–1794), a French mathematician with an amazing gift of prophecy in the Enlightenment. Robert Malthus (1766–1834) ridiculed Condorcet's optimism in his famous *Essay on Population* (1798). Today Malthus is well known, and Condorcet is forgotten. Yet it is Condorcet who has proven to be far more prescient.

In an essay written over 200 years ago, translated as "The Future Progress of the Mind," Condorcet foresaw the agricultural revolution, gigantic leaps in labor productivity, a reduced work week, the consumer society, a dramatic rise in the average life span, medical breakthroughs, cures for common diseases, and an explosion in the world's population.

Condorcet concluded his essay with a statement that accurately describes the two major forces of the twentieth century: the destructive force of war and crimes against humanity, and the creative force of global free-market capitalism. He wrote eloquently of "the errors, the crimes, the injustices which still pollute the earth," while at the same time celebrating our being "emancipated from its shackles, released from the empire of fate and from that of the enemies of its progress, advancing with a firm and sure step along the path of truth, virtue and happiness!"[1]

As we enter the New Millennium, the public has focused on the history of the twentieth century. Condorcet's essay reflects two characteristics of this incredible period. First, the misery and vicious injustices of the past hundred years, and second, the incredible economic and technological advances during the same time.

The Crimes of the Twentieth Century

Paul Johnson's *Modern Times,* by far the best twentieth-century history of the world, demonstrates powerfully that this century has been the bloodiest of all world history.[2] Here is a breakdown of the carnage:

Civilians Killed by Governments

Country	(in Millions)	Years
Soviet Union	62	(1917–91)
China (communist)	35	(1949–)
Germany	21	(1933–45)
China (Kuomintang)	10	(1928–49)
Japan	6	(1936-45)
Other	36	(1900–)
Total	**170 Million**	

Civilians Killed in War

Type of War	(in Millions)
International wars	30
Civil wars	7
Total	**37 million**

Economists use a statistic to measure what national output could exist under conditions of full employment, called Potential GDP. Imagine the Potential GDP if the communists, Nazis, and other despots hadn't used government power to commit those hateful crimes against humanity. Another great French writer, Frederic Bastiat (1801–1850), wrote an essay in 1850 titled "What Is Seen and What Is Not Seen."[3] We do not see the art, literature, inventions, music, books, charity, and good works of the millions who lost their lives in the Soviet gulags, Nazi concentration camps, and Pol Pot's killing fields.

The Economic Miracle of the Twentieth Century

Yet the twentieth century was also the best of times, for those who survived the wars and repression. Millions of Americans, Europeans, and Asians were emancipated from the drudgery of all-day work by miraculous technological advances in telecommunications, agriculture, transportation, energy, and medicine. The best book describing this economic miracle is Stanley Lebergott's *Pursuing Happiness: American Consumers in the Twentieth Century* (Princeton University Press, 1993). Focusing on trends in food, tobacco and alcohol, clothing, housing, fuel, housework, health, transportation, recreation, and religion, he demonstrates powerfully how "consumers have sought to make an uncertain and often cruel world into a pleasanter and more convenient place."[4] As a result, Americans have increased their standard of living at least tenfold in the past 100 years.

What should be the goal of the economist in the new millennium? Certainly not to repeat the blunders of the past. In the halls of Congress, the White House, and academia, we need to reject the brutality of Marxism, the weight of Keynesian big government, and the debauchery of sound currency by interventionist central banks. Most important, ivory-tower economists need to concentrate more on applied economics (like the work of Lebergott) instead of high mathematical modeling. Throughout this book, I have highlighted the outstanding and sometimes astonishing advances of the applied economists in personal finance, business, law, and religion.

As far as a positive program is concerned, the right direction can be found in an essay on the "next economics" written by the great Austrian-born management guru Peter F. Drucker almost 20 years ago: "Capital is the future . . ., the Next Economics will have to be again micro-economic and centered on supply." Drucker demanded an economic theory aiming at "optimizing productivity" that would benefit all workers and consumers.[5] Interestingly, Drucker cited approvingly from the work of Nobel Prize winner, Robert Mundell who is famed for his advocacy of supply-side economics and a gold-backed international currency.

Beware the Enemy

Market forces are on the march. The collapse of Soviet communism has, in the words of Milton Friedman, turned "creeping socialism" into "crumbling socialism." But let us not be deluded. Bad policies, socialistic thinking, and class hatred die slowly. Unless we are vigilant, natural liberty and universal prosperity will be on the defensive once again. We need to deregulate, privatize, cut taxes, open borders, control inflation, balance the budget, and limit government to its proper constitutional authority. We need to teach, write, and speak out for economic liberalization as never before. Let our goal for the coming era be: freedom in our time for all peoples!

Notes

Foreword

1. Letter of Alfred Marshall to C. R. Fay, February 23, 1915, in Arthur C. Pigou, ed., *Memorials of Alfred Marshall* (London: Macmillan, 1925), 489–490.

2. John Maynard Keynes, *Essays in Persuasion* (New York: W. W. Norton, 1963 [1931]), 366–367.

Introduction: A Golden Age of Discovery

1. Diane Coyle, *The Soulful Science: What Economists Really Do and Why It Matters* (Princeton University Press, 2007), 232.

2. Friedrich A. Hayek, "The Pretence of Knowledge," Nobel Prize Lecture (December 11, 1974).

3. Robert J. Barro, "Cut Taxes," *Wall Street Journal* (November 21, 1991).

4. Herbert Stein, "The Age of Ignorance," *Wall Street Journal* (June 11, 1993).

5. Paul Krugman, *Peddling Prosperity* (New York: W. W. Norton, 1994), 9, 24. His previous book, *The Age of Diminishing Expectations,* came out in the early 1990s, just when Third World nations began throwing off socialism and Marxism, and sensed rising expectations for the first time. The decade of the 1990s turned out to be an explosion in economic and stock market growth.

6. J-B. Say, *A Treatise on Political Economy,* 4th ed. (New York: Augustus M. Kelly, 1971 [1880]), xxi, xxxv.

7. Arjo Klamer and David Colander, *The Making of an Economist* (Boulder, Colorado: Westview, 1990), xv.

8. Richard A. Posner, *Law and Literature,* 2nd ed. (Cambridge: Harvard University Press, 1998), 182.

9. Gary S. Becker and Guity Nashat Becker, *The Economics of Life* (New York: McGraw-Hill, 1997), 3.

Chapter 1: Economist Discovers a Painless Way to Triple Your Savings Rate—The $90 Billion Opportunity

1. Testimony of Richard H. Thaler, Graduate School of Business, University of Chicago, before the U.S. Senate Panel, *Helping Americans Save,* March 10, 2004.

2. "Living on Borrowed Time," *The Economist* (November 6, 1999).

3. See Klaus Schmidt-Hebbel and Luis Servén, eds., *The Economics of Saving and Growth* (New York: Cambridge University Press, 1999).

4. N. Greg Mankiw, *Macroeconomics,* 2nd ed. (New York: Worth Publishers, 1994), 86.

5. Dawn Kopecki, "Wrestling for the 401(k) Purse," *BusinessWeek* (September 10, 2007), 60.

6. References to "animal spirits" and "waves of irrational psychology" can be found in John Maynard Keynes, *The General Theory of Employment, Interest and Money* (New York: Macmillan, 1973 [1936]), 161–162.

7. Robert Shiller, *Irrational Exuberance* (Princeton University Press, 2000), 142.

8. Ludwig von Mises, *Theory and History* (New Haven: Yale University Press, 1957), 268. However, Mises refuses to call bad decisions "irrational." He states, "Error, inefficiency, and failure must not be confused with irrationality. He who shoots wants, as a rule, to hit the mark. If he misses it, he is not 'irrational,' he is a poor marksman."

9. Israel M. Kirzner, "Economics and Error" in *Perception, Opportunity, and Profit* (Chicago: University of Chicago Press, 1979), 135.

10. Mark and Jo Ann Skousen, *High Finance on a Low Budget* (Chicago: Dearborn, 1994), *Mark Skousen's 30-Day Plan for Financial Independence* (Washington, D. C.: Regnery, 1998).

Chapter 2: Modern Portfolio Theory: Can You Beat the Market?

1. Burton G. Malkiel, *A Random Walk Down Wall Street,* 5th ed. (New York: Norton, 1990), 24.

2. Warren Buffett, "Remarks," *Berkshire Hathaway Annual Report* (1988).

3. Jack D. Schwager, *The New Market Wizards: Conversations with America's Top Traders* (New York: Collins, 1994).

4. Jack D. Schwager, *Stock Market Wizards: Interviews with America's Top Stock Market Traders* (New York: Collins, 2003).

Chapter 3: Yes, You Can Beat the Market . . . with Less Risk

1. Lawrence Carrel, "Index Wars," *Smart Money,* August 16, 2006.

2. The term *market cap* refers to the total market capitalization of a publicly traded company (price of the stock times numbers of shares outstanding). A market-cap index is a stock index where stocks are ranked according to their market-cap size. Dividend-weight index refers to an index that is ranked according to the dividend each company pays.

Chapter 4: High-Return Investing: Lessons from Yale's Endowment Fund

1. David S. Swensen, *Unconventional Success: A Fundamental Approach to Personal Investment* (New York: Free Press, 2005), 297.

2. Swensen, *Unconventional Success,* 298.

Chapter 5: How Chile Created a Worker-Capitalist Revolution

1. José Piñera, "The Success of Chile's Privatized Social Security," *Cato Policy Report,* http://www.cato.org/pubs/policy_report/pr-ja-jp.html.

2. Milton Friedman, *Capitalism and Freedom* (University of Chicago Press, 1962), 182–89. Friedman later endorsed the Chilean model and favored privatization of Social Security in the United States.

3. Private interview with Arnold C. Harberger at the Mont Pelerin Society meetings in Salt Lake City, August 18, 2004. TIAA-CREF isn't the only pension system in the United States that offers individualized pension accounts. The federal government's Thrift Savings Plan (TSA) offers federal employees a variety of fund choices in their personal retirement accounts.

4. José Piñera, "The Success of Chile's Privatized Social Security," *Cato Policy Report,* http://www.cato.org/pubs/policy_report/pr-ja-jp.html.

5. Rudi Dornbusch, "Dole Blew a Chance to Be Bold," *BusinessWeek,* September 2, 1996.

Chapter 6: The Call for Social Security Reform

1. Vito Tanzi and Ludger Schuknecht, *Public Spending in the 20th Century; A Global Perspective* (Cambridge: Cambridge University Press, 2000), 201.

2. Ludwig von Mises, *Planning for Freedom,* 4th ed. (South Holland, Ill.: Libertarian Press, 1980), 18–35. This argument applies equally to pharmaceutical drugs under Medicare coverage.

Chapter 7: $4,000 a Month from Social Security?

1. William G. Shipman, "Retiring with Dignity: Social Security vs. Private Markets," Cato Institute Policy Analysis (August 14, 1995): http://www.cato.org/pubs/ssps/ssp2es.html.

Chapter 8: How the Private Sector Solved Its Own Pension Crisis

1. Peter F. Drucker, "The Sickness of Government," in *The Age of Discontinuity* (New York: Harper, 1969), 229, 236.

2. Peter F. Drucker, *The Unseen Revolution: How Pension Fund Socialism Came to America* (New York: Harper & Row, 1976). This book was reprinted with a new introduction as *The Pension Fund Revolution* (New Brunswick, N.J.: Transaction, 1996).

3. Andrew G. Biggs, "Social Security: Is It a Crisis That Doesn't Exist?" Cato Social Security Privatization Report 21 (www.cato.org), October 5, 2000, 3.

4. Ibid., 32.

5. Drucker, *The Age of Discontinuity*, 241.

Chapter 9: The Four Sources of Happiness: Is Money One of Them?

1. Bruno S. Frey and Alois Stutzer, *Happiness and Economics* (Princeton, N.J.: Princeton University Press, 2002), 81.

2. See my article "Easy Living—My Two Years in the Bahamas" at www.mskousen.com. Frey and Stutzer, 75.

3. Ibid., 78. In fact, Frey and Stutzer publish a graph showing that "Per capita income in the United States has risen sharply in recent decades, but the proportion of persons considering themselves to be 'very happy' has fallen over the same period" (p. 77).

Chapter 10: Improving the Bottom Line with EVA

1. Al Ehrbar, EVA: *The Real Key to Creating Wealth* (New York: Wiley & Sons, 1998), viii.

2. John Kay, *Why Firms Succeed* (New York: Oxford University Press, 1995), 19.

Chapter 11: How Ludwig von Mises Helped Create the World's Largest Private Company

1. Ludwig von Mises, *The Anti-Capitalist Mentality* (Libertarian Press, 1972 [1956]), 19.

2. John Maynard Keynes, *The General Theory of Employment, Interest and Money* (London: Macmillan, 1936), 383.

3. Charles Koch, *The Science of Success* (New York: Wiley, 2007), 149.

4. Koch, *The Science of Success,* 15.

Chapter 12: Look, Ma'am, No Traffic Jams!

1. Jonathan Leape, "The London Congestion Charge," *Journal of Economic Perspectives* 20:4 (Fall 2006): 157.

2. National Transportation Operations Coalition, *National Traffic Signal Report Card,* 2005.

3. Ted Balaker and Sam Staley, *The Road More Traveled* (New York: Rowman & Littlefield, 2006), xiii.

4. Jonathan Leape, "The London Congestion Charge," *Journal of Economic Perspectives* 20:4 (Fall 2006): 165–166.

5. Quoted in Robert W. Poole, Jr., "HOT Lanes Advance in Seven States," *Budget & Tax News* (Chicago: Heartland Institute, March 2004).

6. Peter Samuel and Robert W. Poole, Jr., "The Role of Tolls in Financing 21st Century Highways" (Los Angeles: Reason Foundation, 2007), Executive Summary.

Chapter 13: Patient Power: The New Consumer-Driven Medical Plan

1. Michael F. Cannon and Michael D. Tanner, *Healthy Competition* (Washington, D.C.: Cato Institute, 2005), 7.

2. Technically, they are Health Reimbursement Accounts (HRAs), which have fewer rules and restrictions than HSAs. Whole Foods Market is considering switching to HSAs in the future.

3. John Mackey, "Whole Foods Markets' Consumer-Driven Health Plan," speech at the State Policy Network meeting, October 2004, Austin, Texas, http://www.world.congress.com/news/Mackey_Transcript.pdf

Chapter 14: Back to Basics: Competition Enters the Classroom

1. Adam Smith, *The Wealth of Nations* (New York: Modern Library, 1965 [1776]), 719.

2. Milton Friedman, "Prologue: A Personal Retrospective," *Liberty and Learning: Milton Friedman's Voucher Idea at Fifty,* ed. by Robert C. Enlow and Leonore T. Ealy (Washington, D.C.: Cato Institute, 2006), x.

3. Adam Smith, *The Wealth of Nations*, 718, 720.

4. Robert C. Enlow and Leonore T. Ealy, eds., *Liberty and Learning* (Cato Institute, 2006), viii, 4.

5. Milton Friedman, *Capitalism and Freedom* (Chicago: University of Chicago Press, 1982 [1962]), 93.

6. Herbert J. Walberg, *School Choice: The Findings* (Washington, D.C.: Cato Institute, 2007), 104.

7. Andrew Coulson, "A Critique of Pure Friedman: An Empirical Reassessment of 'The Role of Government in Education,'" *Liberty and Learning,* 116.

8. Herbert J. Walberg, *School Choice,* 47–49.

9. Herbert J. Walberg, *School Choice,* 51–53.

10. Herbert J. Walberg, *School Choice,* flyleaf.

Chapter 15: Chicago Gun Show

1. Gary S. Becker and Guity Nashat Becker, *The Economics of Life* (New York: McGraw-Hill, 1997), 143.

2. Quoted in David Colander, *The Making of an Economist, Redux* (Princeton University Press, 2007), 190.

3. Becker and Becker, *Economics of Life,* 137.

4. John R. Lott, Jr., Freedomonomics (Washington: Regnery, 2007), 134–135.

5. Lawrence Katz, Steven D. Levitt, and Ellen Shustorovich, "Prison Conditions, Capital Punishment, and Deterrence," *American Law and Economics Review,* 2003 (5:2), 318-343.

6. Adam Liptak, "Does Death Penalty Save Lives? A New Debate on an Old Question," *New York Times* (November 18, 2007), p. 1.

7. Ibid., 32.

8. John R. Lott, Jr., *More Guns, Less Crime* (Chicago: University of Chicago Press, 1998), 5.

9. Ibid.

10. Frederic Bastiat, "What Is Seen and What Is Not Seen," *Selected Essays on Political Economy* (Irvington-on-Hudson, N.Y.: Foundation for Economic Education, 1995 [1850]), 1.

11.

Chapter 16: Economists Catch Auction Fever

1. William Vickrey, "Counterspeculation, auctions, and competitive sealed tenders," *Journal of Finance* 16 (1961), 8–37.

2. Paul Klemperer, *Auctions: Theory and Practice* (Princeton University Press, 2004), 105, 107.

3. Quoted in David Reiley, "Vickrey Auctions in Practice: From Nineteenth Century Philately to Twenty-First Century E-commerce," *Journal of Economic Perspectives* 16:3 (Summer 2000), 183–192.

4. Milton and Rose Friedman, *Two Lucky People* (University of Chicago Press, 1998), 385–386.

5. www.treas.gov/auctions/

6. http://www.cambridge.org/uk/economics/milgrom/reviews.htm.

7. Paul Klemperer, *Auctions: Theory and Practice* (Princeton University Press, 2004), preface.

8. "Why we do what we do on eBay: Economists mine the online auction site to find out why shoppers act irrationally," *Christian Science Monitor* (July 16, 2007).

Chapter 17: If You Build It Privately . . . They Will Come: The Economics of Sports Stadiums

1. Paul A. Samuelson, *Economics,* 6th ed. (New York: McGraw-Hill, 1964), 159.

2. Ronald H. Coase, "The Lighthouse in Economics" in *The Firm, the Market, and the Law* (Chicago: University of Chicago Press, 1988), 213. Coase's article originally appeared in *The Journal of Law and Economics* (October 1974).

3. Mark Skousen, "The Perseverance of Paul Samuelson's Economics," *Journal of Economic Perspectives* (Spring 1997), 145.

4. Paul A. Samuelson and William D. Nordhaus, *Economics,* 16th ed. (New York: McGraw-Hill, 1998), 36n.

5. Peter Waldman, "If You Build It Without Public Cash, They'll Still Come," *Wall Street Journal,* March 31, 2000, 1.

6. Mark S. Rosentraub, *Major League Losers: The Real Cost of Sports and Who's Paying for It* (New York: Basic Books, 1997).

7. Roger G. Noll and Andrew Zimbalist, *Sports, Jobs, and Taxes: The Economic Impact of Sports Teams and Stadiums* (Washington, D.C.: Brookings Institution, 1997).

8. J. C. Bradley, *The Baseball Economist* (New York: Dutton, 2007), 8–9. However, it should be noted that since 1994, the hit batter rates narrowed between the two leagues. Bradley suggests two reasons: the league expansion in the 1990s, which diluted the quality of players, and the "double-warning" rule for hitting batters. See Bradley, *The Baseball Economist,* 10–11.

9. J. C. Bradbury, *The Baseball Economist,* 74–81.

10. J. C. Bradbury, *The Baseball Economist,* 81. See his website, www.sabernomics.com.

Chapter 18: Who Is Henry Spearman? Economics of the Mystery Novel

1. See, for example, Gary Becker, *The Economic Approach to Human Behavior* (Chicago: University of Chicago Press, 1976).

Chapter 19: Eco-nomics Debate: Angry Planet or Beautiful World?

1. Worldwatch Institute, *The State of the World 2002* (New York: Norton, 2002), xvii.

2. Bjorn Lomborg, *The Skeptical Environmentalist: Measuring the Real State of the World* (Cambridge: Cambridge University Press, 2001), 30, 32.

3. See Julian L. Simon, *The Ultimate Resource 2* (Princeton University Press, 1998) and *The State of Humanity* (New York: Blackwell, 1995).

4. Lomborg, *Skeptical Environmentalist,* 33.

5. Lomborg, *Skeptical Environmentalist,* 318.

6. Bjorn Lomborg, *Cool It: The Skeptical Environmentalist's Guide to Global Warming* (New York: Knopf, 2007).

7. Terry L. Anderson and Donald R. Leal, *Free-Market Environmentalism,* 2nd ed. (New York: Palgrave, 2001), 47–58.

8. Garrett Hardin, "The Tragedy of the Commons," reprinted in Garrett Hardin and John Baden, eds., *Managing the Commons* (San Francisco: W.H. Freeman, 1977), 20.

9. Two additional sources written from a free-market perspective are Michael Sanera and Jane S. Shaw, *Facts, Not Fear: A Parent's Guide to Teaching Children About the Environment* (Washington, D.C.: Regnery, 1996), and Ronald Bailey, ed., *Earth Report 2000* (New York: McGraw Hill, 2000).

Chapter 20: The Population Bomb: Economists Enter the Malthusian Debate

1. Julian Huxley, "Too Many People," in Fairfield Osborn, ed., *Our Crowded Planet: Essays on the Pressure of Population* (New York: Doubleday, 1962), 223.

2. Paul R. Ehrlich, *The Population Bomb* (New York: Sierra Club, 1968), preface.

3. Ehrlich, *Population Bomb,* 17.

4. Robert Malthus, *Essay on Population* (New York: Penguin Books, 1985 [1798], 71.

5. Malthus, *Essay on Population,* 67–80, 225.

6. For an alternative view to Malthusianism, see Julian L. Simon, ed., *The State of Humanity* (1995) and *The Ultimate Resource 2* (1996).

Chapter 21: A Private-Sector Solution to Extreme Poverty

1. William Easterly, *The Elusive Quest for Growth* (Cambridge, Mass.: MIT Press, 2001), 291.

2. Recent examples include Paul Craig Roberts and Karen LaFollette Araujo, *The Capitalist Revolution in Latin America* (New York: Oxford University Press, 1997), and James A. Dorn, Steve H. Hanke, and Alan A. Walters, eds., *The Revolution in Development Economics* (Washington, D.C.: Cato Institute, 1998).

3. See P.T. Bauer, *The Development Frontier* (Cambridge, Mass.: Harvard University Press, 1991), *Equality, the Third World and Economic Delusion* (Cambridge, Mass.: Harvard University Press, 1981), *and Dissent on Development* (Cambridge, Mass.: Harvard University Press, 1976).

4. William Easterly, *The White Man's Burden: Why the West's Efforts to Aid the Rest Have Done So Much Ill and So Little Good* (New York: Penguin, 2006).

5. Muhammad Yunus, *Banker for the Poor* (New York: Public-Affairs, 1999), 145–146.

6. Yunus, *Banker to the Poor,* 203–205.

Chapter 22: Poverty and Wealth: India Versus Hong Kong

1. Quoted in William Proctor, *The Templeton Prizes* (New York: Doubleday, 1983), 72.

2. Quoted in Proctor, *Templeton Prizes,* 72.

3. For an excellent survey of India, see "Unlocking India's Growth," *The Economist,* June 2, 2001.

4. P. T. Bauer, "The Lesson of Hong Kong," in *Equality, the Third World and Economic Delusion* (London: Weidenfeld and Nicolson, 1981), 185.

5. P.T. Bauer, "The Lesson of Hong Kong," 189.

6. James Gwartney and Robert Lawson, with William Easterly, *Economic Freedom of the World, Annual Report 2006* (Vancouver, B.C.: Fraser Institute, 2006), 13.

7. Milton Friedman, *Friedman on India* (New Delhi: Centre for Civil Society, 2000), 10.

8. See John Stossel's amazing example in his ABC Special "Is America #1?" available on videotape from Laissez Faire Books, 800-326-0996.

9. The other free-market think tank, the Liberty Institute, is run very capably by Barun Mitra. Shah and Mitra hosted my visit to India in June 2001. Go to www.libertyindia.org.

10. Gita Mehta, *Snakes and Ladders: A Modern View of India* (London: Minerva, 1997), 16.

11. Adam Smith, *The Wealth of Nations* (New York: Random House, 1965 [1776]), 11.

Chapter 23: How Real Is the Asian Economic Miracle?

1. Lee Kuan Yew, *From Third World to First: The Singapore Story, 1965–2000* (New York: Harper Collins, 2000), 291.

2. For an excellent survey of the region, see The World Bank, *The East Asian Miracle* (New York: Oxford University Press, 1993).

3. *East Asian Miracle,* vi.

4. Paul Krugman, "The Myth of Asia's Miracle," *Pop Internationalism* (Cambridge: MIT Press, 1996), 173. Originally published in *Foreign Affairs* (Nov./Dec., 1994).

5. Krugman, "Myth of Asia's Miracle," *Pop Internationalism,* 184.

6. Marshall Goldman, *USSR in Crisis: The Failure of an Economic System* (New York: W. W. Norton, 1983), 2.

7. Lee Kuan Yew, *From Third World to First: The Singapore Story, 1965–2000* (New York: Harper Collins, 2000), 687.

8. Ludwig von Mises, "Capital Supply and American Prosperity," *Planning for Freedom,* 4th ed. (South Holland, Ill.: Libertarian Press, 1980), 214. I highly recommend this talk on economic development, given by Mises in 1952.

Chapter 24: Whatever Happened to the Egyptians?

1. P. T. Bauer and B. S. Yamey, *The Economics of Underdeveloped Countries* (Cambridge: Cambridge University Press, 1957), 157.

2. Claire E. Francy, *Cairo: The Practical Guide,* 10th ed. (Cairo: American University in Cairo Press, 2001), 68. This guidebook is both shocking and indispensable for anyone moving to or studying this unusual nation. I placed exclamation points on practically every page.

3. Import substitution laws are laws passed by the local government to prohibit foreign consumer products in the country, such as shoes, toothpaste, or cars, thus forcing local companies to produce these products at considerably higher prices (and usually less quality).

4. Cited in W. W. Rostow, *Theorists of Economic Growth from David Hume to the Present* (New York: Oxford University Press, 1990), 423.

5. Doug Bandow, "The First World's Misbegotten Economic Legacy to the Third World," in James A. Dorn, Steve H. Hanke, and Alan A. Walters, eds., *The Revolution in Development Economics* (Washington, D.C.: Cato Institute, 1998), 217, 222–223.

6. James Gwartney and Robert Lawson, *Economic Freedom of the World,* Annual Report 2006 (Vancouver, B.C.: Fraser Institute, 2006), 9–10.

Chapter 25: The Irish Economic Miracle: Can We Grow Faster?

1. John Maynard Keynes, "Economic Possibilities for Our Grandchildren," *Essays in Persuasion* (New York: Norton, 1963), 365.

2. Keynes, *Essays in Persuasion,* 365.

3. Quoted in Jerry J. Jasinowski, ed., *The Rising Tide* (New York: John Wiley & Sons, 1998), xxi.

4. James Tobin, "Can We Grow Faster?," in *The Rising Tide,* 44.

5. Robert A. Mundell, "A Progrowth Fiscal System," in *The Rising Tide,* 203–204.

6. Keynes, *Essays in Persuasion,* 367.

Chapter 26: The Marginal Tax Revolution: The Laffer Curve Goes Global

1. Stephen Moore, "Reaganomincs 2.0," *Wall Street Journal* (August 31, 2007), A8.

2. Supply-side economics is the study of how economic growth can be influenced by incentives to produce (supply) goods and services, as opposed to Keynesian economics, which focuses on ways to control the demand for goods and services.

3. Progressive taxation means those who earn more income pay a higher income tax rate.

4. Bruce Bartlett, "Supply-Side Economics and Austrian Economics," *The Freeman* (April, 1987).

5. John Kenneth Galbraith, *The Affluent Society* (Boston: Houghton Mifflin, 1958), 96.

6. Dan Bawley, *The Subterranean Economy* (New York: McGraw-Hill, 1982), 135.

7. William Baumol and Alan Blinder, *Economics: Principles and Policy,* 4th ed. (New York: Harcourt Brace Jovanovich, 1988), 835.

8. Paul Craig Roberts, *The Supply Side Revolution* (Cambridge: Harvard University Press, 1984), 25.

Chapter 27: The Debate over Economic Inequality: The Rich Get Richer, and the Poor Get . . .

1. John Kenneth Galbraith, *The Good Society: The Humane Agenda* (Boston: Houghton Mifflin, 1996), 50.

2. "The Rich, the Poor, and the Growing Gap Between Them," *The Economist,* June 15, 2006.

3. For a critique of the Lorenz curve, see my work *Economics on Trial* (Homewood, Ill.: Irwin, 1991), 187–197.

4. Stanley Lebergott, *Pursuing Happiness: American Consumers in the Twentieth Century* (Princeton, N.J.: Princeton University Press, 1993), 58. It should also be noted that by 2000, over half of couples were sharing housework duties.

5. Lebergott, *Pursuing Happiness,* 117–118. See also Lebergott's work, *Consumer Expenditures* (Princeton, N.J.: Princeton University Press, 1996).

6. Michael Cox and Richard G. Alm, "Buying Time," *Reason Magazine,* August/September 1998, 42. See also their book, *Myths of Rich and Poor: Why We're Better Off Than We Think* (New York: Basic Books, 1999).

7. Gregory Clark, *A Farewell to Alms: A Brief Economic History of the World* (Princeton University Press, 2007), 276, 278.

8. Clark, *Farewell to Alms,* 277.

9. Clark, *Farewell to Alms,* 283–284.

10. Clark, *Farewell to Alms,* 16.

Chapter 28: One Graph Says It All: The Development of the Economic Freedom Index

1. Milton Friedman, "Forward," *Economic Freedom of the World, 1975–1995,* by James Gwartney, Robert Lawson, and Walter Block (Vancouver, BC: Fraser Institute, 1996).

2. Adam Smith, *The Wealth of Nations* (New York: Modern Library, 1965 [1776]), 651.

3. Smith, *Wealth of Nations,* 549.

4. Smith, *Wealth of Nations,* 423.

5. Smith, *Wealth of Nations,* 11.

6. Paul A. Samuelson and William D. Nordhaus, *Economics,* 12th ed. (New York: McGraw-Hill, 1985), 776.

7. Mancur Olson, *How Bright Are the Northern Lights?* (Stockholm: Lund University, 1990), 10.

8. Henry C. Wallich, *The Cost of Freedom* (New York: Collier Books, 1960), 9, 146.

9. Olson, *How Bright Are the Northern Lights?,* 88.

10. See Michael A. Walker, "The Historical Development of the Economic Freedom Index," in James Gwartney, Robert Lawson, and Walter Block, eds., *Economic Freedom of the World 1975–1995* (Vancouver, BC: Fraser Institute, 1996).

Early participants in these meetings included Milton and Rose Friedman, Michael Walker, Lord Peter Bauer, Gary Becker, Douglass C. North, Armen Alchian, Arnold Harberger, Alvin Rabushka, Walter Block, Gordon Tullock, and Sir Alan Walters.

11. James Gwartney and Robert Lawson, *Economic Freedom of the World 2004* (Vancouver: Fraser Institute, 2004), 5.

12. Marc A. Miles, Edwin J. Feulner, and Mary Anastasia O'Grady, *2005 Index of Economic Freedom* (New York and Washington D.C.: *Wall Street Journal.* and the Heritage Foundation, 2005), 58. For the latest index, go to www. heritage.org.

13. Milton Friedman, "Forward," *Economic Freedom of the World, 1975–1995* (1996).

14. Gwartney and Lawson, *Economic Freedom of North America, 2004 Annual Report,* 4.

15. James Gwartney and Robert Lawson, *Economic Freedom of the World, 2004 Annual Report* (Fraser Institute, 2005), 35.

16. Susan Rose-Ackerman, "The Role of The World Bank in Controlling Corruption," *Law and Policy in International Business* (Fall, 1997).

17. Jakob Svensson, as cited in *The Economist* (December 23, 2006), 126.

18. "The etiquette of bribery," *The Economist* (December 23, 2006), 126.

Chapter 29: Amazing Graph: Economists Enter Sacred Territory

1. Gary S. Becker and Guity Nashat Becker, *The Economics of Life* (New York: McGraw-Hill, 1997), 16.

2. Another is Robert H. Nelson, author of two excellent books, *Reaching for Heaven on Earth: The Theological Meaning of Economics* (Savage, Md.: Rowman & Littlefield, 1991) and *Economics as Religion: From Samuelson to Chicago and Beyond* (University Park: Penn State Press, 2001), both of which deal with economics as religion rather than the economics of religion.

3. Adam Smith, *The Wealth of Nations* (New York: Modern Library, 1965 [1776]), 744–748.

4. Lawrence Iannaccone, "The Consequences of Religious Market Structure," *Rationality and Society* (April 1991), 156–177. See also "Adam Smith's Hypothesis on Religion," chapter 10 in Edwin G. West, *Adam Smith and Modern Economics* (Hants, England: Edward Elgar, 1990).

5. Roger Finke and Rodney Stark, *The Churching of America, 1776–1990: Winners and Losers in Our Religious Economy* (New Brunswick, N.J.: Rutgers University Press, 1992), 1.

6. Finke and Stark, *Churching of America,* 32.

7. Finke and Stark, *Churching of America,* 5.

Chapter 30: Peace on Earth, Good Will toward Men: The Case for Religious Competition

1. Adam Smith, *The Wealth of Nations* (New York: Modern Library, 1965 [1776]), 745.

2. Leonard Read, *Anything That's Peaceful,* 2nd ed. (New York: Foundation for Economic Education, 1998), 30.

3. Tim Kane, Kim R. Holmes, and Mary Anastasia O'Grady, *2007 Index of Economic Freedom* (Washington, D.C.: Heritage Books, 2007).

4. Henry Hazlitt, *The Foundations of Morality,* 3rd ed. (New York: Foundation for Economic Education, 1998 [1964]), 339.

5. See Milton Friedman, *Capitalism and Freedom* (Chicago: University of Chicago Press, 1962), chapter 1.

6. Charles Montesquieu, *The Spirit of the Laws* (Cambridge: Cambridge University Press, 1989 [1748]), 338.

7. Albert O. Hirschman, *The Passion and the Interests,* 2nd ed. (Princeton: Princeton University Press, 1997), 72. I highly recommend this brilliant book. For more discussion of the peaceable nature of capitalism, see my book, *The Making of Modern Economics* (New York: M. E. Sharpe, 2001), chapter 1.

8. John Maynard Keynes, *The General Theory of Interest, Money and Employment* (London: Macmillan, 1936), 374. Today we might say, "Better that a person tyrannize over his favorite sports team or his favorite stock than over his fellow citizen."

9. Gerald O'Driscoll, Jr., and Sara J. Fitzgerald, "Trade Promotes Prosperity and Security," Heritage Foundation Backgrounder #1617 (December 18, 2002).

10. Andrew Sullivan, "This Is a Religious War," *New York Times Magazine,* October 7, 2001, 53.

11. Adam Smith, *The Wealth of Nations,* 747–748.

Chapter 31: New Yale Forecasting Model: Has the Irving Fisher Curse Been Lifted?

1. Robert Shiller, *Irrational Exuberance,* 2nd ed. (Princeton University Press, 2005), xii.

2. Irving Fisher was quoted in the October 16, 1929, issue of the *New York Times.*

3. Kathryn M. Dominquez, Ray C. Fair, and Matthew D. Shapiro, "Forecasting the Depression: Harvard Versus Yale," *American Economic Review,* September 1988, 605. The authors ignored the Austrian economists Ludwig von Mises and Friedrich Hayek, as well as the sound money camp of E. C. Harwood and

Benjamin Anderson, who did anticipate economic trouble. See my paper, "Who Predicted the 1929 Crash?" in Jeffrey M. Herbener, ed. *The Meaning of Ludwig von Mises* (New York: Kluwer Publishers, 1993), 247–283.

4. Shiller, *Irrational Exuberance,* xviii.

5. Shiller, *Irrational Exuberance,* 14.

Chapter 32: Forecasting Elections: Economists Do It Better

1. Ludwig von Mises, *Human Action,* 3rd ed. (Chicago: Regnery, 1966), 337–338.

2. Joyce Berg, Forrest Nelson, and Thomas Rietz, "Accuracy and Forecast Standard Error of Prediction Markets," University of Iowa Working Draft, (November 2001), 10.

3. Joyce Berg, Forrest Nelson, and Thomas Rietz, "Prediction Market Accuracy in the Long Run," University of Iowa Working Draft (August 2007), abstract.

4. Berg, Nelson, and Rietz, "Accuracy and Forecast Standard Error of Prediction Markets" (2001), 13.

5. Friedrich A. Hayek, "The Use of Knowledge in Society," *American Economic Review* 35 (1945), 519–530.

Chapter 33: What Drives the Economy and Stocks: Consumer Spending or Business Investment?

1. For more information, see Chapter 2 of my book, *The Making of Modern Economics* (Armon, N.Y.: M. E. Sharpe Publishers, 2001).

2. For more information on Gross Domestic Expenditures (GDE), see my book, *The Structure of Production* (New York: New York University Press, 1990, 2007), which includes a new introduction. Also, see my article, "What Drives the Economy: Consumer Spending or Saving/Investment? Using GDP, Gross Output and Other National Income Statistics to Determine Economic Performance," Backgrounder, 2004, Initiative for Policy Dialogue, http://www-1.gsb.columbia.edu/ipd/j_gdp.html.

3. For information on how the BEA figures Gross Output, go to www.bea.gov and look under "GDP by Industry," then "interactive tables." For the differences between GO, GDE, and GDP, see xv–xvi in the introduction to *The Structure of Production* (2007 edition).

4. Peter F. Drucker, *Toward the Next Economics and Other Essays* (New York: Harper & Row, 1981), 8.

5. Ludwig von Mises, "Capital Supply and American Prosperity," in *Planning for Freedom,* 4th ed. (Spring Mills, PA: Libertarian Press, 1980), 197.

Chapter 34: The Midas Metal: A Golden Comeback

1. Roy W. Jastram, *The Golden Constant: The English and American Experience, 1560–1976* (New York: Wiley & Sons, 1977), 132.

2. Mark Mobius, "Asia Needs a Single Currency," *Wall Street Journal,* February 19, 1998, A22.

3. See my book, *Economics of a Pure Gold Standard,* 3rd ed. (New York: Foundation for Economic Education, 1997), 82. Note how the world monetary stock of gold never has declined between 1810 and 1933, when the West was on the classical gold standard.

4. Jeremy J. Siegel, *Stocks for the Long Run,* 3rd ed. (New York: McGraw-Hill, 2002), 195.

5. For further discussion regarding the inherent volatility of the mining industry, see my work *The Structure of Production* (New York: New York University Press, 1990, 2007), 290–294.

6. "The Song of Bernanke," *Wall Street Journal* lead editorial, August 31, 2007, A8.

Chapter 35: Is Another Great Depression Possible?

1. Milton Friedman, "Why the American Economy is Depression-Proof," *Dollars and Deficits* (Englewood Cliffs, N.J.: Prentice Hall, 1968), 72–96.

2. Benjamin M. Anderson, *Economics and the Public Welfare* (Indianapolis: Liberty Press, 1979 [1949]), and Murray N. Rothbard, *America's Great Depression* (Princeton N.J.: D. Van Nostrand, 1963).

3. Milton Friedman and Anna J. Schwartz, *A Monetary History of the United States, 1867–1960* (Princeton N.J.: Princeton University Press, 1963), 299.

4. Friedman and Schwartz, *Monetary History,* 360–361.

5. Gene Smiley, "Some Austrian Perspectives on Keynesian Fiscal Policy and the Recovery of the Thirties," *Review of Austrian Economics* (1987), 1:146–179, and Mark Skousen, "The Great Depression," in Peter Boettke, ed., *The Elgar Companion to Austrian Economics* (Cheltenham, UK: Edward Elgar, 1994), 431–439.

6. Robert Higgs, "Regime Uncertainty: Why the Great Depression Lasted So Long and Why Prosperity Resumed After the War," *The Independent Review* (Spring 1997), 1:4, 561–590.

7. Robert Higgs, "Wartime Prosperity? A Reassessment of the U.S. Economy in the 1940s," *Journal of Economic History* 52 (March 1992): 41–60. See also Richard K. Vedder and Lowell Gallaway, "The Great Depression of 1946," *Review of Austrian Economics* 5, no. 2 (1991): 3–31.

8. Higgs' papers on the Great Depression have all been compiled into one anthology, *Depression, War, and Cold War: Studies in Political Economy* (Oxford University Press, 2006).

Chapter 36: Today's Most Influential Economist?

1. Daniel Yergin and Joseph Stanislaw, The *Commanding Heights: The Battle Between Government and the Marketplace That Is Remaking the Modern World* (New York: Simon & Schuster, 1998), 15.

2. John Maynard Keynes, *The General Theory of Employment, Interest and Money* (London: Macmillan, 1936), 383.

3. For a good overview of Hayek's works, see *The Essence of Hayek,* ed. Chiaka Nishiyama and Kurt R. Leube (Stanford, Calif.: Hoover Institution, 1984). For a partial autobiography, see *Hayek on Hayek* (Chicago: University of Chicago Press, 1994). A full-scale intellectual biography of Hayek has been written by Alan Ebenstein, *Friedrich Hayek, A Biography* (New York: St. Martins Press, 2001).

4. Peter F. Drucker, "Modern Prophet: Schumpeter or Keynes?" in *The Frontiers of Management* (New York: Harper & Row, 1986), 104.

5. Yergin and Stanislaw, *Commanding Heights,* 141. Also see my book, *Vienna and Chicago, Friends or Foes?* (Washington, D.C.: Capital Press, 2005).

Chapter 37: Economics for the 21st Century

1. Marquis de Condorcet, "The Future Progress of the Human Mind," *The Portable Enlightenment Reader,* ed. Isaac Kramnick (Penguin Books, 1995), 38. Several of Condorcet's writings can be found in this excellent anthology.

2. Paul Johnson, *Modern Times: The World from the Twenties to the Nineties,* rev. ed. (New York: Harper, 1992). The best survey of the horrors of communism is *The Black Book of Communism: Crimes, Terror, Repression* (Cambridge, Mass.: Harvard University Press, 1999), written by six French scholars, some of whom are former communists.

3. Frederic Bastiat, *Selected Essays on Political Economy* (Irvington-on-Hudson, N.Y.: Foundation for Economic Education, 1995 [1964]).

4. Stanley Liebergott, *Pursuing Happiness: American Consumers in the Twentieth Century* (Princeton University Press, 1993), flyleaf.

5. Peter F. Drucker, *Toward the Next Economics, and Other Essays* (New York: Harper & Row, 1981), 1–21.

About the Author

Mark Skousen is a professional economist, investment expert, university professor, and author of over 25 books. Currently he holds the Benjamin Franklin Chair of Management at Grantham University. In 2004–2005, he taught economics and finance at Columbia Business School and Columbia University, Mercy College, an Rollius College. Since 1980, Skousen has been editor in chief of *Forecasts & Strategies,* a popular award-winning investment newsletter (www.markskousen.com). He is also editor of *The Worldly Philosophers,* a weekly e-letter (www.worldlyphilosophers.com). He is a former analyst for the CIA, a columnist to *Forbes* magazine, and past president of the Foundation for Economic Education (FEE) in New York. He has written for the *Wall Street Journal, Forbes,* and the *Christian Science Monitor,* and is a regular contributor to CNBC's *Kudlow & Co.* His bestsellers include *The Making of Modern Economics* and *The Big Three in Economics.* He compiled and edited *The Compleated Autobiography by Benjamin Franklin* (Regnery, 2007). In honor of his work in economics, finance, and management, Grantham University renamed its business school, "The Mark Skousen School of Business."

Index